WITHDRAWN

F
New Sc
1949

D0916018

New Towns
and Urban Policy

New Towns and Urban Policy

Planning Metropolitan Growth

James A. Clapp

DUNELLEN

New York

©1971 by the Dunellen Publishing Company, Inc.
145 East 52nd Street
New York, New York 10022

All rights reserved. No part of this book may be used or reproduced in any manner whatsoever without written permission except in the case of brief quotations embodied in critical articles and reviews.

International Standard Book Number 0-8424-0028-1.

Library of Congress Catalogue Card Number 78-136245.

Printed in the United States of America.

Contents

Preface

Former Federal urban renewal administrator William Slayton remarked at a recent planning conference that "the very mention of new towns or new cities has become an effective way to close a conversation in certain academic and professional circles . . . ." That is probably true, and one need only begin to survey the literature which has mounted on the subject over the years to get the impression that the new town idea may be a "dead horse." At a time when our urban difficulties are more pressing than ever, and more planners urge greater attention to current problems and needs, the utopian-tainted new town concept has seemed worthy of scant attention.

However, if Ebenezer Howard and the new town movement which has resulted in policies for new towns development in many of the advanced nations of the world had never existed, the private sector would probably have come around to discovering the new town anyway. In any event, it is that occurrence which has signaled the rebirth of the new towns debate and added new perspectives to it. The private new town trend and the governmental responses which it has stimulated have led me to undertake a study of the subject.

The central problem to which this study is addressed is that of the planning and control of metropolitan growth and expansion. For the most part, urban planning and land use controls in the United States have traditionally been tied to individual units of government, and these public responsibilities have been separated from authority for development. Furthermore, the myriad of public programs directed at urban problems and needs has not been linked to any coherent or unified national urban public policy or spatial form for urban development.

In theory, the new town concept has offered both a spatial form for urban expansion and a system for implementation which links the authority for planning and development. Basically, the concept encompasses the notions of development in wholes, or unified urban units, and single ownership or control of land.

In recent years, the new town concept and variations of it have been adopted by large-scale private developers and some large industrial corporations. Although the vast majority of private new towns are in the early stages of development, they have stimulated a rebirth of interest in various forms of public new town programs, and, more generally, a wide variety of speculation as to the merits of the new town concept and public new towns policy as a mechanism for introducing order to metropolitan expansion and synthesizing a variety of objectives of different public programs.

This study is basically concerned with an investigation of the relevance and feasibility of new towns policy in the light of the increase of private new town development and a diverse literature on metropolitanism. The methodology employed is fourfold. The subject is approached first through a consideration of the problems to which the new town concept is addressed and investigation of its theoretical assumptions and principal elements. Attention is then turned to the operations of private new town developers. The purpose of this discussion is to identify the characteristics of private new town development, the problems involved, and their implications for public new towns programs. The final two facets of the study are concerned with the feasibility of new towns policy. The first treats the operations of various types of new towns programs at different levels of public involvement in the development process and their relationship to the operations of private developers and to legal and political considerations. The second concern with feasibility deals with the relevance of the concept's objectives to the major social, economic and political forces shaping the metropolitan area.

The writer feels that this approach serves to expose some of the major considerations of an American new towns program. It is recognized that only partial answers to the questions to which this analysis is directed are obtainable, and that to some no single or conclusive answers may be possible. The initial problem inherent in such an inquiry is that of posing the appropriate questions. It has yet to be determined which is the most desirable pattern for metropolitan expansion, or if, indeed, an optimum pattern exists. Many of the proponents of the new town concept claim that the new town can be employed to induce order into metropolitan expansion. The purpose of this study is to examine the validity of this claim, both in theory and operation, in the context of American urbanization. As yet, our limited knowledge of urbanization restricts our ability to examine problems and solutions. These are the limitations with which any student of urban affairs must contend and seek to improve.

In the course of this study I have become indebted to many people. The original impetus came from the late Peter B. Andrews, who encouraged me to undertake a study to propose new towns legislation as a master's thesis at Syracuse University. The time spent on that aspect of the subject served as an introduction to the literature, but was interrupted by my decision to pursue doctoral studies. Since then the private new town trend intensified, the first new towns legislation was introduced, and I decided that a more pertinent effort would be directed to the study of the legislation itself in terms of the operations of private developers and the major issues of metropolitanism.

I owe thanks also to the many persons with whom I corresponded on various aspects of the subject, some of whom are mentioned in the following chapters. Syracuse Professors Max Bloom, Paul Meadows and Robert Bartels provided helpful criticism and suggestions. Particular thanks go to Dean Alan K. Campbell, who was most influential in deepening my interest in urban public policy, and who served as my advisor during the study. Finally, since it is said that "they also serve who stand and wait," special thanks must go to my wife Pat, who sat and typed.

San Diego, California
October 1971

1

The New Town Renaissance

The Identification of Problems

Discussions of solutions to urban problems have a way of turning to Socratic dialogue. The city keeps changing, as do the technology, the people, and the institutions, which leads to new interpretations of urban problems. This process is too fast for some, and too slow for others; it benefits some, and creates disadvantages for others. How one feels about it depends to a great extent on income, education, occupation, color, and age.

Perspective can make a difference in the interpretation of urban problems. Historically, Americans appear to have possessed an anti-urban bias, with a tendency to concentrate on the negative qualities of the city.[1] This ideological antipathy toward cities and urban life is reflected in much of our legal-governmental system, to such an extent that some observers believe that a change from our romantic agrarian perspectives is prerequisite to dealing with the urban realities of today.[2] Still, it is paradoxical that, while supposedly having a great distaste for urban life, people have been

1

flocking to the cities in great numbers since the industrial revolution.

There is little agreement, however, about the effects of urbanization. Human ecologists such as Wirth tend to regard the city as an independent variable which functions as an engine of social disorganization. In contrast, Sjoberg expresses the need for a different perspective on urbanization, one which recognizes ". . . that the city is shaped along certain lines by the broader, embracing society . . .," and that to understand the underlying causes of urban problems one must view the city as a ". . . dependent rather than independent variable, for much of its ecological and social structure are determined by social forces external to it."[3] From this perspective, Wilson questions not only "urban" as an appropriate description (he suggests that "urban" is less relevant than "human"), but also the characterization of our cities as "sick" and crisis-ridden." Rather, he maintains that "Viewed in historical perspective, and taking American cities as a whole, the conditions of urban life have, by most measures, been getting steadily better, not worse."[4]

There are widely divergent positions on some of the particular effects of urbanization. In the literature of the urban crisis, it is frequently asserted that the effect of urbanization (or suburbanization) is an increase in the conformity of behavior, as evidenced particularly by the stereotypical view of the suburban, middle-class family. Again from an historical point of view, it may be argued that the opposite is true: prior to industrialization and urbanization, there was much greater conformity of behavior and life-style in that the society was largely agrarian and was therefore occupationally and ideologically uniform. Thus, the city is seen as a pool for a wide range of different opportunities, causing urban society to be more liberating and varied than rural society. These views are reflected in the different concepts of "community," wherein some observers lament the decline of the traditional, spatially defined community, and others feel that "community" has taken on new, non-spatial forms.

Other examples of differing perspectives might be cited, but they would only belabor the point that people see social change differently, some positively, some in negative terms. But the fact of change itself is indisputable: we have progressed (some would say regressed) from a localized, agrarian society with small isolated urban nodes to a complex and bureaucratized national and international system of cities in a post-industrial society. Increasingly, our most difficult urban problems are national problems. It takes only a bus ride from rural Mississippi to a northern city ghetto to redefine the rural poor as urban poor. The urban economy is intertwined with national and international economies.

No one would dispute that the cities have their problems— not all the same problems, nor to the same degrees—in handling traffic, financing services, reducing crime, disposing of wastes, and providing adequate housing, education, and jobs. These problems are explained and illustrated in considerable detail in a constantly growing literature. However, there is much more consensus on the existence and severity of our problems than there is on our ability to deal with them. As one planner has observed, discussions of our problem-solving capabilities with respect to urban problems have become an "Oh yes we can! Oh no you can't"[5] debate, in which one side argues, for example, that all the elements of a national urban growth policy are already present in existing legislation and only require coordination. The other side retorts that coordination is uncharacteristic of American government, and that it is in the nature of politics and bureaucracy that programs are not brought into concert. The metropolitan government debate runs a similar course.

It is, therefore, in an atmosphere of hazy distinctions between cause and effect, of different perceptions of urban problems and possible solutions,[6] and of insufficient information, that this study is undertaken.

The New Town Concept

Planner Marshall Kaplan has pointed out that, the new town concept lends itself well to two long-standing beliefs which have pre-conditioned planners—"physical determinism" and the "relevance of the general plan."[7] In many ways the new town concept has functioned as the urban planners' model, to which could easily be attached related concepts or ideas such as the physically, socially, or economically balanced community, neighborhood planning, separation of land uses, and optimum city sizes and densities. Established political structures, existing land use patterns, and heterogeneous populations have always served to complicate the application of planning concepts. However, the new town concept has offered the prospect of a unique opportunity to plan the land use arrangement of a community relatively free from the constraints of prior development patterns, local politics, fragmented land ownerships, and other factors which limit freedom of expression and effectiveness in conventional city planning. Explicit or implicit reference to the new town concept or aspects of it can be identified throughout the literature of physical planning and urban design. Much of the influence of the new town idea can be traced to the work of Ebenezer Howard and the resultant Garden City movement.[8]

However, the new town concept has had little influence upon the manner in which cities and metropolitan areas in the United States have developed and expanded. Generally, American urbanization has been unplanned, and where master plans have existed they appear to have had little influence upon urban growth. (It is acknowledged that some cities, such as New York and Washington, D.C., are sometimes referred to as "planned" by virtue of the fact that they were surveyed and laid out; but their eventual development patterns were not the product of comprehensive land use planning.) For the most part, the American development pattern has been the sum of small additions, on a lot-by-lot basis, or, where demand has warranted, on a subdivision-by-subdivision basis. The market characteristics which have dictated, and still do dictate, the manner in which most American urban development takes place are summarized by banker-developer James Rouse:

> Although the business of city building is the largest single industry in America, there is no large corporation engaged in it. City building has no General Motors or General Electric—no IBM, no Xerox; no big capital resources to invest in the purchase of large land areas; no big research and development program unfolding new techniques to produce a better environment. There are no large corporations engaged in the end-product production of the American city. City building—the development of houses and apartments, stores and offices—is the business of thousands of very small corporations, no one of which has within its own resources the financial capacity to invest millions of dollars in land holding to be planned and developed over, say, 10 to 15 years.[9]

The basic features of the new town concept differ significantly from current American planning and land use regulation. First, the development of new towns usually relies upon single ownership or control of large areas of land. Secondly, the successful development of a new town requires a form of development sponsorship of sufficient size and financial resources to undertake long-term, large-scale development. The operations of the American land market and the structure of the building industry have not been consistent with these basic features.

New town development also contrasts with current planning law and practice. In the development of new towns, the objectives set for the community, its planning, regulation, and development all emanate from the same authority. Current American planning practice separates these aspects of the industry; although plans are developed by one authority, the responsibility for the enforcement of regulations (with the exception of subdivision review powers) upon which planning implementation relies belongs to other authorities. With the exception of programming public improvements, development is not initiated by the plan but by market decisions. In addition, it can be argued that public improvements are also conditioned by market decisions.

The Current Interest in the New Town
Concept: Public and Private

Where for the most part American urban planning and private development practices have been incompatible with the basic features of new town development, the current interest in the new town concept is largely a response to departures from traditional planning and development practices. In recent years there has been increasing attention to the new town concept by land developers and builders, large industrial and financial corporations, bankers, governmental officials, and others.*

Several developments appear to have made the new town concept potentially more feasible or acceptable in the United States. The basic underlying influences have been the metropolitan phenomenon and the process of suburbanization, which are results of accelerated population growth and an unprecedented demand for new development. One effect of suburbanization is that all the land use components necessary to assemble new towns are no longer bound to the confines of existing cities.

Specific developments include advances in both public and private planning and development control, particularly the planned unit development and planned community options in some zoning ordinances; the general expansion in financing for new development, both public and private; and the growing interest on the part of large developers and corpora-

---

*There has been since the early part of this century what might be loosely referred to as a new towns or Garden City movement in the United States. Most of its members, however, have come from the ranks of city and regional planners and others associated with the urban planning profession.

tions in the potential profitability of building at the new town scale.

The most striking evidence of these trends has been the significant increase in recent years of large-scale private developments. In 1964, one observer listed a total of seventy-five planned new towns or large community developments of one thousand acres or more which are either projected or under way in the United States.[10] Although opinion varies as to whether many of these developments constitute new towns or are of sufficient size to warrant the name, they at least indicate a greater potential for new towns.

Unlike new town development in other nations, all recent undertaking or projection of American large-scale development has taken place without the direct support or encouragement of the national or state governments. This development does not appear to have been a direct response to the traditional exhortations of planners, who favor publicly-initiated new towns, although the planners have participated in it. Rather, it seems to have been a product of an evolution in the scale of private development, and an increase in participation in large-scale development by both traditional and non-traditional agents.

The impact of the private new towns currently under way or projected may not be determined for several years. However, it is evident that they are potentially significant for the areas in which they are located. Many of these developments will involve thousands of acres and several millions of dollars of private investment. The majority of them will contain populations of several thousand persons (some up to 200 thousand), and could include significant portions of regional economic activity. If these objectives are realized, their impact could be considerable, both for the local jurisdictions and for regional patterns of physical and economic development. Although they are popularly referred to as new towns, new cities, or new communities, by current statistical definitions many would constitute the founding of new metropolitan areas.

The new large-scale developments have rekindled governmental interest in some type of public participation in the establishment of new towns. In the past, the new towns programs of other nations have been viewed with interest, but the operations of these programs have been incompatible with the American institutional and governmental framework. In most cases, foreign programs are based upon a direct governmental involvement in the planning and building of new towns, and have involved broad and heavy controls on the operations of the private market. The few examples of publicly developed new towns in the United States have been the specialized towns which were constructed in conjunction with the operations of Federal agencies such as the Atomic Energy Commission, the TVA, and the New Deal's Resettlement Administration. With the exception of the latter agency's Greenbelt Towns, all of these communities were the necessary by-products of specific public projects and had little relevance to the major trends and issues in metropolitan expansion.

The New Town Concept and Urban Public Policy

In 1964, President Johnson, in a message relating to the administration's housing bills, stated

> The pioneering efforts of progressive and imaginative developers in planning totally new and complete communities indicate some of the exciting possibilities for orderly growth. In the tradition of the long-established partnership between private industry and Government in housing and community development, the Federal Government should encourage and facilitate these new and desirable approaches.[11]

The "new communities" bill was upstaged by the major feature of the housing and urban development bills of that year, the proposal for a Department of Housing and Urban Development. Although it did not survive committee in 1964, the bill marked the first attempt in the United States to introduce a program for public support of the development of new towns. Two years later, a slightly revised version of the new communities bill was enacted by Congress as part of the *Demonstration Cities and Metropolitan Development Act of 1966.*[12]

The new communities legislation is primarily an experimental program for publicly assisted large-scale development. It is a minimal experiment, employing little more than an extension or adaptation of existing parts of other urban development legislation. Only time will disclose whether it is the embryo of an American new towns policy.

The call for a national urban growth policy has a wide-ranging rationale, but basic to it is the magnitude and character of metropolitanization in America. At the turn of this century, metropolitan residents constituted less than one-third of the American population. By 1940, the majority of the population was metropolitan, and it has been pointed out that in the decade from 1950 to 1960 "the population increase in metropolitan areas . . . exceeded the total population living in all such complexes in 1900."[13] The dominance of metropolitan growth is also demonstrated by the fact that in the 1940's SMSA's accounted for approximately 80 percent of the population growth in the United States, and in the 1950's, about 85 percent. During these two decades the population of metropolitan areas increased by 55 percent, compared to an 11 percent increase in the remainder of the nation.[14]

Although there are several other manifestations of metropolitan growth in the United States, such as the increase in the number of governments or dominance in economic activity, the immediately significant fact of metropolitan growth for this analysis is the spatial expansion of metropolitan areas. During the 1950–1960 decade, the majority of metropolitan growth took place outside the central cities.

During this period, central cities of metropolitan areas increased in population by 10.7 percent, including population added through annexations. In contrast, the remaining portion of metropolitan areas increased in population by 17.9 million persons, or 48.6 percent (excluding the 4.9 million persons annexed to central cities during the decade).[15]

The general pattern of metropolitan expansion has been characterized by the centripetal-centrifugal metaphor. Viewed in terms of spatial and locational requirements, most aspects of urban areas have been affected in varying degrees by population growth, space needs, and technological changes. Lack of space in settled areas, increasing use of the private automobile, the desire for home ownership and better schools, highway programs and mortgage insurance (both cause and effect), have both made necessary and enabled the spread of residential development around urban centers. Residential development has been closely followed by suburban development of commercial land uses in the form of shopping centers and strip commercial development, freed of many past locational requirements by the accessibility afforded by the automobile. Manufacturing activities have also been affected. New production methods, greater space requirements, tax considerations, and changing patterns of transport and product distribution have freed or forced many industrial land uses from the bounds of central cities. However, central cities have retained a certain magnetic force. As the major concentrations of manufacturing, service, and industrial activities and as the focus of major transportation routes, they have caused suburban growth to remain accessible to them.

Approaches to the needs and problems created by metropolitan expansion in the United States have evolved largely on an ad hoc basis and have not been framed within any established national or regional development objectives or goals. For the most part, the establishment of programs has been responsive to specific crises such as slums, air and water pollution, and the development problems of suburban communities, and the programs are administered through a large, multi-level, and often uncoordinated bureaucratic system. The nature of these programs and the needs or problems to which they are directed often create situations in which they become part of the problems themselves. In some instances, programs administered by the same agencies function in conflict. The Housing Act of 1949 established a program to eliminate slums and revitalize cities at the same time that other programs were making outside central city areas more attractive to private investment. The Federal Highway Program has made it as easy to get out of the city as to get into it and has opened new suburban neighborhoods, while often fragmenting older city neighborhoods.

Although there have been no attempts to formulate a national urban policy, there have been in recent years some attempts at improved coordination among various programs.[16] Among these have been requirements to improve the coordination of highway and mass transit planning; the recent attempt to coordinate physical and social planning and renewal under the Comprehensive Demonstration (Model) Cities Program; and, at the administrative level, the reorganization of several urban-oriented administrations under the aegis of the Department of Housing and Urban Development.

None of these approaches, however, has been tied to a definable spatial framework for new development or for the metropolitan region as a whole. It will be evident in the following discussion that the new town concept is seen to encompass and interrelate several facets of urban public policies. It is claimed that, in a regional context, the new town concept offers a spatial framework to accommodate increased urban development. Fundamentally, it proposes that new development should be directed into relatively complete and autonomous urban units as opposed to the random pattern of urban development characteristic of most metropolitan suburban areas. Its regional or inter-community community rationale also provides a spatial framework for the physical organization and development of the internal community. Basically, new towns are envisioned as multi-purpose suburban communities (as opposed to dormitory or bedroom communities) which provide for living, working, and recreating within the community. These communities would be socially balanced in terms of their demographic composition and physically balanced in terms of the relationship of their land use composition to community infrastructure. Furthermore, the new town concept proposes (and relies upon) a process or system of development keyed to single ownership or control over new town land during the development period, which permits effective pre-planning and a direct relationship between planning and development.

Both the composition and system of development of the new town concept have been seen to offer significant potential for the satisfaction and interrelation of a variety of public and private objectives for urban development. Among other things, new towns have been promoted as a means for shortening the journey to work, the preservation of open spaces, fostering the development of regional mass transportation systems, creating community identity, and introducing greater variety, innovation, and aesthetic treatment into suburban development. It is also claimed that new towns are potentially beneficial to the central cities of metropolitan regions. Some proponents argue, for example, that new towns could be employed as relocation sites for those displaced from central city urban renewal sites, and that new town development processes might also be employed as a redevelopment measure. Although these claims are not necessarily held in concert or with equal enthusiasm by the various proponents, the new town concept appears to synthesize a number of physical and social objectives within a spatial framework and system of development, and ostensibly offers greater potential for controlling and ordering metropolitan expansion. The following chapters, after providing an historic overview and attempting to deal with the semantic difficulties inherent in the new town concept, elaborate upon these claims and finally analyze them in light of the operations of private developers, existing new towns legislation, and selected political, social, and economic characteristics of metropolitanism.

Notes

1. Morton and Lucia White, *The Intellectual Versus the City* (New York: Mentor, 1962).

2. Joseph S. Clark, "Cities in Crisis: An Ideological Problem," in Jeffrey Hadden, Louis Massotti, and Calvin Larson, eds., *Metropolis in Crisis* (Itasca, Illinois: Peacock, 1967), pp. 125-6.

3. "Theory and Research in Urban Sociology," *The Study of Urbanization,* ed. Hauser and Schnore (New York: John Wiley & Sons, 1965), pp. 157-59.

4. James Q. Wilson, "The War on Cities," *The Public Interest,* No. 3 (Spring 1966), 31. See also Irving Kristol, "It's Not a Bad Crisis to Live In," *The New York Times Magazine,* January 22, 1967, pp. 22ff.

5. Israel Stollman [Editorial], "Oh Yes We Can! Oh No You Can't!" *ASPO Newsletter,* XXXV, No. 2, (February 1969), 1.

6. See, for example, Edward C. Banfield, *The Unheavenly City,* (Boston: Little, Brown and Company, 1970), for some highly controversial perspectives on this point.

7. Marshall Kaplan, "The Roles of the Planner and Developer in the New Community," *Washington University Law Quarterly,* MCMLXV, No. 1 (February 1965), 100.

8. See Ebenezer Howard, *Garden Cities of Tomorrow* (3rd ed.; Cambridge: Massachusetts Institute of Technology Press, 1965). *Garden Cities of Tomorrow* was originally published in 1898 under the title *Tomorrow: A Peaceful Path to Reform,* and was republished under the current title in 1945 by Faber and Faber (London). As Lewis Mumford remarks in the preface to the current edition, "The Garden City Idea and Modern Planning," "*Garden Cities of Tomorrow* has done more than any other single book to guide the modern planning movement and to alter its objectives" (p. 29).

9. U.S., Congress, House, Hearings Before the Subcommittee on Banking and Currency on *Demonstration Cities, Housing and Urban Development, and Urban Mass Transit,* Vol. II, 89th Cong., 2d Sess. (Washington, D.C.: U.S. Government Printing Office, 1966), p. 1048.

10. Robert W. Murray, Jr., "New Towns for America," *House and Home,* XXV, No. 2 (February 1964), 123-30. Since the publication of this article, plans for several other large-scale developments have been announced. Some of these will be discussed in later chapters.

11. U.S., Congress, House, *Drafts of Bills Relating to Housing: Message of the President of the United States Relative to Drafts of Bills Relating to Housing,* Document No. 206, 88th Cong., 2d Sess. (Washington, D.C.: U.S. Government Printing Office, 1964), p. 6.

12. Public Law 89-754, 89th Cong., S. 3708, November 3, 1966, Title IV.

13. John C. Bollens and Henry J. Schmandt, *The Metropolis* (New York: Harper & Row, 1965), p. 13.

14. Ibid.

15. Advisory Commission on Intergovernmental Relations, *Governmental Structure, Organization and Planning in Metropolitan Areas* (Washington, D.C.: U.S. Government Printing Office, 1961), p. 6. These figures are based upon the U.S. Bureau of the Census definition of a Standard Metropolitan Statistical Area: "Except in New England, an SMSA is a county or group of contiguous counties which contains at least one city of 50,000 inhabitants or more or 'twin cities' with a combined population of at least 50,000. In addition to the county, or counties, containing such city or cities, contiguous counties are included in the SMSA if, according to certain criteria, they are essentially metropolitan in character and are socially and economically integrated with the central city."

16. The case for a national urban policy is argued by John Dyckman, "The Public and Private Rationale for a National Urban Policy," *Planning For a Nation of Cities,* ed. S. B. Warner, Jr. (Cambridge: M.I.T. Press, 1966), pp. 23-42.

2 An Historic Overview of New Town Development

The following discussion is a brief review of new town development throughout urban history, in order to identify the changes in purpose and application of new town building. The chapter divides into two periods, roughly separated by the appearance of the Howard thesis.

Many of the developments included would not be considered new towns by current standards. However, they will be referred to as such for the purposes of this discussion since they exhibit two of the fundamental elements of the new town concept—pre-established purposes and pre-planning.

Antecedents of the Modern New Town

The exact beginning of deliberate town planning and building may never be determined. However, the practice of town planning has been traced back to the earliest urban civilizations of different cultures. Recent archeological excavations have unearthed a settlement in India which may be the subcontinent's first, although it is yet to be determined if there are still earlier settlements beneath it. Nevertheless, the discovery of the ancient town of Kalibangan "shows that there was strict town planning in which streets criss-crossed each other, running north and south and east and west . . . [and] . . . there was also evidence of an underground drainage system.[1] In some cases the town plans have been identified in the form of wall paintings.

Evidence of town planning and building for special purposes was discovered in the small town of Kahun, Egypt (about 3000 B.C.). The town was little more than an arrangement of cells in rectangular blocks but is interesting in that it was deliberately laid out and built to house slaves and artisans who were constructing a pyramid. Although it was intended to be a temporary town, there is evidence of forethought in its layout, including drain channels in the center of the narrow streets.[2] Tel-El-Amarna, Egypt, completed about 1000 years after Kahun, was also an ancestor of the "company town," and was erected in a similar manner to provide for tomb-builders. It has also been discovered that a rural belt similar to present-day "greenbelts" which are often associated with new towns was established around the ancient Indian city of Madura.[3] However, many of the towns of antiquity demonstrate that there was little concern for housing conditions. Rather, town-building and site characteristics of this period show that high regard was given to temples, palaces, walls, and moats.

The first new towns founded for special purposes in Europe are reputed to have been constructed by the Greeks some 3000 years ago.[4] The Greeks founded these settlements for purposes of colonization, commerce, and absorption of population increases in the city-states. When the parent polis began to show signs of crowding or inefficiency resulting from population growth, it was customary to dispatch about 10,000 colonists to settle a politically independent new town. This population size appears to have been dictated by the limits of their technology and the food and water potentials of the sites.[5] Speirengen notes that the Greek new town was termed a "neopolis" until it grew large enough to necessitate another new town. The first town was then referred to as a "paleopolis." He adds that "Miletus, the hometown of Hippodamus, is said to have spawned some seventy or more new towns."[6]

Some of the Greek new towns were situated in order to provide ports for the larger cities which had been located inland to avoid attack by sea. Promontories were preferred as sites for these ports; in addition to defense, such locations facilitated escape to the hinterland and reduced the expense of building a complete wall.[7]

Hippodamus, born during the Hellenic period, may have been one of the first theorists of town planning. He is perhaps inaccurately credited with the gridiron street pattern (probably because he employed it indiscriminately), but according to Aristotle he was the first to advance principles regarding wide streets, better groupings of dwellings, and the location of town components around a central market place. Hippodamus may also have been one of the first new town planners, since he is also credited with the plans of the fifth century colonial new towns of Piraeus, Thurii, Rhodes, Selinus, and Cyrene.[8]

The Macedonian period also introduced several new towns, the most notable being Priene, which provided for a population of approximately 4,000 persons. It has been almost wholly preserved, demonstrating the influence of the Hippodamian grid. In contrast to the Greek new towns, those built under the influence of Alexander the Great (there were sixteen Alexandrias) were established for purposes of military strategy and the settlement of newly acquired territories. It has been estimated that nearly sixty new towns were constructed during this period, most of which have long since vanished or been built over with subsequent development.[9]

The advancement of town planning principles up to the end of the Hellenistic period have been summed up by one authority as

> ... predetermined size and design; a reasoned adaption to the physical conditions of carefully chosen sites; clear cut form and

17

protective enclosure; and a comprehensive and attractive communal centre as the focal and general assembly point of the town. It confirmed, moreover, the age-long practice that disposed the residential quarters of cities around the public or civic organization. . . . Their later towns being well planned, self-contained, and beautifully set in country, hillside, by rivers or the sea, there was no need at all for ruralized urbanism.[10]

The age of Roman power continued the new town building tradition of the Hellenistic era. The basis for the Roman boast that "all roads lead to Rome" was in part a string of *castra,* or military camps, that served both for the settlement of new domains and for their control during nearly three hundred years of empire-building. Roman camp-towns, some of which were eventually covered by major cities like London, were austere and generally lacking in aesthetic treatment. The Hippodamian grid evolved into the Roman chessboard with "insulae," or blocks, varying from seventy to two hundred and forty feet square, a layout which had many practical and strategic advantages. Aside from simplifying the task of survey, it was inexpensive to build and was easily policed, supervised, and defended. Most of these towns averaged under a square mile at the outset, but eventually many expanded beyond their original walls.

The Roman architect Marcus Vitruvius Pollio advanced several principles of town planning which are still applicable today. He addressed himself to the "choosing of sites for different purposes," emphasizing the towns' needs, the problems of location, and the suitability of land for different types of development. Vitruvius also reaffirmed the Greek town planning principle that the component parts of a town should be proportioned to the size of its population.[11]

The Dark Ages that followed the fall of the Roman Empire were more a period of city destruction than new town building. However, the eleventh century marked the beginning of some city restoration and expansion into new towns.

Medieval towns were generally small in area and population, but exhibited variety in their design. Most of the early examples demonstrate an irregular layout, although some later towns, most notably those in southern France, indicate that the formal pattern of the Roman new town was still influential. Some of the medieval town builders may have felt that an irregular street pattern would hamper an enemy's progress should the walls be overrun, although there remains some question as to whether these towns were actually irregular by design.

With the reappearance of strong rulers, new towns once again became a necessity, both to maintain control over conquered territories and to establish a system of commerce—generally in that order. Most of the new towns of this time were established around monasteries, feudal estates, and particularly bastides founded by the crown. There were some "neustadts" such as Aachen (Aix-La-Chapelle), Germany; but more is known of the part which planning played in the development of the French and English new towns.

The "villeneuves" of France were representative of both the formal and informal types of designs. An example of the former was the pre-planned bastide, Montpazier, founded in southern France in 1284. Montpazier was a totally rectilinear town planned in the tradition of the Roman-style camp with a centralized market place and arcades. The internal order of this bastide, as that of others in southern France, was fixed by definite military principles, which employed main thoroughfares from the central area to the main gates of the town. The founding of French new towns of that era has been described as a process whereby

> A site was first acquired and a name chosen, a rectilinear or square site being selected whenever possible; then the founder marked the central point of the new settlement. The new town was always protected by a wall and a ditch, but rarely by a citadel or castle in addition. [12]

Eventually the planning and building of new towns became a policy of some rulers. One English prince initiated about thirty new towns in France and many in England. For new town planners he sought

... the most clever and able, and those who best know how to divide, order and arrange a new town in the manner that will be most beneficial for us and for the merchants; and who shall be ready and willing to go for that purpose wherever we may send them.[13]

New town building in England lagged behind that in France, and it was not until the English prince returned from France to reign as Edward I that any large-scale efforts were undertaken. Prior to this there were a few examples in England and Wales, the Welsh towns bearing similarity in plot allotments to the bastides of southern France. There was always a garrison near the English new towns, and settlers were attracted by land grants and other economic and social privileges. Most new town settlement at this time was encouraged by barons and other regional potentates.

Edward, who had developed a considerable talent for site selection from his experience with the French new towns, attempted to relate new towns to regional purposes. He replaced some of the less efficient existing towns with new planned developments, again employing his French experience to attract settlers. On discovering that an old town, Winchelsea, was falling into the sea, he replaced it with a new one in a more suitable location. He also founded Kingston-Upon-Hull, where he personally selected the site, arranged for land acquisition, and provided for the diversion and construction of highways to service the port.[14]

The advent of the Renaissance marked a decline in the vast amount of new town building that had prevailed during the Middle Ages. With some exceptions, attention turned primarily to the expansion and improvement of existing urban centers. Most notable among these exceptions were new developments such as Richelieu, France (which was completely pre-planned), Mannheim and Karlsruhe, Germany, and St. Petersburg (Leningrad), Russia. Emphasis upon defensive features remained as the dominant characteristic in many towns, which largely conformed to the polygonal fortifications of the Vitruvian model. Karlsruhe demonstrates the influence of formalistic baroque design, as do others which were established to depict the authority of monarchy.

As a period of new thought and rebirth in intellectualism, the Renaissance fostered new thinking along the lines of model and ideal towns. For the most part, these ideas were related to military or social goals, ranging from practical solutions such as Scamozzio's heavily fortified town, Da Vinci's workers' satellite towns, and greenbelts for Milan to philosophical approaches such as More's Utopia.[15]

But it was perhaps more the general spirit of curiosity engendered by the late Renaissance that gave rise to conditions necessitating more new towns. Achievements in science and exploration generated changes in social, economic, political, and religious thinking. A new colonialism arose out of need for expansion, exploitation and escape. More important, the concomitant beginnings of the industrial revolution instigated a new force for urbanism.

Early settlements in America assumed many of the features of the European new communities. The gridiron pattern was the most dominant feature in their layout, but in some cases a radial pattern was used, either separately or superimposed over the grid. Some of the best known examples include Williamsburg, Virginia; Annapolis, Maryland; Savannah, Georgia; Philadelphia, and New Orleans. Williamsburg, settled in 1693 to provide a capital for the Virginia colony, had an original population of about three to four thousand. Both Philadelphia, laid out in 1682 by Thomas Holme, and Savannah, planned by James Oglethorpe in 1733, display a rigid adherence to the gridiron pattern spotted with equally spaced squares.

During the colonial expansion and up to the Revolution, the building of new towns continued in the settlement of gradually acquired territories. Of particular interest with regard to its design and purpose is Washington, D.C. The founding fathers, after much deliberation, selected the Potomac site in order to avoid the commercial environment of many of the already established cities. Its grand design and scale, which were originally determined by Pierre L'Enfant and later revised by Andrew Ellicott, appealed to aristocratic tastes and also affected the design of other new settlements such as Buffalo (1800), and Detroit (1807). As a new town, Washington was probably the largest up to that time, and its layout of broad radial boulevards superimposed over a grid invited expansion.[16]

The New Towns Movement

With industrialization, the city changed fundamentally from what it had been for over 5,000 years. As Mumford phrased it, the city had burst its container. The transformation from ruralism to urbanism is perhaps most striking in terms of the rate at which it took place. Kingsley Davis states,

> By 1801 nearly a tenth of the people of England and Wales were living in cities of 100,00 or larger. This proportion doubled in 40 years and doubled again in another 60 years. By 1900 Britain was an urbanized society. In general, the later each country became industrialized, the faster was its urbanization. The change from a population with 10 percent of its members in cities of 100,000 or larger to one in which 30 percent lived in such cities took about 79 years in England and Wales, 66 in the U.S., 48 in Germany, 36 in Japan and 26 in Australia.[17]

What is often described as the new towns movement had its beginnings in the era of the industrial city near the end of the nineteenth century. No attempt is made here to summarize the urban conditions at that time nor the sweeping social and economic changes which took place and were manifested most dramatically in the growth and change of the city. It is only stated that the new towns movement, like the city planning movement of which it is a part, had its roots in the reform era which arose as a reaction to the physical, social and economic conditions of the late nineteenth century.[18]

Ebenezer Howard (1850—1928)

The origins of the new towns movement can be found in writings of many reformers, but as Rodwin points out, "the notion of recasting our urban environment in the form of garden cities owes its contemporary formulation to Ebenezer Howard.[19] The Howard thesis probably had more influence on new town development and city planning than any other single approach to urban problems.

What made Howard the progenitor of the new towns movement and distinguished him from many other social reformers of his time was his pragmatism. He not only set his ideas down in some detail, but actively promoted them through the formation of the Garden Cities Association[20] and later in the promotion of the Garden Cities of Letchworth and Welwyn.

Howard's Garden City idea was conceived to bring together the best elements of town and country life, as expressed by the author in his metaphor of the three magnets:

> There are in reality not only, as is so constantly assumed, two alternatives—town life and country life—but a third alternative, in which all the advantages of the most energetic and active town life, with all the beauty and delight of the country, may be secured in perfect combination; and the certainty of being able to live this life will be the magnet which will produce the effect for which we are all striving—the spontaneous movement of the people from our crowded cities to the bosom of our kindly mother earth, at once the source of life, of happiness, of wealth, and of power. The town and the country may, therefore, be regarded as two magnets, each striving to draw the people to itself—a rivalry which a new form of life, partaking of the nature of both, comes to take part in.
>
> Town and Country *must be married,* and out of this joyous union will spring a new hope, a new life, a new civilization. It is the purpose of this work to show how a first step can be taken in this direction by the construction of a Town-country magnet; and I hope to convince the reader that this is practicable, here and

now, and that on principles which are the very soundest, whether viewed from the ethical or the economic standpoint.[21]

Convinced of the validity of his general theme, Howard proceeded to set down a detailed formula for the Garden City in physical, and particularly, fiscal terms. Although he presented the physical scheme for Garden City in symmetrical form (on which he noted "A diagram only—plan must depend upon site selected."),[22] he included many features found in current new towns. Garden City was divided into six wards, or neighborhoods, which faced inward upon parks and contained a school at their center. The wards were bounded by radial boulevards and a circumferential railway. In many respects Howard's wards were the prototype of the "neighborhood superblock" which was later refined in the Stein and Wright plan for Radburn, N.J.[23] Industries were to be located at the periphery of the town within easy access of the neighborhoods and serviced by the circumferential railway.

By Garden City, Howard meant "a city in a garden" rather than a city of gardens. He proposed to provide the physical boundaries for the town with his greenbelt, within which he placed the hinterland activities for the support of Garden City and envisioned sites for such diverse uses as convalescent homes and farms for epileptics.

However, the main purpose of the Garden City scheme appears to have been to provide a visual foundation for major discussion in his book—the economics of the building and operation of Garden City. Howard entered into considerable detail in discussing the economics of his scheme, but he also provides his reader with a summary of his argument:

The economies with which we have thus dealt are, it will be seen, effected by the two simple expedients we have referred to. First, by buying the land *before* a new value is given to it by migration, the migrating people obtain a site at an extremely low figure, and secure the coming increment for themselves and those who come after them; and secondly, by coming to a new site, they do not have to pay large sums for old buildings, for compensation for disturbance, and for heavy legal charges.[24]

Howard's primary intention was to secure the "unearned increment" in the rising value of Garden City land for the residents of the community. The land upon which Garden City was to be erected would be "held in trust for the community." Although he allowed that rents might still rise considerably in the new town, Howard asserted that the incremental value given to land by those migrating to the community would be applied in relief of rates. The rising value of the land would become the property of the community rather than that of individuals.[25]

The second feature of Howard's economic scheme refers to his comparison of the costs of improving "any old city like London" and building a new town. For example, he notes that land acquisition costs for the London School Board, "including old buildings, business-disturbance, law changes, etc.," averaged £ 9,500 per acre, compared to £ 40 per acre in Garden City.[26]

Through the combination of these advantages in Garden City, Howard calculated that the total cost of all land in the publicly acquired 1,000-acre townsite could be reduced to less than one shilling and one penny annually for each of the town's 30,000 residents. The cost of the acquiring the land under his scheme would be almost totally recaptured by the community.[27]

Howard also felt that planning would provide further economic justification of the Garden City idea. Although he admitted that the fact that Garden City would be a planned community was "an element of economy which will be simply incalculable," he was convinced economies would be realized through better planning. He argued that the planning of the town would "be the work of many minds—the minds of engineers, of architects and surveyors, of landscape gardeners and electricians," but that it would be planned as a whole with "unity of design and purpose." Growth would be staged to provide for unified development throughout the building process.

More specifically, Howard emphasized that

> Garden City is not only planned, but it is planned with a view to the very latest of modern requirements, and it is obviously always easier, and usually far more economical and and completely satisfactory, to make out of fresh material a new instrument than to patch up and alter an old one.[28]

Howard's book and his views attracted considerable attention and favorable review, and in 1903 a company, First Garden City Limited, attempted to demonstrate the feasibility of the Garden City idea in the building of Letchworth, about 34 miles from London. Rodwin points out that this location, coupled with managerial and financial problems, caused the town to grow slowly. It did not provide its investors the expected return, but apparently these difficulties did not deter Howard from securing in 1920 a site for a second Garden City, Welwyn, about 14 miles closer to London. The second Garden City also encountered difficulties, particularly financial. Two managerial reorganizations produced very little profit for shareholders. Despite its problems, Welwyn grew to a population of 18,500 by 1948, at which time its development was taken over by a public development corporation under the new towns program.[29]

Although the two Garden City experiments pointed up some of the difficulties of transfering Howard's general scheme to reality, it is evident that the initial objectives of the enterprises were successful. As Rodwin observes:

> Despite all the mistakes and obstacles, the towns were built; and because they were built, they have provided an enduring three-dimensional expression of the general ideas for all the world to see. In the process of development, the towns also pioneered some significant planning innovations, including use and density zoning, a form of ward or neighborhood planning, employment of an agricultural greenbelt to control urban size, and unified urban land ownership for the purpose of capturing rising land

values for the benefit of the residents. A body of experience was also accumulated which gave some inkling of the difficulties ahead and some of the necessary conditions for execution of any larger program.[30]

Thus developed in a relatively short period of time a synthesized philosophy for the treatment of urban expansion at both the regional and local level, a formal organization for its promotion, and two demonstrations of its application. The more general outgrowth of the Garden City idea was a recasting of the new town idea in terms of both existing and emerging needs and problems of urban expansion. The Garden City movement had its strongest impact as a major influence in the formulation of the United Kingdom's new towns policy, the first comprehensive attempt to utilize the new town idea as a framework for metropolitan and regional development.*

New Towns in Other Nations

It is difficult to assess the impact of the Garden City and the British program upon other nations, but the international appeal of Howard's ideas is witnessed by the fact that, by 1913, there were Garden Cities associations in seven countries other than the United Kingdom and an international federation. So-called Garden Cities were built in several nations, but as Osborn points out, the principles of the idea were often misinterpreted and misapplied. He observed that many of these developments, particularly those constructed up to World War II, were actually little more than planned dormitory suburbs, either by design or as a result of

*This is not to suggest that the New Towns Act of 1946 was passed solely on the merits of the Howard thesis or the efforts of new town enthusiasts. It was, in fact, a confluence of circumstances and problems to which the new town idea offered reasonable solutions which led to the national policy. Overcrowding in cities, the loss of agricultural land from urban expansion, the bombings during the war, and the postwar victory of the Labor party combined to produce the necessary needs and political climate.

circumstances which inhibited their development into more complete new towns.[31]

The varied applications of the new town idea make generalization difficult. New towns have been or are now being built in over fifty nations. The purposes for which they are being founded vary within a single country as well as among nations. Moreover, some countries have national programs.

The Soviet Union has probably founded more new towns than any other nation, reputedly more than 800 between 1926 and 1963. About one third of these have been situated in totally undeveloped areas, with the majority in the eastern regions of the nation. Russian new towns have been developed for a variety of purposes, but they can generally be catagorized as part of broad schemes for national development and decentralization of industry. Many of the earlier Soviet new towns were connected with extractive industries and hydro-electric power projects, and later expanded with the development of manufacturing.

The majority of Soviet new towns have populations around 50,000; however, about 100 are larger, some having developed as regional centers with populations of 300,000 to 500,000.[32] However, despite demographic policies and strong control by the state, the use of satellite new towns to control growth in major urban centers has been unsuccessful, particularly around Moscow.[33]

A country which has more recently embarked upon a program of planned decentralization is Israel. Three urban centers contained most of the new nation's population, which was expected to double from immigration. These conditions prompted the establishment of Israel's national new towns program.

Originally, Israel had intended to build thirty new towns, relatively small, to serve as regional centers for the Kibbutzim. Ashdod, the largest, was established to create a new port to relieve Haifa. However, because of difficulties in attracting industry, lack of amenities, and unattractive locations of some of the new towns, the decision was made to concentrate upon construction of only four or five new towns with larger planned populations. Ashdod was re-designed from a planned population of 150,000 to an ultimate population of 350,000, and other towns were re-planned for lower populations.[34]

Like those in the United Kingdom, most of the new towns in the highly urbanized Netherlands are intended to relieve population pressures on major urban centers. Most of the postwar new towns were situated as planned expansions; however, newer developments are intended to spread growth into less developed areas and into the polders.

Other countries in which several new towns have been built or are under construction are:

Canada: mostly single-enterprise new communities built by industrial companies associated with mining and production of paper and aluminum. Canadian new towns vary from the completely planned Kitimat, British Columbia to towns which have been simply surveyed and subdivided.[35]

Germany: several industrial new towns associated with heavy industry and automobile production.

France: concentration upon planned extensions of existing cities and satellite towns. Plans are currently being developed to establish several large new towns near Paris.

South Africa: several new towns built around gold-mining, industry and chemicals.

Sweden: new towns built in association with mining and industry, and the renowned Stockholm planned satellites.

New Towns in America

In 1939, case studies were made by Wehrly and Comey for the Urbanism Committee of the Natural Resources Committee of "144 of those comparatively few communities which, unlike the ordinary city, have actually been constructed from the start according to a more or less comprehensive physical plan."[36] Few of the communities studied were complete new towns; many were actually satellites to existing cities or planned communities within cities or company towns. The main criterion for selection in the study was that they were in varying degrees pre-planned. However, the Committee's findings are useful here since they emphasize the types of developers and their objectives. The authors state that

> Of the communities studied, those founded by industry constitute over one-half (53.3 percent) of the total; by private developers for urban residential purposes, over one-fourth (27.7 percent); and for rural and agricultural residential purposes, over one-tenth (10.4 percent). War housing towns and villages make up 7.6 percent; and miscellaneous developments, 2.8 percent.[37]

Due to the large number of planned communities which have been founded in the United States, any survey must be selective. The following discussion classifies planned communities and new towns according to the auspices under which they were founded and constructed in order to identify general trends.

Towns Founded by Industry

Industry had an early dominant role as a founder of communities in America. Many of the old-fashioned "company towns" which were built during the early days of American industrial development were completely owned and dominated by their founding industries. Total ownership of land, housing and facilities was usually maintained to control employees and not necessarily to insure orderly development of the land.

The new towns of industrial enterprises varied; examples are to be found among them which have both advanced and retarded the development of town planning techniques. Some were single industry towns, while others have attracted several industrial tenants. They also differed in plan, type of housing, extent of community facilities, land ownership, and control over development. However, the industries generally involved, at least initially, tended to be concerned with early stage production or extraction processes. Consequently, many industrial new towns, like many of other nations, appeared to be more resource- than market-oriented.[38]

However, several industrial new towns changed after the period of the company town. With the demands of the labor movement, increasing competition, population mobility, and other conditions affecting their monopolistic or semi-monopolistic positions, many industries found an interest in the community life to be a valuable fringe benefit to offer existing and potential employees. Well-planned and administered communities created more mutually satisfying labor-company relations, and increased competitive advantages for technically trained personnel. Moreover, many industries grew large enough to be financially able to invest in community building. Community planning and land use controls were employed to protect both these investments and the interests of employees.[39]

The single ownership of land in most of the industrial new towns also provided a strong control over the development of the plan. As Henry Churchill observed:

> These industrial towns and projects seem to definitely demonstrate the value of unified and strong control of land use. The appearance and integrity of the character of the development is rapidly lost in towns which have reverted to "normal" municipal practices, such as Kingsport, and Longview. Company-owned villages such as Hopedale, or even Alcoa (where most of the land is still company-owned although the government is normal), tend to retain the advantages of their plan.[40]

Churchill's observation is appropriate in the case of Kingsport, where inadequate land use controls resulted in an additional 5,000 population living around the periphery in shack housing. In contrast, Alcoa Aluminum Company obtained and retained title of land at the periphery "to form an effective physical barrier to undesirable growth."[41]

Although many new industrial towns have been constructed in North America, observers of new town development have given most attention to the Aluminum Company of Canada's Kitimat, British Columbia, founded in 1952. In the development of its master plan, the Kitimat staff of consultants included not only planners, architects and engineers but also authorities on government, administration, and conservation and experts on climatology, education, family life and community living.

> . . . a unique double command was set at the head—a consultant and his aides concerned with over-all policy and guidance, only, paralleled by a physical planning team concerned with implementation. Both were greatly aided by a company planning division created for liaison and continuing action . . . continuity was assured by retention of the planners as consultants.[42]

In designing Kitimat, planners drew heavily upon past experiences with the "neighborhood unit principle," the planned industrial park, the Radburn scheme for traffic separation, the greenbelt principle, and some of the development practices of the British new towns. These features were undoubtedly influenced by the presence on the staff of Clarence Stein, an admirer of the British new towns and planner of Radburn. Kitimat is planned for a population of about 50,000 which, by means of a staged process of development, is to be routed into successively developed neighborhoods. Since Alcan hopes to attract other industrial tenants, the fourth phase of development is based upon the population growth which would result from their addition.

Towns Founded by Government

The United States has never had a national policy for the development of new towns such as those of Great Britain, the Soviet Union, and Israel. Rather, the communities founded directly by the U.S. Government and its agencies are products of particular needs. Although the agencies of government involved have undertaken various types of development, very few of their developments have reached the scale of new towns. With regard to size and location, the majority are roughly comparable to those founded by industries. Both of these factors are closely related to their special purposes. The most dominant of these purposes have been for or in connection with: wartime industry and housing (Brooklawn, N.J., Cradock and Hilton, Va., and Fairlawn, N.J.); strategic operations (Oak Ridge, Tenn., Los Alamos, N.M., and Richland, Wash.); and regional resource development (Norris, Tenn., and Boulder City, Nevada). Others, particularly the Greenbelt Towns of the Resettlement Administration, are most accurately classified as demonstration or experimental projects.

Owing to their special purposes, the community function of many of these towns (with the exception of the Greenbelt Towns) was ancillary to the particular government projects with which they were associated. Planning and development of community facilities were given detailed consideration in most cases insofar as the immediate needs related to the special project were concerned, but since many communities were intended to be temporary, long-range planning for expansion was usually not included. For some, such as Oak Ridge and Los Alamos, a transition from temporary to permanent status was successful due to well-conceived extensions and updating of the original plans. In view of the rapid pace at which the AEC towns were developed, they are considered to have been well-planned. Also, they grew much larger than previous towns related to wartime projects. After ten years their populations were: over 31,000 at Oak Ridge, about 23,000 at Richland, and about 13,000 at Los Alamos.[43]

Another example of a specific purpose new town founded by a government agency was Norris, Tenn., planned by the Land Planning and Housing Division of TVA in 1934. In many respects, Norris was similar to the war housing and AEC towns: it was related to a specific government project (the first of the TVA dams); it was small (population by 1938 was only 1,250); and its immediate objective was provision of housing for project workers. However, Norris was planned as a permanent town from the outset, and was eventually auctioned and incorporated by its residents.[44]

Perhaps the most renowned of all the new towns founded by agencies of government are the Greenbelt Towns, which came closest to utilizing the principles of the Garden City idea. Originally, the Greenbelt project was to have included eight communities, but after budget cuts only four were planned. Of these, three were eventually constructed: Greenbelt, Maryland; Greendale, Wisconsin; and Greenhills, Ohio. Officially, the purposes of the Greenbelt projects were:

1. to give useful work to men on employment relief,
2. to demonstrate in practice the soundness of planning and operating towns according to certain Garden City principles,
3. to provide low rent housing in healthful surroundings, both physical and social for families that are in the low income brackets.[45]

The planning of the Greenbelt Towns was based on the application of three basic principles: the Garden City, the Radburn Idea, and the Neighborhood Unit. However, each town was planned by a different team, and their treatment of these ideas varied. The greenbelt principle, from which the program derived its name, also became an integral part of the plans for these towns and was intended to provide a balance between urban and rural land use areas, a geographic limitation for the size and density of the community, and a wall of protection from external encroachment.[46]

The last Greenbelt Town was sold to private interests in 1954. Individually and as a group they were a financial loss to the Federal government, returning only about 53 percent of their combined cost of $36,200,910.[47] With their sale appears to have ended the brief direct role of the Federal government in the planning and building of new towns not for specific projects.*

*The most recent example of a potential government-sponsored new town in connection with a specific project is the Nevada Test Site Community, which is

34

One other pre-World War II planned community, Radburn, N.J., merits special mention because of its relationship to the Garden City idea and its influence upon principles of new town design. Radburn's planners, Clarence Stein and Henry Wright, were greatly influenced by Howard, and undertook the project (sponsored by The City Housing Corporation of New York) with the intention of designing America's first Garden City. Basically, the Radburn plan employed the "superblock." Stein and Wright also inverted the greenbelt by placing the green areas within the residential areas. The superblocks provided for a specialized internal traffic system of their own and afforded a nearly complete separation of pedestrian and vehicular traffic. Isolation of vehicular traffic was made possible through the use of cul-de-sac streets which penetrated into the periphery of the superblocks from collector roads. Houses faced upon interior parklands containing elementary schools and activity areas, rather than upon streets. The superblocks were interconnected by a series of over- and under-passes. Although the Depression kept Radburn from ever being completed as planned, the influence of these design concepts is to be seen in several British and American new towns.

Other Sponsors of New Towns

In recent years, a new phase of new town building has developed, characterized particularly by the advent of the large-scale land developer and the renewed interest of large industrial corporations in the financial and experimental advantages of new town development. Large increases in population growth, higher incomes, increased mobility, and the expansion of credit appear to be the underlying factors of this trend.

intended to be located at or near the Nuclear Rocket Development Station, 90 miles from Las Vegas. Bills were introduced in Congress in 1963 (H.R. 8003 and S. 2030, 88th Cong., 1st Sess.), to authorize the community. Hearings were conducted by the Joint Committee on Atomic Energy, but no further action has been taken on the bills.

Although a few postwar private new town developments are the forerunners of large-scale private new town development, the trend, for the most part, has been a phenomenon of the 1960's. In the past few years, new town development in various parts of the country has constituted what some observers consider to be a significant portion of U.S. building activity. Murray states, for example, that

Across the U.S. there are at least 75 completely planned communities of 1,000 or more acres where developers are creating facilities to house more than 6 million people. And by 1985 when these new towns should be completed, their aggregate built-up value will probably exceed $75 billion . . . equal to more than three years' total U.S. housing production. Yet these big new communities are in or on the edge of metropolitan areas, most particularly in areas of the greatest population growth. In five years, these new towns may well account for 9 percent of our annual housing output.[48]

This trend, which has generated widespread discussion and speculation as to the potential of the new town concept as a major component of national and metropolitan development plans, is discussed in detail in Chapter 5. The following chapter attempts to deal with some of the semantic hurdles which arise to plague any discussion of this subject.

Notes

1. "India Unearths Old Civilization," *The New York Times,* August 30, 1964, p. 8.

2. U.S. National Resources Committee, *Urban Planning and Land Policies,* II of the Supplementary Report of the Urbanism Committee to the National Resources Committee (Washington, D.C.: U.S. Government Printing Office, 1939), p. 12. Part one of this report was prepared by Arthur C. Comey and Max S. Wehrly.

3. Ibid., p. 14.

4. Cecil Stewart, *A Prospect of Cities* (London: Longmans-Green, 1952), p. 4.

5. Arthur Gallion and Simon Eisner, *The Urban Pattern* (Princeton: Van Nostrand, 1960), p. 19.

6. Paul D. Speirengen, *Urban Design: The Architecture of Towns and Cities* (New York: McGraw-Hill, 1965), p. 5.

7. Stewart, op. cit., pp. 13-14.

8. U.S. National Resources Committee, op. cit., pp. 12-13.

9. Stewart, op. cit., pp. 18-19.

10. Fredrick Hiorns, *Town-Building in History* (London: Harrap, 1956), p. 44.

11. Thomas Adams, *Outline of Town and City Planning* (New York: Russell Sage, 1935), pp. 73-76.

12. Ibid., p. 86.

13. Ibid., p. 88 and relevant note.

14. Ibid., pp. 91-96.

15. U.S. National Resources Committee, op. cit., p. 15.

16. Carl Feiss, "New Towns for America," *Journal of the American Institute of Architects,* XXXIII, No. 1 (January 1960), 86.

17. Kingsley Davis, "The Urbanization of the Human Population," *Scientific American,* CCXIII, No. 3 (September 1965), 43.

18. See, for example, William Petersen, "The Ideological Origins of Britain's New Towns," *Journal of American Institute of Planners,* XXXIV, No. 3 (May 1968), 160-170.

19. Lloyd Rodwin, *The British New Towns Policy* (Cambridge: Harvard University Press, 1956), p. 9.

20. The Garden Cities Association was later renamed The Garden Cities and Town Planning Association, and is presently known as the Town and Country Planning Association, publishers of *Town and Country Planning.* For an account of the history and influence of the Town and Country Planning Association, see Donald L. Foley, "Idea and Influence: The Town and Country Planning Association," *Journal of the American Institute of Planners,* XXVIII, No. 1 (February 1962), 10–17.

21. Ebenezer Howard, *Garden Cities of Tomorrow* (3rd ed.; Cambridge: M.I.T. Press 1965), pp. 45-46 and 48.

22. Ibid., pp. 52–53.

23. Humphrey Carver, *Cities in the Suburbs* (Toronto: University of Toronto Press, 1962), p. 34.

24. Howard, op. cit., p. 75.

25. Ibid., p. 59.

26. Ibid., p. 73.

27. Ibid., pp. 66-67.

28. Ibid., p. 77.

29. Rodwin, op. cit., pp. 13-15; F. J. Osborn and A. Whittick, *The New Towns* (New York: McGraw-Hill, 1963), p. 52.

30. Rodwin, op. cit., p. 15.

31. Osborn and Whittick, op. cit., pp. 137-138.

32. V. Shkvarikov, M. Haucke, and O. Smirnova, "The Building of New Towns in the USSR," *Ekistics,* XVIII, No. 108 (November 1964), 307.

33. R. H. Anderson, "Soviet Urban Sprawl Defies Official Efforts to Curb the Growth of Cities," *The New York Times,* November 13, 1966.

34. Lord Silkin, "Israel's New Town Programme," *Town and Country Planning,* XXXV, No. 3 (March 1967), 146-147. For a detailed account of the Israeli program see Erika Spiegel, *New Towns in Israel* (Stuttgart: Verlag, 1966).

35. Harry A. Walker, "Canadian 'New Towns,' " *Community Planning Review,* IV (1954), 80-87.

36. U.S. National Resources Committee, op. cit., p. 3.

37. Ibid.

38. Ibid.

39. Christopher Tunnard, *The City of Man* (New York: Scribner's, 1953), pp. 158-175.

40. Henry S. Churchill, *The City is the People* (New York: Norton, 1962), pp. 76-77.

41. U.S. National Resources Committee, op. cit., pp. 21-24; 35-39.

42. "Industry Builds Kitimat," *Architectural Forum,* CI, No. 1 (July 1954), 130.

43. Carroll A. Towne, "Atomic Energy Community Developments," *Landscape Architecture,* XLIII, No. 3 (April 1953), 119-120.

44. John H. Kyle, *The Building of TVA* (Baton Rouge: Louisiana State University Press, 1958), pp. 15-18.

45. Clarence Stein, *Toward New Towns for America* (New York: Reinhold, 1957), p. 119.

46. Lewis Mumford, in introduction to O. Kline Fulmer, *Greenbelt* (Washington, D.C.: American Council on Public Affairs, 1941), p. 2.

47. Paul K. Conkin, *Tomorrow a New World: The New Deal Community Program* (Binghamton: Cornell University Press, 1959), p. 325.

48. Robert W. Murray, Jr., "New Towns for America," *House and Home,* XXV, No. 2 (February, 1964), p. 123. Out of context, Murray's statement would appear to suggest that new towns have emerged in

many parts of the nation. Actually, as discussed in a chapter to follow, the pattern of private new town development has not been that geographically widespread.

3   Elements of the New Town Concept

The primary purpose of this chapter is to discuss the elements of the new town concept as a basis for reference and comparison in the following analysis. There does not appear to be, at this writing, any single or universally accepted definition or description of what constitutes a new town. The following discussion does not purport to establish such a definition; rather, it attempts to distill from other descriptions what the writer feels are the major elements of the new town concept and how those elements distinguish the new town from other forms of urban development.

The Problem of Definition

Part of the problem in defining "new town" is the matter of perspective; it has been described from a number of varying points of view. This problem, however, is not unique to new towns. The word "city," for example, has never been defined to general satisfaction. As Wirth observed in 1938:

> Despite the preponderant significance of the city in our civiliza-
> tion . . . , our knowledge of the nature of urbanism and the

process of urbanization is meager. Many attempts have indeed been made to isolate the distinguishing characteristics of urban life. Geographers, historians, economists, and political scientists have incorporated the points of view of their respective disciplines into diverse definitions of the city.[1]

The difficulties associated with establishing an inclusive definition of the city led Wirth to qualify his own definition, in which he concluded that "for sociological purposes a city may be defined as a relatively large, dense, and permanent settlement of socially heterogeneous individuals."[2] However, as Sjoberg has pointed out, the matter of a widely acceptable definition among sociologists is by no means settled.[3] Weber's institutional definition of a "full urban community" contrasts temporally as well as conceptually with Wirth's—"1) a fortification, 2) a market, 3) a court of its own and at least partially autonomous law, 4) a related form of association, and, 5) at least partial autonomy and autocephaly. . . ."[4] Other major variables in definitions are political, economic, demographic, and environmental.

Problems of definition are also compounded by the creation of descriptive terminology to distinguish among the characteristics of urban areas. For example, Webber observes:

In the literature and the popular mind, the idea of a city is imprecise: the terms "city," "urban," "metropolitan," and the various other synonyms are applied to a wide variety of phenomena. Sometimes we speak of the city as though it were simply an artifact—an agglomeration of buildings, roads, and interstitial spaces that marks the settlements of large numbers of people. On other occasions we refer not to the physical buildings, but to concentrations of physical bodies of humans, as they accumulate in nodal concentrations at higher densities than in "nonurban" places. At other times we refer to the spatial concentration of the places at which human activities are conducted. At still other times we mean a particular set of institutions that mark urban systems of human organization, where we mean to identify the organizational arrangements through which human activities are related to each other—the formal and the informal role allocating systems and the authority systems controlling human behavior. In turn, we sometimes refer to patterns of behavior, and sometimes we mean to distinguish the social value systems of those people and groups that are "urban" from those that are "nonurban."[5]

New towns, as forms of urbanization, present similar problems of definition. Most people appear to define or describe "new town" to suit their particular viewpoint. A definition may emphasize physical, social, environmental, legal, or organizational factors. Some definitions tend to be more philosophical than descriptive, others tend to set down precise formulae for the establishment of new towns.

To some degree, as in the case of the city, understanding is obscured by the different terms used to describe new towns or developments. "New communities," "planned communities," "satellite towns," "new cities," "greenbelt towns," and "garden cities" are some of the alternative labels for large-scale planned developments. Although "new town" is the most common rubric, these terms are in some cases employed interchangeably. In other cases, it is felt that certain distinguishing characteristics warrant the use of a term other than "new town."* A commonly accepted label may not be a necessity, but the variety of terms used is indicative of the confusion which often surrounds discussion of the subject. The proceedings of a recent conference concerning new towns in the United States illustrates that the definition problem often defies solution. It reported that

> The two-day conference on "New Towns" wasted no time in pinpointing two basic problems of New Towns: What are New Towns? Isn't there a better name for them? After each of those described his interest in New Towns, generally, by telling something about his own current project, the meeting sought to find a working definition. It proved elusive.[6]

*The writer has chosen to use "new town" because it is the most common term used. However, it will be noted that the literature used throughout this analysis employs other of the above terms. In most cases no distinction will be made by the writer unless it would clarify the discussion.

A second point of confusion arises from the fact that, as Secretary Weaver has noted

> Regretfully, one notes that much that has been written on the subject in this country describes European experience and then proposes a reproduction of it in the United States. Without going into details at this point, let it be noted that we cannot successfully recreate in this nation approaches and programs which have evolved out of a somewhat different European environment. Recognition of this fact led me a year ago to speak of "new communities" rather than "new towns" in America.[7]

Weaver's decision to use the term "new community" appears to have been primarily to allay fears which in the past have arisen at the mere mention of "new towns," in that the latter meant to some the adoption of Federal control over development and other "socialistic" characteristics of the British new towns policy. The purpose of the new term seems to be to distinguish the governmental processes which would be involved rather than to indicate any difference in the towns themselves.

Much misunderstanding arises from the nature of the new town concept itself. It is one that has always held a unique attractiveness, that of offering the opportunity to apply fresh solutions, relatively unencumbered by existing development. There has been a tendency on the part of some proponents of the idea to regard new towns as a panacea for urban problems. Consequently, it is sometimes viewed by others as a utopian or socialistic scheme, or as a fad, rather than as a serious proposal.

Some Definitions of the New Town

The variety of existing terms is indicative of the lack of a commonly accepted definition of the new town concept.

Ebenezer Howard, who is sometimes referred to as the progenitor of the idea, often used the term new town interchangeably with the term Garden City, and offered a definition which summarized the major elements of his thesis:

A Garden City is a town designed for healthy living and industry; of a size that makes possible the full measure of social life, but not larger; surrounded by a rural belt; the whole of the land being in public ownership or held in trust for the community.[8]

Some more recent definitions of new towns exhibit greater detail and more precise requirements. One, for example, states that

By "new towns" we mean first of all towns built on a site without any urban concentrations—towns which are large enough to have an independent existence, in other words, self-contained towns with commercial, educational, social and cultural institutions that satisfy all the needs of families and individuals alike; above all, the towns must have a sufficient number of industrial enterprises to create a wide labor market. Such towns are fundamentally different from "satellite towns," where workers are dependent upon another urban centre which may, or may not, be easily accessible, or from towns enlarged by new districts, which meet other needs and raise other problems. They are also different from towns that have been almost entirely destroyed and have been rebuilt on the same site. . . .[9]

Secretary Weaver, in testimony on the 1964 housing bills, offered the following description of a "new community":

A new community is distinguished even from a large subdivision partly by size and location. It should, normally, be planned for a population of 25,000 or more, and some are now being planned for populations of 100,000 or more. It need not be established on wholly undeveloped land, and may even be built around the nucleus of a small existing community, but it requires large tracts of land and, unlike the usual subdivision, will as a practical matter usually be found some distance beyond the nearest built-up area. More basically, however, the new community differs from the usual subdivision by reason of the fact that it is planned so as to provide within its limits, more of the amenities and services required for daily living.[10]

However, the definition submitted in the *Drafts of Bills Relating to Housing* in 1964 differed from Secretary Weaver's definition. Omitting the matter of suggested population ranges and distinctions from conventional subdivisions, the bill stated that

> The term new community means a locality so established and planned as to provide, on a balanced and internally cohesive basis, the housing, facilities, services, and amenities suitable for appropriate living.[11]

Another definition sets aside the question of a common label and raises a fundamental question concerning the new town as a tool of public policy. Feiss offers that

> A new town or for that matter a new village or new city, is in contemporary terms, any completely designed and built new community in which are to be found all the elements of a complete urban settlement regardless of size. This means that there would be within such a new community not only residence but also commercial and industrial areas, schools and recreation areas, and all services and facilities necessary for the establishment and maintenance of a full-time, full-scale, administrative, economic, and social unit. A new town may be built by public or private means or a combination of both. It may be located as a satellite community to a central urban area or it may be in an isolated location. It may be an isolated area within a greenbelt surrounded by urban sprawl. A new town may be of any size, any mixture of percentages of types of residential and industrial uses. It may be designed or undesigned depending upon the nature of the sponsorship and the interest of the people involved. There is nothing complex about the concept of the new town. The only complex problem is to find the reason why the new town idea is not acceptable to the American people.[12]

Feiss's definition contrasts with the more rigid and precise definition above of Suquet-Bonnaud cited above and contains a number of internal inconsistencies. For example, it states initially that a new town is ". . . any completely designed and built new community . . ." and later states that a new town may be ". . . designed or undesigned . . ." Furthermore, it raises but does not answer the question as to what point a development may be considered to be a new town, or when can it be distinguished when a new town of ". . . any size, any mixture of percentages of types of residential and industrial uses . . ." constitutes a ". . . full-time, full-scale, administrative, economic and social unit."

Others feel that the distinguishing feature of new towns must be an advancement of urban design or a quality of up-to-dateness. Geer, for example,

> . . . would like to limit the term "new towns" to those which have contributed in some considerable measure to our knowledge of better urban living. Most new towns, because they are consciously designed, have produced better urban results than we have obtained by adding a thousand little subdivisions to an existing city. We should include as part of our definition of the term "new town" a statement of design concept, procedures and standards.[13]

Eichler and Kaplan feel that the major difference between European new towns and American "new communities" revolves around the "degree of 'self-sufficiency'." They emphasize that ". . . a new community is much less self-sufficient than a new town."[14]

Several other definitions might be referred to here, but they would only belabor the point that there is no generally accepted definition of the new town, and that many definitions tend to emphasize a particular point of view. The variety of definitions for "new town," like that of "city," appears to indicate that a widely acceptable definition of the new town is probably unattainable. As with any dynamic process, definitions or descriptions of the physical manifestations of urbanization, in whatever form, can only reflect a limited perception at a point in time.

Elements of the New Town Concept

The following discussion will attempt to distill from the diversity of thought on the subject some of the basic features of the new town concept. The approach focuses upon the nature of new town development—that is, characteristics of the development of new towns which appear to distinguish them from other forms of urban development. The general approach draws upon and seeks generalizations from past and present experience in new town development.

The Purposes of New Towns

Probably the most distinguishing characteristic of new towns is that they are always founded for some pre-established purposes or objectives. The objectives determine the major planning characteristics of any new town, such as size, location and composition of land uses.

The purposes for which new towns are founded are numerous and serve to demonstrate the flexibility of the concept.* New towns have been built, for example, to establish capital cities (Brazilia, Canberra); for military or strategic purposes (Oak Ridge, Tenn., Los Alamos, N.M.); in connection with public works projects (Norris, Tenn., New Mannford, Okla.); to exploit natural resources (Ciudad Guayana, Venezuela, Kitimat, B.C.); as demonstration projects (Greenbelt, Md., Greenhills, Ohio, Greendale, Wisc.); to relieve urban congestion in established centers (Harlow, Stevenage, Cumbernauld, U.K.); to revive declining areas (Peterlee, U.K.); as educational centers (University City, Calif.); and as private land development enterprises (Park Forest, Ill., Reston, Va., Litchfield Park, Ariz.). New towns

*It may be argued that many cities and towns which are generally not considered to be new towns exhibit special purposes or functions. In many cases, however, these cities and towns were not purposely built for these functions, but the functions evolved into dominant activities through competitive advantages or resulted from other circumstances. In other cases the purposes of some cities were pre-established, but their development has differed from other features of the new town development process.

have also been founded for colonization, as ports, to relocate the populations of existing towns, and as planned extensions of existing towns. In many cases the purposes for which new towns are built overlap, or some other function may be served which is incidental to the major purpose for which a town is founded. Also, the purposes for some new towns may be established by the broader objectives of national development plans.

Sponsorship of New Towns

In most cases, the purposes for which new towns are founded reflect the auspices under which they are sponsored. The creation and development of a new town may be undertaken by government, private enterprise, or a combination of both forms of sponsorship. Brazilia, the new capital of Brazil, for example, is a completely public-sponsored new town. The new towns of the United Kingdom are publicly sponsored by the national government and developed by corporations chartered by the government's Ministry of Housing and Local Government. All of the new towns proposed or currently under way in the United States are sponsored by single private developers and development corporations, large landholders, or large industrial and financial corporations.

Single Ownership or Control

Related to the fact that new towns are purposely founded under some form of sponsorship is that new town sites are generally held in some form of single ownership or control during the development process. Most observers and theorists of new towns appear to be of the opinion that single ownership or control of new town land is a vital requirement for the assurance of plan implementation.[15]

However, the precise control mechanism may vary with the type of sponsorship, the permissiveness of the legal framework, or with the relationship between the developer and builder.* Whatever method of ownership or development control is employed, single ownership or control over new town land, at least during the development process, is one of the fundamental characteristics of new town planning and development.

New Towns as Pre-planned Communities

Another distinguishing feature of new towns is their planning. The new town master plan is usually developed before the building process is actually begun;[16] whereas the more familiar master plans for existing communities are often prepared after much of the community has already undergone development. Moreover, conventional master plans are often strongly influenced by pre-existing land use patterns and problems. Consequently, much of conventional city planning in the United States has been as much concerned with the re-planning of prior growth as with planning new growth.[17] By contrast, new towns are more accurately pre-planned communities.

There are also notable differences in the methods by which new town plans and city plans are implemented. The essential difference, as discussed above, is that the new town sponsor usually controls the title or development rights to new town land during the development process. This direct link between planning and land use control contrasts with that of conventional city planning, wherein the city planner must rely upon political acceptance and the discretion of the board of zoning appeals or planning commission to promote and enforce the principles of the plan. In the development of new towns the roles of planner and developer are combined.*

*These considerations are discussed in more detail in later chapters.

*This is not to say that the new town developer always has complete freedom in planning and land use control. For example, new towns in the United States are subject to the land use controls of the governmental units in which they are located and, in most cases, release from local restrictions must be obtained in order to develop a new town. This matter is discussed in further detail in a later chapter.

Planning and Design Principles

Since each new town should be planned according to its own requirements with respect to purpose, location, and projected size, there are no set design principles which govern the planning of new towns. The general guiding procedures advocated by most proponents of new towns do not differ significantly from what is generally termed comprehensive planning. That is, new town plans should be based upon thorough analysis of the town's location, physical characteristics, relationship to the regional transportation system, projected population size and land use needs, and relationship to other communities.[18] It is generally agreed that the planning of new towns should not simply meet the technical requirements of pre-planning. Wehrly and Comey point out that:

> . . . "planned" should mean comprehensively planned, in accordance with all the modern conceptions of city planning, but not necessarily so planned in all respects. A community with a mere rectangular street plan, though technically meeting the requirements of pre-planning, does not ordinarily indicate the application of modern planning technique . . . nor is a community consisting of successive "additions" or "subdivisions" of blocks and lots, each planned separately with comparatively little thought for the community as a whole.[19]

Beyond this point, however, it is difficult to translate the requirements of some definitions of the new town into a general definition. For example, Stein would add highly subjective requirements to new town planning.

> What do I mean by New Towns? Not merely that they are newly created. Many towns have been and are being built that are immediately obsolete and out-dated. They may have been fitted to an age long past; but they have nothing whatsoever to do with the life people now want to live, or would if they thought it were attainable.
>
> New towns are contemporary. This does not necessarily mean that they should have any particular type of "New Look," a different type of architectural style or veneer. By contemporary I

mean towns that are planned, built, and operated to serve present day needs and conditions.[20]

The matter of what is up-to-date, contemporary, or "good" community planning is, of course, difficult to evaluate. However, many advocates of new towns feel that the concept can or should be employed to produce innovations and improvements in urban planning and design,[21] and some feel that the new town offers opportunities for a combination of forms of physical and social planning.[22] Nevertheless, Geer's suggestion that a statement of a design concept should be part of a definition of a new town also appears to be impractical in view of the varied and changing design concepts currently being proposed or employed in new towns. Although there are hazards in generalizing about the designs of new towns, the most common design scheme employed in new towns in the United States and the United Kingdom has been described as a "flower pattern," or a compact central area surrounded by a series of neighborhoods.[23] However, some recent plans in both countries employ or propose "linear" and "cross-shaped" new towns or central areas. Cumbernauld, the proposed new town of Hook, U.K., and Litchfield Park, Ariz. are some examples exhibiting linear design.[24]

The changing new town planning concepts in the United States and the United Kingdom suggest that there are no standard design concepts for new towns. As in the case of Radburn, some design features are likely to gain wide acceptance and be repeated in other developments. However, the inclusion of specific design approaches as part of the new town concept would appear to be inconsistent with the claim that new towns should be developed to foster innovation and variety in urban development.

The Components of New Towns

Arguments over what is or is not an "authentic" new town often rage over whether the development in question is a "complete" new town in the sense of containing an appropriate range of land uses. Although there is a general consensus among definitions which refer to this matter, it is an aspect of the concept which is difficult to express explicitly, since there exist no general or specific standards as to what components are necessary for a city, town, or any urban area.

Generally, the components of new towns are expressed in three ways: by the use of descriptive phrases; through a general enumeration of functions or land uses considered to be essential; or both.

Self-Sufficient and Balanced Communities

The descriptive phrases most commonly employed to indicate what a new town should include are "self-sufficient" (or "self-contained") and "balanced." Although these phrases are subject to interpretation, they do give a general indication of the criteria for new towns. For example, O'Harrow states "if [new towns] are not to be sprawled, they must be reasonably self-sufficient and self-contained."[25] Another definition states that:

> new towns . . . are large enough to have an independent existence, in other words self-contained towns with commercial, educational, social and cultural institutions that satisfy all the needs of families and individuals alike; above all, the towns must have a sufficient number of industrial enterprises to create a wide labour market.[26]

The point at which any community may be considered to be self-contained is debatable and is largely dependent upon the criteria selected. All urban settlements are in one way or another dependent upon other urban areas for the satisfaction of some of the needs of their inhabitants. In most cases, the existence of new towns is dependent upon other centers of population. Most of the British new towns and nearly all of those proposed or being constructed in the United States are located near major metropolitan areas. To the extent that they are intended to participate in or absorb the expansion of these areas and the decentralization of industries and commercial facilities they are dependent for their growth and "self-sufficiency" upon them.

As was evident in a number of the definitions quoted above, several observers claim the degree of "self-sufficiency" to be the principal difference between British and American new towns. At this time, this is easily verified. Local employment in the new towns is a matter of British policy and the great majority of new town workers have local jobs. Most American new town developers do not stress employment opportunities within their projects, and some may avoid it because of the stigma on industry in some areas. Still, some American developers hope to provide local employment and include industrial areas within their plans. With respect to these latter developments, comparisons with British new towns may be unfair because they contrast intentions with results. In time, some American new towns may come to provide significant amounts of local employment, but that result will probably owe more to a fortunate location and promotion that to government policy.

The use of the terms "self-sufficient" and "self-contained" appear to be generally employed to convey the notion that new towns should be developed as relatively self-sustaining communities which should not be totally dependent upon a parent city for employment of its work force. The distinction is made by some writers that communities which depend upon other centers are "satellite towns" rather than new towns.

A further criterion is often conveyed in the phrase "balanced community." This term is usually employed to describe a variety of desired relationships in new towns. One interpretation, for example, derives from the Garden City concept of the wedding of advantages from urban and rural life. As Mumford puts it:

> If new cities were deliberately founded, as reservoirs are formed
> in flood areas, the uncontrolled flood of population which

plunged so devastatingly into the metropolis would be abated; there would be a chance to build a new type of civilization. The new type of regional center would combine the hygienic advantages of the open suburbs with the social advantages of the big city, would give an equal place in its scheme to the urban and the rural possibilities of modern life; in short, it would be a balanced environment.[27]

However, the term "balance" is more frequently employed to describe the physical and social composition and arrangement of new towns, usually to convey the notion that new towns should not be simply dormitory suburbs or residential satellites for other centers of employment, but that they should provide for both living and working. For example, O'Harrow's definition calls for "employment opportunities for at least 90 percent of the labor force" and a range of residential facilities for all economic classes,[28] the latter requirement at least implying a variety of employment opportunities. Similar requirements are submitted by Hurd, who feels that new towns

> . . . must be planned to provide a mix of age groups and economic levels, for the New Town is designed to be a small but complete city, and not a white collar, middle income ghetto.
>
> Industry is an integral part of the New Town, and is critical to its success. Companies of various types must be attracted, and must be located so as to be convenient yet separate from, and not a nuisance to, the residential and community areas of the city.[29]

In terms of the arrangement of land uses within the sub-areas of the new town, one California new town planner states that "the villages are planned as 'balanced communities,' that is, containing a mixture of land uses including single-family and multiunit residences, neighborhood shopping areas, parks, churches and offices. . . ."[30]

In general, "the balanced community" sums up the basic distinction and assumption which is drawn between new towns and other suburban developments—that new towns are composed of a variety of land uses related to the traditional

55

functions of the city, and that this balance between land uses both necessitates and makes possible communities which are socially balanced. In many definitions where this requirement is not phrased explicitly, it is often indicated by requirements that new towns should provide for a variety of housing styles and price ranges and a diversified labor market.[31] These varied uses of the term "balance" to describe the internal functions and composition of the new town are summed up by Albert Mayer: "They are conceived internally as integrated or balanced in terms of: jobs and workers in varied occupations; economic and social groups; open space and development."[32]

Most of those who define new towns appear to avoid an enumeration of minimum land use requirements for new towns. However, those which include them provide further indication of the uses that are generally considered to be necessary for the composition of a "complete" new town. McDade, for example, submits that a new community in America should be

A development of substantial acreage of land under direction of a single entity in relation to a master plan which provides for and interrelates at least the following land uses.

Residential—from single-family detached housing through multiple housing (both rental and sales), providing for complete life cycle.

Institutional—with civic buildings, schools, churches, open spaces, recreational and other facilities for public and common uses.

Commercial—from neighborhood shopping through to a community shopping center and possibly a regional shopping center . . .

Industrial—complementary to its region and not necessarily the exclusive or predominant economic base of the community.[33]

Citing similar requirements, O'Harrow states that

In order to be self-sufficient they must be large enough to contain and support:
a) a commercial center;
b) a reasonable range of cultural activities (short of grand opera and such);

c) a reasonable range of recreational facilities;

d) sufficient medical and health facilities to include a general hospital and a psychiatric clinic-hospital;

e) all necessary public facilities, such as schools, water, complete sewage treatment, etc;

f) a range of residential facilities to accommodate all economic classes;

g) a range of residential types, from the free-standing house to the apartment building (but not necessarily five-acre lots, nor high-rise flats); and

h) employment opportunities for at least 90 percent of the labor force.[34]

Despite the fact that these terms and norms connote some ideal physical and social composition for the new town, their general intent is not unclear. Whatever their faults may be, the terms "self-sufficient," "physically, economically and socially balanced," and the enumerations of functions which new towns should contain convey the notion that new towns are not single-class or single-function communities, but that their occupational structure and residential composition should provide internally for a mixture of socio-economic groups and economic activities. In general, they are envisioned as multi-functional developments which provide not only for residential and commercial facilities, but also for the employment, recreation and education of their inhabitants.

Size and Density

In those definitions or descriptions which treat the matter, prescribed sizes of new towns are usually expressed in terms of population ranges or critical lower limits. However, despite Huxtable's assertion that "accepted criteria call for a population of at least 20,000,"[35] there does not appear to be any consistency among definitions as to minimum or maximum populations. Moreover, there appears to be some discrepancy among theoretical sizes and between theoretical sizes and practice. For example, Osborn notes that

> . . . the New Towns (Reith) Committee, after exhaustive consideration and deliberation, suggested as an 'optimal normal range' 30,000 to 50,000 people in the built area—almost exactly Howard's proposed size . . . of 32,000 in the initial garden city and its rural belt and 58,000 in a later town to be central to an associated group of towns. . . ."[36]

However, the Reith Committee's optimum range has not been observed in new towns in the United Kingdom. New town population ranges appear to be set or amended by the particular needs of each new town, its purposes, and its growth potential. Five of the eight new towns in the London area, for example, have proposed populations ranging from 80 to 120 thousand persons, and five currently have populations ranging from 59 to 70 thousand.[37] A recently designated new town in North Buckinghamshire is expected to have a population of 250,000 by the end of the century.[38]

New towns in the United States also exhibit a wide range of target populations. Rather than being related to any ideal conceptions as to population size, their target populations appear to be more a function of the particular developer's goals, land holdings, market evaluations, or financial capabilities.*

Although most definitions avoid reference to specific population ranges or sizes, those which do contain them appear to emphasize that some lower limit must be attained to provide for or justify the inclusion of required new town components or land uses. However, opinion varies. O'Harrow argues that "in order to be self-sufficient, the new town will necessarily be housing a population on the order of 50,000.[39] From the same point of view, Hurd claims that

> [a new town] must provide sufficient industrial, commercial and residential space to support a population of 100,000 or more in

*The projected populations of new towns in the United States are discussed in the following chapter.

order to provide and support all of the institutions commonly found in a city: libraries, music, museums, art, drama, clubs of various types, opportunity for higher education and other attractions generally available only in a city of 100,000 people.[40]

As quoted earlier, Secretary Weaver has stated that new towns "should, normally, be planned for a population of 25,000 or more."[41]

The breadth of these population ranges not only indicates that opinion on the subject is varied but also raises the question of whether there is any critical minimum which must be met in order to assure a community self-sufficient status or a diversified labor market. These factors may be subject to a number of variables other than or in addition to population size alone. For example, location may be a significant variable as it affects the components of a new town. A community of five or ten thousand may attract a regional shopping center or a large industrial plant if it is located near other centers of population which would add to the accessible shopping market area or labor pool area, whereas new towns in more isolated areas may have to depend more upon the attractiveness and location factors which they themselves provide. Although there may be some minimum population sizes necessary to justify the presence of a particular activity or land use, such a minimum may not be consistent with other factors, such as efficiency in certain municipal services. Duncan, in his study of the effects of different city sizes upon several variables ranging from municipal efficiency to selected psychological characteristics of population, concluded that

> The optimum size of cities is quite different from the standpoint of certain criteria from what it is on the basis of others. It is found that even an apparently unitary criterion—e.g., health may give conflicting indications of the optimum. There is no immediately obvious way in which these various optima may be objectively equilibrated, compromised, weighted, or balanced to yield an unequivocal figure for *the* optimum population for a city. Any

numerical choice of a figure for the optimum population is involved in subjective value preferences and impressionistic weighting systems. Most theorists proposing a size or size range as the optimum adopt this procedure, or the alternative one of confining attention to a few of the many criteria of optimum city-size that have been exposed in the literature.[42]

It seems, therefore, that absolute population minimums or maximums are questionable aspects of a general new town definition and that any notion of population size must be related to the purposes of the new town and its location. One Soviet planner states

> The optimum size of a town is determined by the pattern of production it is to have, the way it is to be laid out, and the feasibility of providing community services at a high standard and making effective use of industrial building methods.
>
> It is clear from the foregoing that the optimum size for a town is not a constant; according to the data assembled by Soviet town planners, it varies in terms of population between 150,000 and 250,000. The optimum size for a satellite town ranges from 50,000 to 100,000 inhabitants.[43]

This is not to say, however, that population sizes or ranges are not set for specific new towns. In practice, planning for some predetermined population size or range is considered to be a critical and essential part of the new town development process. As Mayer explains,

> Our [American] new towns will not be of any standard size—they can well vary from 50,000 to several hundred thousand, appropriate to the individual location, function, and outlook. But each will be of an approximately pre-determined size modified by "tolerances," because only so can utilities and city structure be economically provided and maintained, only so can we forestall the same fringification all over again, only so can we keep "open water" or open green between towns or between town and city. . . .[44]

Most definitions make no reference to specific or required densities for new towns, probably because of problems similar to those of absolute populations sizes—that is, densities can only be meaningful relative to other factors. Like optimum sizes of cities, the optimization of any two factors may not necessarily be a function of the same level of density.[45]

Consideration of densities appears to have shifted in the course of the development of the new town concept. Under Howard and his disciples the rationale for new towns was strongly influenced by the high densities and over-crowded conditions of existing cities. Howard envisioned in a "marriage" of town and country more commodious settings for the inhabitants of new towns, although they were still to be relatively compact urban settlements. Reiterating Howard's standards, Mumford states that

> Thirty thousand people were to live on those thousand acres; 30 per gross acre as compared with 57 per gross acre in the present congested, park-destitute county of London. Parks were provided within the Garden City on the basis of a little more than nine acres per thousand; well above the four acres suggested in the new plan for London, but not so much higher than the six that Westminster normally boasts.[46]

Current proponents of new towns, however, reacting to what is considered to be too low a density in typical suburban development, more often argue the case for new towns as a means for the conservation and efficient use of land as opposed to "urban sprawl."[47]

Density in new towns appears to be more of a theoretical issue in the United Kingdom than in the United States, probably due to the difference in land areas available for development. However, within the United Kingdom, some of the dispute over desirable densities also appears to be the result of friction between traditionalists (as embodied by the Town and Country Planning Association) and planners of the more recent British new towns.[48] Thus in the United Kingdom increases in density appear to be measured against some prescribed limits and tend to be met with opposition by disciples of Howard. In the United States, under current new town development practices, densities set by conventional zoning are crucial to the developer and are more controlling than any considerations of ideal or optimal density compositions.

Location

Although the particular locations of new towns may be influenced by such factors as availability of land, location of major transportation routes, or the physical characteristics of an area, the major considerations in their general locations are the purposes for which they are built. Most definitions, therefore, make no specific reference to appropriate locations for new towns. To the extent that the matter of location is treated in any detail in definitions, it is usually a reflection of the author's emphasis upon a particular purpose for new towns. For example, Hurd feels that

> The New Town should be in a location which has the following attributes:
> a) It must be in a legal jurisdiction capable of permitting sound local government and sound planning and zoning.
> b) It must be near population, a source of supply of inhabitants.
> c) It must have adequate means of transportation by highway and rail to attract industry as well as people.
> d) It must have a reasonably attractive climate.
> e) It should be reasonably easy and inexpensive to develop topographically.
> f) It should be capable of water orientation, either natural or man-made.
> g) It should be capable of having proportions developed into recreational facilities—boating, golf, bridle trails, parks, etc.[49]

In practice, new towns have been and are being constructed in a variety of locations. For example, Brazilia, Kitimat, and Lake Havasu City are located in quite isolated areas; Reston, Columbia and the majority of the British new towns are within commuting distance of major metropolitan centers; and Le Mirail (France) and Redwood Shores (California) are being constructed as planned extensions to existing cities. Some new towns in the United Kingdom were planned and located to include existing villages within them, and it has recently been suggested that new towns might even be located within existing cities.[50]

Any discussion of principles or requirements for the location of new towns, therefore, would have to distinguish the purposes which the new town or towns are intended to serve. It is axiomatic that a new town intended to absorb overspill population from metropolitan centers has significantly different locational requirements than one intended to colonize sparsely developed or undeveloped areas.

Most definitions, because they focus on the new town as a separate entity, make no reference to location within the context of or in conformance with a regional plan as a requirement for new towns. Hurd, for example, places emphasis upon those locational factors which he believes are important to the success of the new town alone.[51] Although the need has been expressed for regional planning for new towns or the conformance of new towns with metropolitan or regional plans,[52] it would appear to be a disputable element of a general definition of the new town. That is, it would seem improper to reason that a community which conforms to the internal requirements of the new town concept is not a new town because it may not have been located and constructed within the framework of an area-wide plan.

Summary

Fundamentally, the new town concept appears to maintain that new urban development should be organized into integrated units, or wholes. Although this notion was originally formulated as a reaction against the increasing size and congestion in existing cities, it is envisioned today as a means for organizing scattered and low-density development around metropolitan centers. In addition to this general purpose, new towns have also been constructed to serve a variety of specific functions.

A second identifiable feature of the new town concept is that it proposes a system or process by which the objectives of the new town may be satisfied. Single ownership or control over new town land permits a direct linkage between planning and development. Therefore, new town development usually takes place under some form of sponsorship.

Third, new towns are pre-planned; that is, they are planned entirely in advance of land development and construction, as contrasted with most conventional city planning.

Fourth, new towns are intended to be multi-purpose settlements which provide for traditional urban functions within their borders. That is, they are intended to achieve a functional balance, as opposed to being bedroom communities. It appears from the literature surveyed here that this condition may be met within a wide range of populations and densities. However, for planning purposes, some population size or range for individual new towns is usually established.

Fifth, new towns are envisioned as socially balanced communities which provide housing and employment for all socio-economic groups.

The purpose of this chapter has been to identify the major elements of the new town concept as they have appeared in various definitions and descriptions of that concept. Also, it has attempted to demonstrate that there is at present no widely accepted single definition of the new town.

The problem of formulating a general definition of the new town from existing developments which are generally considered to be new towns is similar to that of defining the city from the same approach. It is evident that existing new towns exhibit a wide variety of purposes and functions, locations, sizes, and mixtures of land uses. This variety makes questionable the selection of any one type of new town as a model.[53] Consequently, there is considerable variety in definitions and descriptions of the concept. Some definitions are rigid and precise in their construction, whereas others are more loosely constructed and less definitive.

It is quite evident that there probably will never be a

widely acceptable definition of the new town concept, since it will continually be redefined to fit new purposes and problems. People tend to define new towns to suit their own values and visions, and it may well be that, conceptually, new towns will always reflect hoped for improvements in the status quo.

The lack of a widely accepted definition of the new towns concept has not restrained enthusiasm for new towns development or public policies to promote them. Rather, it appears to have invited a great variety of speculation as to the utility of new towns for dealing with a wide variety of urban problems. These claims are treated in the following chapter.

Notes

1. Louis Wirth, "Urbanism as a Way of Life," *Cities and Society*, ed. Hatt and Reiss (Glencoe: The Free Press, 1961), pp. 47–63.

2. Ibid., p. 50.

3. Gideon Sjöberg, "Theory and Research in Urban Sociology," *The Study of Urbanization*, ed. Hauser and Schnore (New York: John Wiley and Sons, 1965), pp. 157–89.

4. Max Weber, *The City* (New York: Collier, 1962), p. 59 (Prefatory Remarks by Don Martindale).

5. Melvin Webber, "Order in Diversity; Community Without Propinquity," *Cities and Space*, ed. Lowden Wingo (Baltimore: Johns Hopkins Press, 1963), pp. 26–27.

6. National Association of Home Builders, *Report: New Towns: A Conference*, at the National Housing Center, June 29-30, 1964, p. 1.

7. Robert C. Weaver, *Dilemmas of Urban America* (Cambridge: Harvard University Press, 1965), p. 13. This writer notes, however, that despite the use of the term "new communities" in the administration's proposed legislation in 1964 and as part of the title of the Title IV program in 1966, they were often referred to throughout Congressional hearings on the bills as "new towns."

8. Ebenezer Howard, *Garden Cities of Tomorrow* (3rd ed.; Cambridge: M.I.T. Press, 1965), p. 26. Although the term "Garden City"

was most often used to describe Howard's proposal, one of his major disciples, F. J. Osborn, notes that the term "satellite town" was used as an alternative description (Ibid., p. 27).

9. Definition of A. Suquet-Bonnaud as quoted in Jean Viet, *New Towns: A Selected, Annotated Bibliography,* (France: UNESCO, 1960), p. 16.

10. U.S., Congress, Senate, *Housing Legislation of 1964,* Hearings Before a Subcommittee of the Committee on Banking and Currency, 88th Cong., 2nd Sess. on S. 2468 and other bills to amend the Federal Housing Laws (Washington, D.C.: U.S. Government Printing Office, 1964), p. 368.

11. *Drafts of Bills Relating to Housing,—Message from the President of the United States Relative to Drafts of Bills Relating to Housing,* 88th Cong., 2nd Sess., 206, (Washington, D.C.: U.S. Government Printing Office, 1964), p. 22. It should also be noted that terms such as "balanced" used in this definition are also in dispute, as is discussed in this and later chapters.

12. Carl Feiss, "New Towns for America," *Journal of the American Institute of Architects,* XXIII (January 1960), 85.

13. David S. Geer, "Oak Ridge: A World War II New Town," *Journal of the American Institute of Architects,* XV, No. 1 (January 1951), 16.

14. Edward P. Eichler and Marshall Kaplan, *The Community Builders* (Berkeley: University of California Press, 1967), p. 24. This same distinction appears to have been adopted by the Advisory Commission on Intergovernmental Relations. See Advisory Commission on Intergovernmental Relations, *Urban and Rural America: Policies for Future Growth,* Report A-32 (Washington, D.C.: U.S. Government Printing Office, 1968), pp.63-64.

15. See, for example, Ada Louise Huxtable, " 'Clusters' Instead of 'Slurbs,' " *The New York Times Magazine,* February 9, 1964, p. 44; Foley, "Idea and Influence: The Town and Country Planning Association," *Journal of the American Institute of Planners,* XXVIII, No. 1 (February, 1962), p. 11; and U.S. National Resources Committee, *Urban Planning and Land Policies,* II of the Supplementary Report of the Urbanism Committee to the National Resources Committee (Washington, D.C.: U.S. Government Printing Office, 1939), p. 8; ACIR, *Urban and Rural America,* op. cit., p. 64.

16. Viet, op. cit., p. 21. This distinction is also emphasized in *Current Municipal Problems,* "A New Concept in Pre-City Planning," X, No. 3 (February 1969), 253-264.

17. Other distinctions on this point, though somewhat lacking in objectivity, are made by Clarence Stein, *Towards New Towns for America,* (New York: Reinhold, 1957), pp. 220-21.

18. See, for example, Huxtable, op. cit., p. 44; United States National Resources Committee, op. cit., p. 8; and John Nolen, "New Towns vs. Existing Cities," *Journal of the American Institute of Planners,* II, No. 2 (1926), 75.

19. U.S. National Resources Committee, op. cit., p. 8.

20. Stein, op. cit., p. 217. Similar viewpoints are expressed in Geer, op. cit., p. 16, and in W. J. Conklin, "Planning Approaches to New Towns," *Building Research,* III, No. 1 (January/February 1966), 18, 20.

21. See, for example, Wayne E. Thompson, "Prototype City— Design for Tomorrow," *New Towns: A New Dimension of Urbanism* (Chicago: International City Managers Association, 1966), pp. 38-43.

22. Paul V. Lemkau, "Human Factors in the New Town," *Building Research,* III, No. 1 (January/February 1966), 29-32.

23. Some of the general design principles of new towns in the United States and the United Kingdom are related in Conklin, op. cit., p. 18f.

24. *The Sunday* (London) *Times* March 22, 1964, p. 7; London County Council, *The Planning of a New Town* (London: London County Council, 1961); F. J. Osborn and A. Whittick, *The New Towns* (New York: McGraw-Hill, 1963), p. 312; *Litchfield Park Plan,* Litchfield Park Properties n.d. In some cases the design of a new town may be employed to express a particular theme. The Costa plan for the new capital city of Brazilia, for example, was intended to be symbolic of "the national power and integrity which the Capital embodies." [David E. Snyder, "Alternative Perspectives on Brazilia," *Ekistics,* XVIII, No. 108 (November 1964), 328.] However, such dominance of a design theme appears to be rare in new town planning.

25. Dennis O'Harrow, "New Towns or New Sprawl," *American Society of Planning Officials Newsletter,* XXX, No. 9 (October 1964), 105.

26. Viet, op. cit., p. 16.

27. Lewis Mumford, *The Culture of Cities* (New York: Harcourt, Brace and Co., 1939), p. 396. See also diagram and description in Howard, op. cit., p. 41f.

28. O'Harrow, loc. cit.

29. R. M. Hurd, "City Problems Require Building New Towns," *Urban Land,* XXV, No. 3 (March 1966), 16. It should be added that

Hurd also feels that the new town should not be entirely dependent upon local industry and that it is desirable to have some cross movement of workers between the new town and other centers of employment (ibid).

30. Henry K. Evans, "Transportation Planning Criteria for New Towns," *Planned Communities,* Highway Research Record No. 97 (Washington, D.C.: Highway Research Board, 1965), p. 40.

31. See, for example, Robert M. Gladstone, "Does Building a City Make Economic Sense," *Appraisal Journal,* XXXIV, No. 3 (July 1966), 410. The term has also been employed with reference to "fiscal viability based on balanced development patterns" in Robert M. Gladstone, "New Towns Role in Urban Growth Explored," *Journal of Housing,* XXXII, No. 1 (January 1966), 32.

32. Albert Mayer, "Ingredients of an Effective Program for New Towns," *Proceedings of the 1964 Annual Conference,* Newark, August 16-20. (Washington, D.C.: American Institute of Planners, 1964), p. 187.

33. Thomas McDade, "New Communities in America: A New Context for Institutional Innovation," text of speech given by the Director of Urban Studies, Housing and Home Finance Agency, to the Eighth Annual Organization of the Cornell Planners, Cornell University, Ithaca, N.Y., October 17, 1964, p. 8.

34. O'Harrow, loc. cit.

35. Huxtable, op. cit., p. 44.

36. Osborn and Whittick, op. cit., p. 12.

37. Based on figures published in *Town and Country Planning,* "Progress of the New Towns to December, 1966," XXXV, No. 1 (January 1967), 40-41.

38. *Official Planning and Architecture,* XXX, No. 2 (February 1967), 266.

39. O'Harrow, loc. cit.

40. Hurd, loc. cit.

41. U.S., Congress, Senate, *Housing Legislation of 1964 . . .,* op. cit., p. 368.

42. O. D. Duncan, "The Optimum Size of Cities," *Cities and Society* (Glencoe: The Free Press, 1957), p. 772. See also United Nations, *European Seminar on Urban Development Policy and Planning, Warsaw, September 1962 (Report)* (Geneva: U.N., 1962), p. 10.

43. N. V. Baranov, "Building New Towns," Background Paper No. 11, *Round Table Conference on the Planning and Development of New Towns* (New York: United Nations, 1964), p. 3.

44. Mayer, op. cit., p. 188.

45. There is a diverse literature relating to the differential effects of urban sizes and densities from various points of view. See, for example, Ruth L. Mace, *Municipal Cost-Revenue Research in the United States* (Chapel Hill: University of North Carolina Press, 1961); Edward Higbee, *The Squeeze* (New York: William Morrow & Co., 1960); R. C. Schmitt, "Density, Health, and Social Disorganization," *Journal of the American Institute of Planners,* XXXII, No. 1 (January 1966), 38-39.

46. Howard, op. cit., p. 24.

47. See O'Harrow, op. cit., pp. 105-106.

48. See, for example, F. J. Osborn, "Just How Dense Can You Get," *Town and Country Planning,* XXXIII, No. 3 (March 1965), 113-114.

49. Hurd, loc. cit.

50. Harvey S. Perloff, "New Towns Intown," *Journal of the American Institute of Planners,* XXXII, No. 3 (May 1966), 155.

51. Hurd, loc. cit.

52. See, for example, United Nations, *Report of the United Nations Symposium on the Planning and Development of New Towns* (New York: United Nations, 1966), p. 3 ff; and Daniel Mandelker, "Some Policy Considerations in the Drafting of New Towns Legislation," *Washington University Law Quarterly,* MCMLXV, No. 1 (February 1965), 72 ff. Regional planning for new towns is discussed in a later section.

53. Secretary Weaver has deplored the fact that many proponents of the new town idea in the United States have proposed the British new towns as a model of what American new towns should be (see *Dilemmas of Urban America,* p. 13 ff). However, even as the British new towns differ in many respects, with significant differences in planning between the first and second "generation" (Mark I and Mark II) new towns. See, for example, J. R. Atkinson, "Washington New Town, England," *Washington University Law Quarterly,* MCMLXV, No. 1, (February 1965), 56-57.

4 The Case for New Towns

In Chapter 3 it was demonstrated that many people tend to define the new town concept to suit their own attitudes, values and visions. In a somewhat similar fashion, this observation applies as well to the rationale for some sort of a new towns program in the United States. The case for new towns and a policy for their development in this country consists of a variety of arguments and claims rather than a unified argument. The arguments range from extreme speculation on the potential advantages of a new towns policy to more cautious appraisals of current urban development and the potential utility of new towns. The purpose of this chapter is to outline the case for new towns and a new towns policy as argued from different points of view. Counter-arguments are reserved for later discussion.

The Development of the Case for New Towns

As was indicated in the historical review of new town development, the case for new towns was first formally articulated by Ebenezer Howard at the beginning of the nineteenth century. To a large extent, many of the arguments which comprise the case for new towns in the United States today paraphrase or reflect Howard's thesis. Basically, Howard's proposals emerged from his disgust with the squalor and congestion of large industrial cities at the turn of the century. He felt that an alternative to these conditions could be created by bringing together what he considered to be the best ingredients of urban and rural life in pre-planned communities in outlying areas. Since his thesis was based upon conditions which existed prior to widespread suburbanization, Howard's case rested upon a scheme for the decentralization of existing cities into planned towns in the countryside.

With the dawn of the era of suburbanization, a new dimension was added by Howard's followers and others to the case for new towns. The advent of the automobile enabled large populations to exercise the option between city and suburbs more freely, and proponents of new towns based their arguments upon re-centralization of spreading and unplanned suburban growth rather than decentralization. Although the shift in emphasis from city to suburb is not totally separable, it is evident that the major thrust of the case for new towns in the United States today proposes the new town as a solution to unplanned suburban growth.

Upon these basic arguments have since been built numerous other claims as to the merits of new towns. New towns have been seen or proposed as solutions (or partial solution) to the problems of community and area-wide planning, local and regional transportation problems, suburban sprawl, the revitalization of central cities, preservation of open space, racial problems, the prolonged journey to work, and defense against nuclear attack. They are also considered advantageous in meeting quasi-urban problems such as the decline of a sense of "community" and urban aesthetics. These arguments are voiced with varying enthusiasm and accuracy by the many converts to the new town idea and publicly assisted new towns programs. For the most part, they are the arguments of the traditional supporters of the new town concept—planners, architects, and landscape architects—but they have also received the attention of a number of public officials, developers, journalists, engineers, and members of a variety of other professions. The list of endorsers of the new town concept expands almost daily. It includes such diverse bodies and individuals as Urban America, Inc., the American Institute of Planners, the Advisory Commission on Inter-governmental Relations, the Council of State Governments, the National Association of Counties, the United States Conference of Mayors, the National League of Cities, former President Johnson, Vice-President Agnew, and a variety of members of the Federal, state, and local governments.

There is no single way to classify the various arguments in the case for new towns; however, some distinction can be made between those aspects which emphasize what might be termed the "intra-community" and those which emphasize the "inter-community" advantages of new towns. In the former, emphasis is placed upon those advantages which, it is claimed, would obtain in a community planned from the ground up; in the latter, upon the regional role of new towns organizing and accommodating urban expansion. The distinction is not a tidy one, since several aspects of the case rely upon both lines of reasoning, but it does serve to highlight the diversity of opinion behind the new town idea.

New Towns as a Community Philosophy

One need not delve too deeply into planning literature and promotional material which explains and enumerates the advantages of new towns to discover an inherent nostalgia for the traditional urban community.* Most of the "com-

---

*The term "community" has been used and described in a variety of ways and is subject to all the difficulties of definition which confront those who attempt to define the "neighborhood," the "city," or any other entity comprised of a complex set of interrelated variables. In new town literature it is often employed in a casual manner, but it is evident that (1) it is part of the underlying rationale for

munity" rationale for new towns relates to what might be termed the geographic or spatial aspects of the urban community. This rationale is traceable to Howard and the Garden City movement, but it is also in evidence in much of new town planning and promotional literature today. In essence, this facet of the case for new towns leans heavily upon the claim that the modern city has evolved to a size and scale which has continually diminished the sense of identity with community as a place, or a spatial entity. With some distinctions, it is applied to both urban and suburban areas.

With respect to cities, or highly urbanized areas, the reference to "community" is primarily in terms of scale. The underlying theme of this argument appears to be that the individual in the large, densely developed urban area tends to become dominated, oppressed, and diminished in importance in relation to his environment—that, rather than controlling his environment, urban man is controlled by it. Howard, for example, stated that "These crowded cities have done their work; they were the best which a society based on selfishness and rapacity could construct, but they are in the nature of things entirely unadapted for a society in which the social side of our nature is demanding a larger share of recognition—a society where even the very love of self leads us to insist upon a greater regard for the well-being of our fellows."[1]

Howard, of course, was addressing himself to the urban conditions at the end of the nineteenth century, before the forces of urban compaction were technologically loosened. Nevertheless, there has been a persistence of allusion to the alleged de-personalizing aspects of city life, notably among urban sociologists such as Wirth, who have contrasted contempory urbanism with the spatially more simple, and

the intra-community case for new towns, and (2) it is employed to refer to several different, but related, aspects of new town development and structure. No attempt is made here to offer an additional definition for "community;" rather, the purpose is to analyze the various ways in which the term has been employed in the case for new towns.

smaller, folk community. In stating his arguments for new towns, Clarence Stein, one of the founders of the new town movement in the United States, argues in his book, *Toward New Towns for America,* that "Man is submerged in the colossal human swarm, his individuality overwhelmed, his personality negated, his essential dignity is lost in crowds without a sense of community."[2] There is a strong relationship between the proponents of new towns and those sociologists and others who consider the process of urbanization as primarily one of social disorganization which has weakened kinship bonds, family life, and neighborliness and created anonymity and transitory personal relations.

The response of the new town advocate and the planner to this disorganizing view of the city was correspondingly in terms of scale. Howard alluded to it in his definition of the Garden City: a town "designed for healthy living and industry of a size that makes possible the full measure of social life, but not larger."[3] The implied scale advantages have been embellished by later planners such as Albert Mayer:

> On the social side, and on the side of citizens' political stake and alertness, the new town offers a whole gamut of advantages and freshened viewpoints. It is on a total scale—also in the crystallized communities composing it—in which the citizen can feel some degree of significance, identification, influence as compared with big-city frustration and remoteness.[4]

Orlans states in a study of the British new towns that new town planners contended that "sociability and community activity could be organized, or, at least, encouraged by a congenial physical environment and genuine social reform which would counteract the consequences of industrialism, occupational specializations, and class segregation and conflict.[5]

The Suburban Community

Although an anti-big-city bias is still evident in the views of some of the proponents of new towns, it is clear that the major emphasis in the new town "community" rationale today is upon what are felt to be the disorganizing consequences of suburban development, both physically and socially. Wood observed this new emphasis in his study of suburbia.

> In light of the information available at the time, Bryce, Wells, Geddes, and Howard based their doctrines of reform on apparently irrefutable facts which indicated the disappearance of the small community. And today, modern reformers and planners can present impressive evidence and reasoned arguments to show that the modern suburb possesses none of the vital prerequisites for community life as it is commonly understood.[6]

Where the early proponents of new towns saw the industrial city of the late nineteenth century as an oppressive entrapment for its inhabitants, current proponents of the concept view suburban growth as lacking the "place" and physical identity of community. It is felt that the haphazard and unplanned manner in which the components of the community are established in suburban areas has created a pattern of urbanization which the individual can scarcely identify as a spatial community. Considerable emphasis is placed upon the fact that the community has become spatially disorganized and balkanized. It is further argued that the components of urban areas are scattered, disorganized, and spread in a manner which diminishes social contact by inhibiting frequent social interaction and necessitating a heavy reliance upon the automobile. Jobs and residence are no longer juxtaposed, and the journey to work deprives the worker of leisure or productive hours. There is no sub-community unit, at least in traditional terms, such as the neighborhood.

With respect to the suburban community, it is clear that the new town concept is primarily posited as a framework for the spatial reorganization of scattered community elements. It is evident that it is offered on the assumption that a "community" is a spatially identifiable entity, and that its physical configuration is determinant of some undefined level of community identity and social interaction between its inhabitants and institutions. Perloff and Hanson have testified, for example, that

> The 'new town' idea has been receiving a great deal of attention in recent decades because of the advantages that a newly constructed community on open land can offer. Its design can be geared to the new technologies, it can offer more modern public services and facilities, more and better recreation, and, most of all, a greater sense of community.[7]

Taken in concert, then, these assertions claim that the new towns concept offers in its process of development and physical organization more than a balance between town and country, but a balance between frequent social contact and privacy, a balance in daily activities such as work and leisure, and a balance between people and institutions. These balances are undefined, but are believed attainable given the conditions and power to affect new town development.

The "Sprawl" Argument

The case against urban sprawl, suburban sprawl, or urban scatteration is unquestionably the most dominant theme in the case for new towns and a new towns policy in the United States. As was indicated above, there has been a shift in the case for new towns from what might be termed the "anti-big-city argument" to an indictment of the pattern of suburban growth. However, the sprawl argument, like the case against big cities, stresses the spatial characteristics of suburban development as they relate to a number of physical and social variables.

Since World War II, a vast literature has amassed on a variety of aspects of suburban development. The value-heavy terms which are often employed to describe the phenomenon—"sprawl," "slurbs," "the suburban dislocation," "disturbia," etc.—indicate the general disfavor with which many observers have viewed this form of development. The majority of comment upon suburban development and the suburban way of life tends to convey the general impression that the whole process has been a lamentable phase in American urbanization. The case for new towns has both fed upon and fueled these pejorative views.

A sampling of the commentary on suburban development illustrates that virtually every aspect of suburbanization has been viewed with dismay and concern. *New York Times* architecture critic Ada Louis Huxtable is unrestrained in her criticism:

> Suburban Christmas is a cheap plastic Santa Claus in a shopping-center parking lot surrounded by asphalt and a sea of cars. Suburban spring is not a walk in the awakening woods, but mud in poorly built roads. Suburban life is no voyage of discovery or private exploration of the world's wonders, natural and man-made; it is cliche conformity as far as the eye can see, with no stimulation through quality of environment.[8]

Several books have popularized the notion that the suburban way of life has disintegrated the American family unit and has resulted in a host of interpersonal problems including sexual promiscuity, juvenile delinquency, role confusion, status-seeking, and an assortment of psychological stresses, anxieties and neuroses. One case study of eight families in a "typical" American suburb paints a picture of a seemingly unavoidable psychological entrapment for the suburbanite. The authors report that

> The picture is distressing and even frightening. Bergan's [County] delinquency rates look like those of a city—where life is perceivably more stressful than in the country. The movers who have contributed so much to the building of America, who are its backbone and its future, have apparently created for themselves a way of life that is dangerous to them. It is important to find exactly where and how this disturbed modern community—this archetype of the mobile world, this Disturbia—has gone wrong.[9]

Spatial and physical characteristics of suburban development have been viewed with equal alarm. Where some observers of interpersonal behavior have apparently discovered a disintegration of family life and social patterns, planners and architects have observed a parallel (and implicitly related) disintegration of the physical urban pattern. It is with respect to the physical pattern of suburban development that the case for new towns draws its heaviest emphasis, although there is a prevalent strong implication that the physical pattern has definite personal and social ramifications. The implied relationship between the spatial arrangement of land uses in suburbia and the physical identification of "community" is the most recurrent theme. For example

> The U.S. has virtually ceased creating new settlements that have focal points of the traditional type, with stores, offices, schools, and churches closely linked to sidewalks. Instead the elements of community are flung at random over a wide area; here a housing subdivision, a mile away a row of drive-in stores, and so on.
>
> Baltimore developer James Rouse calls today's new settlements "Non-communities—formless places without order, beauty, or reason."[10]

Gutkind makes a similar observation:

> The last vestiges of a community have disappeared. They are hardly anything else than an agglomeration of innumerable and isolated details, of human atoms, and rows of boxes, called houses, intersperced between the industries. It is a total victory of laissez faire insensibility and recklessness over organic growth and even over organized development.[11]

When the case against urban sprawl is distilled further, it is expressed strongly in terms of inefficiency and waste and the foregone opportunity to create a more desirable urban environment. As Weaver expresses it

> Urban sprawl has brought ugliness and botched land uses. It has wasted land. It has stifled opportunity and minimized choice for minorities and low income people. It has hindered rational development of transportation systems to serve needs of central cities and their suburbs. Its scattering has spawned fiscal problems and eroded the central cities' economic base.[12]

A similar indictment is made by William H. Whyte, Jr.

> Sprawl is bad aesthetics; it is bad economics. Five acres are being made to do the work of one, and do it very poorly. This is bad for the farmers, it is bad for communities, it is bad for industry, it is bad for utilities, it is bad for the railroads, it is bad for recreation groups, it is even bad for developers.[13]

There have been many solutions proposed for the elimination of suburban sprawl, but none appear as encompassing as the new towns proposal. As one article points out, "Suburban sprawl is the direct opposite of planning satellite centers or self-contained new towns, each surrounded by its own greenbelt."[14] In explaining the rationale for the experimental new communities program, Secretary Weaver states that "new communities are one way to eliminate the waste and disorder of urban sprawl."[15]

As it relates to the phenomenon of suburban sprawl, the case for the establishment of new towns in metropolitan regions can be reduced to a relatively simple tenet: if suburban sprawl disintegrates the elements of community in such a fashion as to destroy the physical identity of the community, and results in the uncontrolled development and uneconomic use of land and unnecessary costs for suburbanites, then the logical solution would appear to be to initiate policies to bring the elements of community together into unified and relatively concentrated planned settlements. The common theme, it has been pointed out, to most proposals for the elimination of suburban sprawl is that "future developments should be conceived in terms of wholes—that they must be determined on the basis of essential physical, social, economic, and human needs. Future development, in other words, must be thoroughly planned."[16]

New towns as a case against suburban sprawl, then, is a contrast between what are considered to be the advantages of complete, planned communities over the unplanned and scattered elements of the community characteristic of suburban sprawl. Where the new town as a philosophy of community stresses some of the social advantages which are attached to the new town concept, the case against suburban sprawl stresses advantages in terms of the physical expansion of the metropolis by relating it to a number of physical growth problems which result from sprawl.

New Towns and Metropolitan Transportation

One of the major elements in the sprawl argument in the case for new towns is the relationship of the new town to the problem of transportation throughout the metropolis. No attempt is made here to state or analyze the metropolitan transportation problem; rather, the purpose is to point out the manner in which proponents of new towns view the problem, and the factors which influence this perception.

Basically, proponents of new towns (and others) see suburban sprawl as the cause of an inefficient and inadequate system of responses to the need for access to the various parts of the metropolitan area. Central to this view is that the spread of urban development around the central city necessitates a transportation network which must attempt to connect a broad and relatively uncompacted area with the central city. Such a system is considered undesirable because it necessitates excessive expenditure for highways, and because the pattern of sprawl precludes the use of media other than the private automobile.

It is argued that the new town, or a constellation of new towns, can offer decided advantages in solving the transportation problem occasioned by sprawl. By initiating policies to concentrate populations at strategic nodal points in the metropolitan region, a transportation network could be established to provide more direct access between larger suburban populations and the central city. Basically, it is reasoned that development according to strategically located nodal centers would obviate the need for an ubiquitous regional transportation network and simultaneously permit the development of efficient regional mass transit systems.*

To some extent the new town concept has also absorbed the anti-automobile bias which characterizes much of the criticism of suburban sprawl. It is argued, for example, that one of the advantages of completely pre-planned settlements is the opportunity to arrange land uses in such a way as to minimize dependence upon the automobile for many daily activities within the community. By organizing the town into well-planned neighborhoods, for example, daily needs such as shopping and school trips could be reduced to walking distances.[17] A related factor is that higher densities and better planning afford greater opportunities for local mass transit systems than spread patterns of development.[18]

Probably the most consistent claim for new towns as it relates to both intra-community and inter-regional transportation concerns the journey to work. One of the major goals of the new town concept is the establishment of relatively self-contained communities with local employment for a large share of workers.[19] Local employment opportunities in new towns therefore help reduce the burden on regional transportation systems, eliminate many wasted hours absorbed in commuting, and could serve to alleviate some of the traffic congestion and parking problems in central cities.

New Towns and Community Utilities

The rationale behind the transportation advantages of towns are somewhat paralleled with respect to the advantages of economy and efficiency in the development of public utilities and community facilities claimed for new towns. Basically, the contrast with suburban sprawl is drawn on the basis of three factors: density, balance, and pre-planning.

With respect to density, the argument paraphrases that for transportation. Like roads, provisions of water and sewer

*This is the basic rationale behind the principles of the National Capital Plan, which is discussed and analyzed in greater detail in a chapter to follow.

facilities under conditions of sprawl necessarily involve higher per unit costs for installation of utilities because of the distance between dwelling units of subdivisions which must be covered. Under the higher densities envisioned for new towns, it is argued, these costs could be reduced and more efficient utility linkages provided between the residential neighborhoods and between residential areas and other land use areas. It is expected that additional economy would result from the orderly phasing of new town development into successive neighborhoods and other land use areas, and from analysis and determination of the most efficient balances between levels of demand which are built into the land use plan and the design capabilities of the utility systems.[20]

Open Space and Land Conservation

One of the major criticisms of suburban sprawl concerns its absorption of the fixed supply of land in metropolitan regions. Concern over the supply of land and dwindling open space in metropolitan areas has been voiced from many quarters, ranging from conservation groups to land developers, resulting in the identification of numerous causes, solutions, and points of view.[21]

The new town concept has had a longtime relationship to concern over land supply and open space, beginning with the Howard thesis. Howard's proposal for the grouping or clustering of new towns surrounded by greenbelts and separated by areas of open countryside, for example, is not fundamentally different from regional plans for the Washington, D.C. and Baltimore metropolitan regions.[22] These plans employ the general principles of the new town concept and have as major goals the conservation of land resources and the establishment of open and recreational spaces in the metropolitan region.

From a regional point of view, the primary characteristic of the new town concept which has won favor as a method for conserving land resources and preserving open spaces is the clustering of urban development. The reasoning is twofold and rather axiomatic: first, nucleation of new urban development (if adequate controls are exercised over areas not designated for urban uses) would reduce the amount of space usurped by urbanization; second, and also resulting from concentration, open areas of land would be more readily accessible under such a pattern.[23] From a related point of view, it is also suggested that the internal planning in new town development can provide more sensitively for the relationship between urban land uses and open spaces, parks, and recreation areas.[24]

New Towns and Social Balance in Suburbia

One of the most familiar characterizations of the metropolitan area has become that of a central city increasingly dominated by the poor, the aged, and minority groups, surrounded by more affluent suburban areas. Suburban areas themselves often tend to become balkanized among different socio-economic groups. If anything, this characterization appears to be increasing in accuracy in a number of the larger metropolitan areas.

The new town concept has always embraced the desirability of "social balance," out of the traditional perception of the new town as a full-fledged microcosm of the parent city. However, in recent years, new towns have come to be seen as a means for resolving some of the social imbalances and disparities of metropolitan areas. Because of the difficulties associated with this objective, such uses of the new town concept are usually linked with some form of public sponsorship or control over development, but even some private developers claim social balance as one of their objectives and are working to achieve both profitable and open communities.[25]

Since the degree of control over the development of new towns presumably holds potential for social as well as physical planning and experimentation, some proponents claim that new towns located on outlying land will avoid some of the resistance to lower socio-economic groups which is often encountered in established suburbs and that, once demonstrated, social balance in the suburbs will come to greater acceptance.[26]

In recent years it has become increasingly evident that the problem of providing decent jobs, homes, and living environments for the poor and blacks is almost insurmountable if inner city ghettos are the only alternatives to rural areas. In many of the larger, older metropolitan areas, manufacturing has steadily deserted the central city for cheaper and more spacious suburban sites, and most new plant location is largely avoiding the center city.[27] These trends have had massive impact on central cities and suburbs. One of the most significant aspects is that manufacturing shifts from inner city to suburban areas have made it more difficult for inner city workers to find, keep, and commute to jobs. For example, a study of the impact of plant relocations in the Boston area disclosed that of the workers in relocated plants who were interviewed ". . . for those who live in the core area commuting time increased by over two-thirds. Those residing in the suburbs shortened only slightly."[28]

New towns are envisioned as a highly useful vehicle for providing low-cost housing in suburban areas and for matching housing to job locations. A number of different strategies have been proposed in recent years. For example, a national population distribution strategy proposed by Planners For Equal Opportunity calls for ". . . relatively self-contained new towns . . . starting with government ownership and development of land . . ." in three types of locations throughout the country:

> First, in depressed areas such as Appalachia and the Mississippi Delta. In these areas, new cities could halt the march of the poor to our overcrowded metropolises.
>
> Second, already overpopulated and congested metropolitan areas could be relieved. Where ghettos are huge and overcrowded as in New York, Washington, Chicago, and the San Francisco Bay Area, new cities could materially reduce pressures on the ghettos

and bring people and jobs back into some proximity with each other.

Third, and most important in the long run, are cities built in presently unpopulated areas.[29]

Weissbourd and Channick have proposed a more detailed five-year program for ghetto dispersal ". . . aimed at the elimination of the ghetto and the creation of a desegregated society."[30] There are three basic elements in their strategy:

1. A massive ten-year program of development of New Towns in outlying areas to accommodate projected Negro and white population growth.
2. The construction in these New Towns of some additional 350,000 subsidized housing units each year for ten years. This will allow the ultimate replacement of urban substandard housing and create a temporary housing surplus.
3. The withdrawal of public expenditures for housing subsidies, sewers, water, roads, and mass transportation from ordinary subdivision development and their rechanneling into New Towns—virtually eliminating the competition of segregated housing development.[31]

One of the more recent developments in the case for new towns has been the call for so-called "black new towns." As expressed by Galantay, the black new town proposal embraces a number of objectives. Galantay also recognizes that the economic action in metropolitan areas is shifting in directions unfavorable to many central cities, and that blacks must have the opportunity to obtain suburban homes and jobs if the ghetto cycle of poverty is to be broken. He further recognizes the importance of so-called "ghetto enrichment" policies, as well as policies aimed at suburban integration. But he claims that black new towns offer the additional opportunity for blacks ". . . to control their own destinites . . . [and] . . . be masters of their own life and shape their own environment."[32]

For the most part, however, new towns have been promoted as a means of fostering social balance in suburban areas more by association with broader objectives for increasing housing opportunity throughout the metropolitan area than as a result of any inherent capacity of the new town development process to effect social balance (other than the ability to plan more sensitively for the integration of different housing prices and styles. In an intra-community, sense they are seen to provide opportunities for both physical and social innovation and experimentation which can further the objectives of socially-balanced communities.[33]

New Towns and Regional Planning

Many proponents of the new town concept consider it a potentially significant means for ordering urban development on a regional or area-wide basis. Gladstone submits, for example, that "At stake is the chance to create more appropriate solutions to problems of urban growth and extension while sustaining central city strength through a balanced regional development pattern."[34]

Lloyd Rodwin, who has scrutinized the British New Towns Policy and is often regarded as one of the critics of the new town concept, concludes in his study that

> ... new and expanded towns can be one of the means for increasing the range of choice of living patterns, both in central areas and elsewhere. By their existence they alter the form of the metropolis. By providing satisfactory alternatives for those who are displaced, they can facilitate the reconstruction of central areas. By experimentation they can also contribute to innovations adopted by others. Indirectly, therefore, they can make substantial contributions to greater variety in metropolitan form, density, and appearance.[35]

The particular appeal of the new town concept as a mechanism for regional planning is attributable to the fact that it may be readily translated into a desired spatial form for the organization of metropolitan growth, and that it is a multi-purpose concept. As opposed to scattered and small-scale development, new towns are considered to offer to create greater potential for the organization of substantial amounts of private development at strategic points in the region, and are conceptually linked with other regional objectives such as the preservation of open space and planning of regional transportation systems. Some of these advantages have been enumerated in the regional plan for the National Capital:

> This [new town] alternative offers a number of advantages. It would make a more efficient use of land, each resident in the Region could find housing suitable to his needs within a reasonable distance of his job; and conversely, each would have a variety of job opportunities within easy reach of his home. This, combined with the concentration of high density housing near large shopping districts, would reduce the amount of travel that takes place. The suburban communities would offer a much greater range of social, recreational and cultural resources than today's suburbia; and the new business districts would provide for greater choice, be better to look at and more pleasant to visit than most commercial areas of present day suburbia. This approach to regional development would make it much easier to preserve open spaces, and to reserve land for future needs, than in the case of all-encompassing sprawl. Finally, well-defined urban communities containing most of the economic, social and cultural institutions of a large city could encourage wide-spread citizen participation in government and civic affairs.[36]

In addition to these advantages, it is also evident that the new town concept is appealing as a possible solution to the difficulties, both conceptual and practical, which have confronted past attempts to plan and control the use of land at the metropolitan or regional level. The most serious shortcoming of regional planning has been the diffusion of land use control authority among a great number of individual units of government comprising the planning region. Through new town development, regional planning authorities would be able to deal more directly with large-scale developers or public development agencies whose projects have heavy impact upon regional development patterns.

New Towns and Local Planning

Some of the characteristics of new towns development relevant to local planning and land use control have already been touched upon in the discussion of the elements of the new town concept. (Local planning in this case is used to denote the internal land use planning of communities as opposed to the more traditional connotation of land use planning for existing communities.)

With respect to local planning, the major advantage of the new town concept appears to be that it proposes a system of planning and development control which differs from the auspices for traditional planning and development control by establishing a direct link between planning and execution of development. Although local land use plans and land use control regulations may exist in a new town development area, the new town development plan takes the process one step closer to execution. The most common operation of current American new town planning and development within the framework of local land use control powers follows the process whereby the developer's initiative is accommodated by planned unit development or planned community ordinances, and results in what has been referred to as "public planning." Typically, local land use regulations are developed after the land use pattern of the community has been determined. Although planning and land use controls are established by public authorities, the initiative for actual development rests largely in the hands of private land developers and builders. New town development under the more flexible planned development regulations can function to bring greater coordination to these separated stages. Moreover, under the mechanics of such an arrangement, compromises between the market considerations of private developers and the public objectives of local planning authorities may be more readily effected. The process also results in a more definitive system of land use control because the developer's detailed plans may be incorporated into local zone plans. Single ownership or control of large areas of land to be developed under a unified plan can result in less uncertainty on the part of local planning authorities as to future private development intentions (aside from market uncertainties which affect both parties). The effect, then, is a system under which local authorities can deal more directly in their local planning decisions with a single land owner whose development intentions are more predictable.*

New Towns and the Renewal of the Central City

Although the new town concept emerged as a result of dissatisfaction with the conditions of large existing cities, a part of the new town rationale today focuses upon the relationship of the new town to central city problems. There appear to be two major themes in the case for new towns which are related to the problems of renewal and revitalization of the central cities of metropolitan regions. The first of these is somewhat defensive. Although the creation of new towns obviously promotes a form of suburban growth, it should not be considered as a policy to hasten the decline of existing cities by aggravating decentralization of economic activity.[37] The argument is based on the line of reasoning that, because of space needs, population growth, and a variety of other factors, decentralization is an established and inevitable trend. Thus a policy for regrouping industry, population and commercial activities is intended to respond to rather than exacerbate decentralization.

The second theme is related to the first: by pre-planning suburban development into new towns, it is argued that a new towns policy is a preventative measure for urban re-

*As will be discussed in the following chapter, new town developers have been relatively successful in convincing local officials of the advantages of dealing with a large developer.

newal.[38] The reasoning in this case emphasizes that by promoting better planning in suburban developments, new towns can lessen the necessity for urban renewal in the future and, at the same time, would function to free financial resources for the more urgent problems of renewal in older urban areas. Gladstone offers that, given a new towns policy which takes cognizance of the interrelationship of the entire metropolitan region, "rather than competing with central cities, in a rational distribution of the region's activities, new communities would complement them."[39]

Others have advanced the notion that the new towns could be employed directly in the renewal of central cities. One proposal advocates that cities be empowered to enter into the operation of new town construction themselves by acquiring and disposing of exurban land in a manner similar to urban renewal.[40] Other proposals suggest that new towns could be constructed within existing cities.[41]

Other Regional Objectives

Related to the potential afforded by the new town concept for regional planning are arguments as to the advantages of new towns with respect to civil defense and the revitalization of depressed areas. Although these facets of the case for new towns are only indirectly related to the central focus of this study, they serve to illustrate the breadth of the case for new towns and are frequently employed to add weight to the new towns thesis.

New Towns and Civil Defense

For the most part, the deployment of new towns as a means of urban decentralization for defensive purposes appears to have declined in forcefulness. Most considerations of the subject would appear to agree with Augur who, although he claims that there are significant defensive advantages to urban dispersal via new towns, admits that it would be difficult to justify an effective commitment to a new towns policy solely on the basis of defense against nuclear attack. However, he does claim that the issue is not really in dispute, because new towns can be justified on other grounds as well. As he states the case,

> If a decrease in the nation's vulnerability to attack were the only thing to be achieved, either type of argument might have weight. But it happens that a sound program of dispersal for our cities would improve our position for a life of peace at the same time that it improved our chance of averting war and surviving one if it came. The same features of urban organization that make a modern nation strong for war also make it strong for peace. And a start in that direction can be made at once and carried forward vigorously without upsetting the established machinery of urban life or the national economy that it supports.[42]

It is interesting that Augur's assertion was precisely the issue submitted to analysis in a comprehensive study commissioned by the Office for Civil Defense in 1963. In brief, the study first set out to determine a pattern of urban dispersal which would not disrupt the basic economic functions of the metropolitan region, but which would also significantly reduce the effects of nuclear attack. The study configuration submitted to analysis consisted basically of a constellation of new towns of 75 to 100 thousand in population, separated by four to seven miles of open space.[43]

The second phase of the study reiterates many of the arguments for new towns, noting that:

> . . . it is certainly appropriate to observe that the urban configuration under examination here is consistent with the most influential, durable, and practically oriented line of thought in the ideal community tradition: the new towns movement. The latter will not stand or fall, of course, with the results of this study. On the contrary, the appeal here is to the weight of authority of a number of powerful and persuasive social thinkers. . . .[44]

The implementation phase of the study, however, corroborates Augur's earlier assertion.

Those who would seek acceptance by the public of ordered sprawl [the term used to describe the study configuration] and the strategies required to achieve it will have to do more than cite the underlying rationale of the endeavor; reduction of urban vulnerability is unlikely to strike large numbers of citizens as sufficient justification for undertaking a restructuring task of such magnitude.[45]

In practice, it appears that the new town concept has been employed more directly and may have greater utility in the offensive aspects of nuclear warfare. Ironically, specialized new towns such as Oak Ridge and Los Alamos have played a direct and dramatic role in the development and practical application of nuclear weaponry.[46]

New Towns and Depressed Areas

Basically, the advantages seen for new town development in depressed areas revolve around goals for concentrating existing resources within depressed regions into new communities which would render economies in the development of needed community facilities and assemble pools of available labor as an attraction to industry. In the preface to a study considering the mechanics needed for a new towns program for the Appalachian region, Grady Clay remarks that

The major function of a new town will be to provide that concentration of labor transport, capital, education and productive facilities which creates wealth. Without concentration there can be no wealth, few jobs, little education. Without concentration men fritter away their efforts singly, alone. It is in the New Town—communities of at least 50,000 population as a goal—that the people of Appalachian Kentucky can begin to find a choice of new jobs, and new opportunities for their children. It will be in these New Towns that employers will find concentration of people eager and able to work.[47]

New Towns as a Public Policy Response

The President's message on the housing bills of 1964 (Supra, p. 1) illustrates another facet of the case for a new towns policy. Basically, this aspect recognizes potentials for quid pro quo arrangements in the trend in the private sector toward large-scale development. As the statement illustrates, innovation and a concern for planning are observed as desirable characteristics of this trend, and it is felt that it is an appropriate role of government to enforce and bolster it with its assistance.

Subsequent statements by administration members indicate other facets of the rationale for the entry of the Federal government into the area of assistance to private new towns. Secretary Weaver states, for example, that the role of government is clearly to initiate assistance programs which can enhance the desirable aspects of this trend by providing incentives to private developers to incorporate public objectives into their communities.

> At this time, when we are just beginning to produce new communities, it is imperative that there be some demonstrations of the feasibility of housing low-income, moderate-income, and high-income families in well-designed and attractive communities which excite people's imagination and promise to afford a new form of suburban living. Without federal assistance and federal standards, few, if any, will emerge.[48]

Federal officials have also promoted the need for a new towns assistance program on the basis of regional planning objectives. Gordon Edwards, former Chief of the Planning Branch of HUD's Office of Metropolitan Development, offers the following rationale:

> What is the need for the [new communities] program? New towns are being built today. Land assembly has not been a major problem for private developers. But without this program the planning of new communities will be determined too often by fortuitous circumstances with little thought given to their impact upon existing urban areas, or upon existing local plans.
>
> This program will provide a mechanism by which developers, who are interested in the objectives of sound development in cooperation with responsible local governments, can act so as to

secure the assistance that will permit them to undertake the development of well-balanced communities within the context of metropolitan planning. I think it is clear that we need assistance for land development if this objective is to be realized.[49]

It is apparent from most of the literature and Congressional testimony on Federal proposals for assistance to developers of new towns that Federal officials believe that the trend of large-scale private community development can be manipulated through incentives to serve a variety of public objectives. Although there has been limited discussion of the prospect of a federal new towns program for several years, the impetus for recent discussion has clearly been provided by the operations of the private sector. Federal interest in the latter case has therefore been of a responsive nature, and one which will attempt to create a quid pro quo relationship between the government and the developer. The fact that an inevitable impact upon suburban development is recognized, and that many of the characteristics of the private developments are, at least in principle and plan, aligned with certain public objectives for metropolitan planning has generated the opinion that public assistance is both desirable and necessary. As Secretary Weaver has testified in hearings on the 1964 bill,

> The need for the Government program is dual. First, it is to accelerate this type of new community development; second, it is to get certain amenities in these types of development that are in the public interest; adequate open spaces; economical public facility development that anticipated future need. . . . We also want to have diversity in the economic levels of families for which these communities provide housing.[50]

Urban Growth

In addition to the "official" governmental position, a rationale for a new town program has come from a variety of other quarters. These arguments are often based upon broader perspectives than those which have already been treated. An increasingly popular argument for new towns is related to national population projections. Many discussions of the need for a new towns program in the United States are prefaced by reference to metropolitan expansion, the inevitability of burgeoning urban populations, and the imperative need to accommodate and order this growth. The general reasoning appears to be that the urgency of spatial and social problems of dealing with urban growth requires some type of national policy for urban expansion and settlement. The new town concept, which embraces all of the basic components of urban areas and has both local and regional implications, has probably received more attention than any other proposal at this level of consideration.

It may therefore be considered that one of the advantages of the new town concept is that it constitutes a comprehensive scheme for the development of the entire metropolitan region which has a relatively well-defined conceptual base. The major implication here is that, although it is generally recognized by most advocates of a new towns policy that new towns cannot provide the only scheme for urban expansion, the establishment of a new towns policy would provide a relatively uniform and definable process for ordering and directing growth. Gladstone argues, for example, that "urgently needed now is a comprehensive metropolitan development system that can effectively relate all the parts of the region to appropriate components of development, balancing the interests of the central city with new outlying developments."[51] As a scheme for metropolitan organization, then, the new town concept offers a spatial pattern and process, which at least in principle interrelates several urban development criteria.

The Scale of Components

Related to the comprehensiveness of the new town concept as a scheme for metropolitan order is the argument that changes in the form and scale of urban components have made the pursuit of new towns more feasible in terms of the operations of the private sector. It is argued, for example, that developments such as the suburban regional shopping center, the industrial park, large integrated public school complexes, and increasingly larger subdivision developments have created a series of "coagulants," which given the proper coordination and assistance can be effectively brought together into a community setting.[52] Increased suburban industrial development in recent decades has freed one of the essential elements of the new town concept from central city locations, and thereby made more feasible the assembly of more complete or "semi-self-sufficient" suburban communities.

Administration officials have also received the exhortation and support of some elements of the private sector, which believe that certain public goals could be furthered through private means if support were available. The Committee for a National Land Development Policy, composed of bankers, builders, and real estate interests and headed by a developer, has urged that such a policy be based upon the construction of 25 "new cities," each of one million population.[53] Several large developers appear to be of the opinion that, although the capabilities of the private sector to engage in development at the new town scale have increased significantly both financially and technologically, public support is necessary to reduce risk and insure the incorporation of certain facilities.[54] Developer James Rouse claims that public assistance is essential to the mobilization of the vast number of smaller developers and builders into coordinated large-scale development.[56]

Urban Development Laboratories

As was pointed out above, much of the traditional attractiveness of the new town concept to planners derives from its provision of a unique opportunity to plan urban development on a relatively clean slate. Connected with this appeal has been the claim that the new town concept requires sufficient demonstration and should be approached as a vehicle for innovation and experimentation.

In recent years, these attributes of the new town concept have been embellished and speculated upon not only by planners, but also by various public officials, technicians, and social scientists. Wheaton argues, for example, that new towns must become the models for achievement of traditional urban ideals.

> The United States alone among the major nations of the world has failed to adopt and implement some sort of new towns policy. As a consequence, we have no examples of the convenience, amenity, and economy characteristic of the high-quality new city design performance found in Scandinavian countries. We particularly need planned new cities to set design standards for a population which has come to accept scattered, unorganized growth as the norm. We have few distinguished examples of how beautiful an urban area can be. Thus, we urgently need 50 to 100 standard-setting models.[56]

In a similar vein, Thompson claims that "American industry needs an 'urban test tube' in which they can exercise free thought and ingenuity—unfettered by the shackles of tradition, political obstacles, and outmoded special interest municipal plants." He explains further that

> By establishing a satellite city under experimental conditions American industry would have a unique opportunity to exercise its ingenuity and resources in building a new community incorporating innovations in public facilities, home building and equipment, and amenities for good living never before available in one community.
>
> As a "laboratory city," this community will also test ideas for the solution of urgent economic as well as social problems of the central city.[57]

Other writers have been moved to consider various ways in which an experimental program in urban development might be undertaken. Rubel claims that the technologies and methods of problem analysis which have been developed in the aerospace program could be applied to urban development.

> The "new city projects" would provide a truly unique opportunity not just to plan or to analyze, but to apply the results of planning and analysis—actually experimentation—and to modify these in light of actual results. It is precisely such feedback that makes the concept of the "systems approach" meaningful when applied to socio-economic matters of such magnitude and gravity.[58]

Some writers are also of the opinion that new towns can supply an empirical base for research into various social, economic, and political aspects of community development, providing a unique opportunity to observe the process of community organization and establishment from its inception in relation to both the form and process of its physical organization. Gans points out, for example, that the "entire network of relationships we call community" may differ in a new town (as opposed to established communities) because of "its newness, its social organization and culture, and its social and ecological independence."[59]

Summary

The purpose of this chapter has been to discuss the case for new towns as it evolved from the varied literature on the subject. It is at first evident that the case for new towns has been argued from a variety of points of view. However, in general the case is not a uniform one. The claims of some new town enthusiasts would probably be unacceptable to others. Some recent converts to the new town idea have based their support for the concept rather narrowly on one or a few American examples by private developers.[60] Others have been more cautious and insist that government must take initiative. It is also clear that many of the arguments, or at least the manner in which they have been presented, are based on narrow criteria or are value-heavy and impressionistic.

In general, the new town concept appears to function today as it has in the past—as a vehicle for defining and synthesizing a variety of proposals for the improvement of specific problems of environment, and as a philosophy of the requirements of urban life in general. Historically, one of the characteristics of the new town concept has been a means for maintaining some sort of equilibrium in the form of urban development. Its original form, the Garden City idea generated from reaction against the congestion of existing cities at the turn of the century and a general anti-urbanism. The Garden City idea proposed lower densities and reversed the single-family home on larger lots.[61] Today, this form of development has become more the rule than the exception, and many modern proponents of the new town concept scorn the monotony of suburbia. In this light, the Garden City idea may not be out of keeping with prevalent housing tastes and aspirations.

It is also evident that much of the new town argument is phrased in terms of the potential for achievement of its objectives, given sufficient ability to create them and control their development. The recent crop of privately developed new towns, although in their early stages of development, indicate to some that the new town and its objectives may be achievable in the context of the entrepreneurial framework of American urban development.

Chapter 5 examines the motives and operations of American new town developers.

Notes

1. Ebenezer Howard, *Garden Cities of Tomorrow* (3rd ed.; Cambridge: M.I.T. Press, 1965), p. 46.

2. Clarence Stein, *Toward New Towns for America* (New York: Reinhold, 1957), p. 218.

3. Howard, op. cit., p. 26.

4. Albert Mayer, "Ingredients of an Effective Program for New Towns," *Proceedings of the 1964 Annual Conference,* Newark, August 16-20 (Washington, D.C.: American Institute of Planners, 1964), p. 186.

A similar viewpoint is expressed by Tracy Augur (Untitled Paper on New Towns), *Report of the Milwaukee Proceedings, 46th Annual Conference of the American Institute of Planners*, (Washington, D.C.: American Institute of Planners), p. 161.

5. Harold Orlans, *Utopia Ltd.* (London: Routledge and Kegan, 1952), pp. 99-100.

6. Robert C. Wood, *Suburbia, Its People and Its Politics* (Boston: Houghton-Mifflin, 1958), p. 92.

7. Harvey S. Perloff and Royce Hanson, "The Inner City and a New Urban Politics," *Urban America: Goals and Problems*, materials compiled and prepared for the Subcommittee on Urban Affairs of the Joint Economic Committee, Congress of the United States (Washington, D.C.: U.S. Government Printing Office, 1967), p. 165.

8. Ada Louis Huxtable, " 'Clusters' Instead of 'Slurbs,' " *The New York Times Magazine*, February 9, 1964, p. 37.

9. R. E. Gordon, K. K. Gordon, M. Gunther, *The Split-Level Trap* (New York: Dell, 1960), p. 24. For similar observations see A. C. Spectorsky, *The Exurbanites*, (New York: Lippincott, 1955); John Keats, *The Crack in the Picture Window* (Boston: Mifflin, 1957).

10. E. K. Faltermayer, "We Can Cope With the Coming Suburban Explosion," *Fortune* LXXIV, No. 4 (September 1966), p. 147.

11. E. A. Gutkind, *The Expanding Environment* (London: Freedom Press, 1953), as quoted in Edward P. Eichler and Marshall Kaplan, *The Community Builders* (Berkeley: University of California Press, 1967), p. 7.

12. Robert C. Weaver, "Federal Proposals May Solve City Problems," *New Towns: A New Dimension of Urbanism* (Chicago: International City Managers Association, 1966), p. 36. See also *House and Home*, XVIII, No. 2 (August 1960), 116; and *House and Home*, XXVI, No. 3 (September 1964), 41 ff.

13. William H. Whyte, Jr. "Urban Sprawl," *The Exploding Metropolis*, Editors of Fortune (Garden City: Doubleday, 1957), p. 17.

14. *House and Home*, Special Issue on Land, XVIII, No. 2 (August 1960), p. 114. See also National Capital Planning Commission and National Capital Regional Planning Council, *The Nation's Capital—A Plan for the Year 2000* (Washington, D.C.: U.S. Government Printing Office, 1961), p. 38.

15. Weaver, op. cit., p. 34.

16. Eichler and Kaplan, op. cit., p. 8. For similar observations, see James Dahir, *Communities for Better Living* (New York: Harper, 1950); E. Cartsonis, "New Towns: A Challenge to Partnership of Pri-

vate and Public Enterprise," *Planning 1967* (Chicago: American Society of Planning Officials, 1967), p. 175; and Serge Chermayeff and Christopher Alexander, *Community and Privacy* (New York: Doubleday, 1963), p. 72.

17. Mayer, op. cit., p. 187.

18. Some new towns currently under development, such as Columbia, will attempt to establish local bus systems. See also Secretary Weaver's discussion of local and regional transportation advantages of new towns in Robert C. Weaver, "Planned Communities," *Planned Communities,* Highway Research Record No. 97 (Washington, D.C.: Highway Research Board, 1965), pp. 1-6.

19. G. H. Perkins, "New Towns for America's Peacetime Needs," *Journal of the American Institute of Architects,* XV, No. 1 (January 1951), 14.

20. Maryland National Capital Park and Planning Commission, . . . *On Wedges and Corridors* (Silver Spring, 1964), p. 18. See also Perkins, op. cit., p. 12.

21. See, for example, Roger Willcox, "Trend of Development in the New York Region," *Planning 1948* (Chicago: American Society of Planning Officials, 1948), Whyte, op. cit., and "New Towns: Are They the Best Answer to the Land Use Problem," *House and Home,* XXVI, No. 3 (September 1964), 64-70.

22. Maryland-National Capital Park and Planning Commission, op. cit.; National Capital Planning Commission and National Capital Regional Planning Council, op. cit.; Baltimore Regional Planning Council, *Metrotowns for the Baltimore Region—Stages and Measures,* Planning Report No. 2, Baltimore: Maryland State Planning Department, 1962.

23. See, for example, Stanley Tankel (untitled paper), *Open Space and the Metropolis,* Selected Portions of the Proceedings of the Fourth Annual Conference of the Organization of Cornell Planners, 1960, p. 53. See also the recommendation of that report, p. 94.

24. Shirley Siegel, *The Law of Open Space* (New York: Regional Plan Association, Inc., 1960), p. 58. See also Mayer, op. cit., p. 187.

25. Attention appears to be focused on the new town of Columbia, Maryland in this regard, where most of the progress appears to be taking place. See, for example, the articles dealing with low-income housing and foreign-born members of the community in the developer's magazine *Columbia Today,* III (April/May 1970).

26. Edgardo Contini, "New Perspectives for Urban America," *Urban America: Goals and Problems,* p. 266.

27. See, for example, Advisory Commission on Intergovernmental Relations, *State-Local Taxation and Industrial Location,* Report A-30 (Washington, D.C.: U.S. Government Printing Office, 1967) pp. 19-22.

28. Everett J. Burtt, Jr., *Plant Relocation and the Core City Worker* (Washington, D.C.: U.S. Government Printing Office, 1967), p. 4. See also John F. Kain, "Coping With Ghetto Unemployment," *Journal of the American Institute of Planners,* XXXV, No. 2 (March 1969) pp. 80-89; and Jeanne R. Lowe, "Race, Jobs, and Cities: What Business Can Do," *Saturday Review,* January 11, 1969, p. 27.

29. Planners for Equal Opportunity, *New Cities for Black and White* (New York: Planners for Equal Opportunity, 1970), p. 8. See also the statement of Joseph P. Lyford in U.S. Congress, Senate, *Federal Role in Urban Affairs,* Hearings Before the Subcommittee on Executive Reorganization of the Committee on Government Operations, 89th Cong., 2nd Sess., Part 6 (Washington, D.C.: U.S. Government Printing Office, 1966), p. 1334.

30. Bernard Weissbourd and Herbert Channick, "An Urban Strategy," *The Appraisal Journal,* January 1970, p. 101.

31. Ibid., p. 102.

32. Ervin Galantay, "Black New Towns: The Fourth Alternative," *Progressive Architecture* XLIX, No. 8 (August 1968), pp. 126-127. The author goes on to spell out how a black new town strategy might be put into operation, including using land from military reservations.

33. See, for example, David S. Arnold, "What New Towns Ought to Be," *New Towns: A New Dimension of Urbanism* (Chicago: International City Managers Association, 1966), p. 52.

34. Robert Gladstone, "Planned New Communities and Regional Development," *Proceedings: 1965 Government Relations and Planning Policy Conference* (Washington, D.C.: American Institute of Planners, 1965), p. 44. See also G. H. Perkins, "The Regional City," *The Future of Cities and Urban Redevelopment,* ed. Coleman Woodbury (Chicago: University of Chicago Press, 1953), p. 39.

35. Lloyd Rodwin, *The British New Towns Policy* (Cambridge: Harvard University Press, 1956), p. 176.

36. National Capital Planning Commission, op. cit., p. 38.

37. Robert C. Weaver, *Dilemmas of Urban America* (Cambridge: Harvard University Press, 1965), p. 36.

38. See, for example, the discussion of the Community Builders Council, *The Community Builders Handbook* (Washington, D.C.: Urban Land Institute, 1960), p. 189; and Wolf Von Eckardt, "New Towns in America," *The New Republic* October 26, 1963, p. 18.

39. Robert M. Gladstone, "New Towns Role in Urban Growth Explored," *Journal of Housing,* XXXII, No. 1 (January 1966). Similar views are expressed in Perkins, "New Towns . . . Needs," p. 93; and James Rouse, "The City of Columbia, Maryland," *Taming Megalopolis,* ed. H. W. Eldredge (New York: Praeger, 1967), II, p. 843.

40. Governor's Advisory Commission on Housing Problems, *Housing in California* (n.d.), Summary (unpaged).

41. Harvey S. Perloff, "New Towns Intown," *Journal of the American Institute of Planners,* XXXII, No. 3 (May 1966), pp. 155 ff; Perloff and Hanson, op. cit., p. 162 ff.; and Mayer, op. cit., p. 92.

42. Tracy Augur, "The Dispersal of Cities As a Defense Measure," *Journal of the American Institute of Planners,* Summer 1948, p. 31. Similar viewpoints are expressed in William L. C. Wheaton, "New Towns for American Defense," *Journal of the American Institute of Architects,* XV, No. 1 (January 1951), 4-5; and Albert Mayer, "A New Town Program," *Journal of the American Institute of Architects,* XV, No. 1 (January 1951), 8-9. Rodwin, op. cit., p. 176-177, suggests that the defensive aspect of new towns may be exaggerated, and notes that it has become less of a consideration in new town size, density, and location in Britain.

43. H. R. Woltman and E. C. Goodrow, *Civil Defense Implications of Current and Future Urban Configurations,* prepared for the Office of Civil Defense (Los Angeles: Planning Research Corporation, 1963).

44. H. R. Woltman et al., *The Economic Feasibility of Decentralized Metropolitan Regions,* prepared for the Office of Civil Defense (Los Angeles: Planning Research Corporation, 1965), pp. iv-v.

45. Keith R. Blunt et al., *Implementation of an Ordered Sprawl Urban Configuration,* prepared for the Office of Civil Defense (Los Angeles: Planning Research Corporation, 1967), p. 147.

46. See David S. Geer, "Oak Ridge: A World War II New Town," *Journal of the American Institute of Architects,* XV, No. 1 (January 1951); and Carroll A. Towne, "Atomic Energy Community Developments," *Landscape Architecture,* XLIII, No. 3 (April 1954). Similar uses of the new town concept may be forthcoming as Congress considers legislation to create community development legislation for a test site community in Nevada. U.S., Congress, Senate, *Nevada Test Site Community,* Hearings Before the Subcommittee on Legislation and Subcommittee on Communities of the Joint Committee on Atomic Energy, 88th Cong., lst Sess. on H.R. 8003 and S. 2030 (Washington, D.C.: U.S. Government Printing Office, 1963), part I.

47. Department of Architecture, University of Kentucky, *New Towns for the Appalachian Region* (Lexington, 1960), p. 2. See also D. B. Steele, "New Towns for Depressed Areas," *Town Planning Review,* XXXIV, No. 3 (October 1963); and *Progressive Architecture,* "New Town-New Hope for Mississippi," XLVII, No. 9 (September 1966),192-94; University of Louisville, Urban Studies Center, *New Community Development As A Means For Realizing Urban and Rural Opportunities* (Louisville, 1968).

48. Weaver, *Dilemmas* p. 36.

49. Gordon Edwards, "The Proposed Federal Program," *Planning 1964* (Chicago: American Society of Planning Officials, 1964), p. 157. The particulars of the proposed Federal program are discussed in a later chapter.

50. U.S., Congress, Senate, Housing Legislation of 1964, op. cit., p. 101.

51. Gladstone, "New Towns Role" pp. 32-33.

52. Carl Feiss, "New Towns for America," *Journal of the American Institute of Architects,* XXIII (January 1960), pp. 87-88.

53. "U.S. Asked to Help Build New Cities," *The New York Times,* July 31, 1966, p. 87. See also *Architectural Forum,* CXXIV, No. 6 (June 1966), 87.

54. Maggie Bellows, "He'd [William J. Levitt] Mass Produce Whole New Cities at $1 Billion Each," *The Democrat and Chronicle,* Rochester: July 31, 1966, p. 1.

55. U.S., Congress, House, *Demonstration Cities, Housing and Urban Development, and Urban Mass Transit.* Hearings before the Subcommittee on Banking and Currency, 89th Cong., 2nd Sess. (Washington, D.C.: U.S. Government Printing Office, 1966), pp. 1050-51.

56. William L. C. Wheaton, "Form and Structure of the Metropolitan Area," *Environment for Man,* ed. William Ewald, Jr. (Bloomington: Indiana University Press, 1967), p. 174.

57. Wayne E. Thompson, "Prototype City—Design for Tomorrow," *New Towns: A New Dimension of Urbanism* (Chicago: International City Managers Association, 1966), p. 39. Similar needs and potentials have been speculated upon in a series of articles published in the *Democrat and Chronicle* (Rochester, N.Y.) by A. Spilhous, "The City of Tomorrow . . .," beginning March 19, 1967, p. 1H.

58. John H. Rubel, "The Aerospace Project Approach Applied to Building New Cities," *Taming Megalopolis,* ed. H. W. Eldredge, (New York: Praeger, 1967), p. 374.

59. Herbert Gans, "The Sociology of New Towns: Opportunities for Research," *Sociology and Social Research,* XL (March/April, 1956), p. 232. Gans has subsequently followed up on the research opportunities which he indicates above, and to some extent refutes his earlier contentions. The relevant literature for new towns is reviewed in Chapter 7 of this study.

60. See, for example, Wolfgang Langewiesche, "Look At America's 'New Towns,' " *Reader's Digest* (March 1967), pp. 140-145.

61. Donald L. Foley, "Idea and Influence: The Town and Country Planning Association," *Journal of the American Institute of Planners,* XXVIII, No. 1 (February 1962), p. 14.

5 Some Characteristics of American New Town Developers and Developments

As noted in Chapter 1, the primary impetus to the recently enacted new communities program and the rebirth of interest in public support for new town development has come from the significant increase in private new town and large-scale community development since 1960. For the most part, although these developments have received increasing attention from various quarters, there has been relatively little research into the operations of private new town developers, largely because of the nascency of the trend and, hence, the lack of an established empirical base.*

The purpose of this chapter is to discuss the characteristics and operations of private new town developers. It will treat specifically the types of new town developers, their motivations, objectives, financial backing, and relationships with

*The only comprehensive research known by this writer to be under way is being conducted by the Community Development Project of the University of California at Berkeley under a $250,000 grant from the Ford Foundation. Some of the findings of this research have been published and will be drawn upon in this chapter. However, this discussion will also draw upon a variety of promotional material and other sources.

local governments, and the sizes, locations and compositions of their projects. Understandably, this discussion focuses for the most part upon the initial phases of private new town development. These characteristics will be related to current legislation and legislative proposals in the following chapter.

The New Town Developers

The motivations, objectives, operating strategies and other characteristics of new town developers in general in the United States have led some observers to characterize them as a "new breed" in the private sector of urban development.[1] As will be discussed below, in view of the new combinations of traditional agents in urban development with new sources of interest and financial backing, this characterization appears appropriate.

Motivations and Objectives

Although different aspects of the motivations and objectives of private developers are emphasized in various discussions of private new town development, Kaplan points out that basically all new town developers in the United States "would agree that making money is one of their prime objectives."[2]

Private community building provides a wide range of profitable enterprises in which developers may choose to become involved. A sampling is provided in the following reference to Park Forest, a community begun by American Community Builders south of Chicago in the late 1940's.

> The basic premise was that a subdivider or builder creates many values on which he does not realize. He takes his quick profit on the main items, land and buildings, but neglects the buying power newly created in the community. American Community Builders envisioned a larger operation, with a substantial number of rental units under long-term ownerships, a profitable shopping center,

several sidelines, on the theory that this was the way to profitable operation with successive income from one single item, say rents.[3]

Eichler and Kaplan point out that sometimes the current American new town developer desires to build some structures as "income property" because "by owning not only a parcel of land but the buildings on it as well, he can get a much more favorable tax treatment on his income tax than if he were to sell the buildings." The major advantage to the developer is the likelihood that the sale of land and improvements at a later time can be ruled under current tax laws as a capital gain rather than ordinary income, the capital gain tax rate being only 25 percent for ordinary corporate profit.[4]

But Kaplan points out that most of ACB's successors are at least beginning with the intention of a less extensive involvement in all phases of community development.

> Most developers seek to confine their activities to acquiring land, planning the community and then pre-servicing the land with water, sewer, and other public facilities. They are not true community builders, and they hope, in effect, to market finished lots to builders. Expectations are that the primary source of profit will emanate from land appreciation accruing to the development because of its planned community image and the availability of community services. Additionally, they see the builder as willing to pay a premium to be buffered from local political pressures.[5]

Still, most American new towns exist primarily on multicolored paper, since most of the projects are in the planning phases, or in early stages of development. However, these plans and their various uses provide further insight into the motivations and operations of developers. For example, in their promotional uses, new town master plans contrast the advantages of the planned new town environment with the disadvantages of the city and more conventional suburban areas. The aesthetic attributes of the new town as opposed to "blighted and smog-bound cities" or "chaotic and sprawling suburban subdivision and commercial development" are invariably stressed. Contrasts often allude to the preservation of natural features of the landscape in new towns, the accessibility and adequacy of planned community facilities, well-located schools, the eventually shortened journey to work, the abundance of recreation and open spaces, and a variety of other features. Since the features of most new towns are aimed at a suburbanizing population, the contrast places greater emphasis upon the planned new town as opposed to unplanned suburban development. The major point of the developers' promotion appears to be that since the new town is "planned" these features will be instituted.

It appears that new town developers have been influenced to a significant degree by criticisms of stereotypical American suburban development and by the alternatives posed by the Garden City idea and its more current versions. Paraphrasing the Garden City idea, promotional literature for the new town of Valencia states that: "Here on the eastern portion of the vast and historic Newhall Ranch, we are creating the new town of Valencia . . . a community which will combine the best of town and country life . . . the best of old and new.[6]

It would be difficult to assess the impact of planners and architects upon developers, but it nevertheless appears that new town developers and builders have become convinced that the new town concept can be a profitable commodity. If the nature of their claims is indicative, most developers feel that both they and the residents of new towns will profit from new town planning and development.

It would also be difficult to determine a clear dividing line between idealism and business practice in the promotion of new towns by their developers, but the adoption of the concept by some private developers appears to have been spurred by a form of practical idealism. This has been most vigorously promoted by Columbia developer James Rouse, who is convinced that "the surest way to make the American city what it ought to be is to demonstrate that it's enormously profitable to do it a better way.[7]

110

Types of Developers

Kaplan distinguishes the types of developers involved in the construction of new towns according to what he terms "the expansionists" and "the non-expansionists." His basic distinction is between those developers and corporations who "perceive themselves as having developed sufficient expertise to operate in a wide number of development areas" and those developers which appear to concentrate their financial commitments in new towns to a single undertaking. The expansionist group would be characterized by such developers as Sunset International Petroleum Company (Sunset City, California) the Del Webb Corporation (several large developments throughout California), and the Janss Corporation (Conejo, near Los Angeles). The second group is characterized by a more personal and philosophical approach to new town building. Kaplan would cast these developers in the roles of missionaries "determined to bring to America a better way of life," among them James Rouse (Columbia, Maryland), and Robert Simon (Reston, Virginia). These developers, he feels, are more inclined to stress and experiment with community design and social facilities in their projects.[8] Although this distinction appears to be generally appropriate with regard to the types of developers currently active in new town development, simple classification obscures some of the combinations of investors and the varieties of investment resources which have been attracted to or are considering new town development. For example, in some cases, large industries have acted as financial backers for traditional land developers; in others they have functioned more directly as developer (or intend to eventually); and in still others, they have combined with or bought out land development corporations. Consequently, several different types of developer interests may be involved in a given new town, among them traditional land developers, large financial institutions, large industries, oil companies, mortgage lenders, and large land owners. In practice, the management responsibilities may vary in a given project and also may change during its development. However, some general categories are evident.

Developer-Builders

The majority of American new town developers are from the larger members of the land development and home-building industries. These include companies with past land development experience and often multiple participation in the construction of new towns. Among the most active are: the Horizon Land Corporation (Horizon City, Texas; Paradise Hills, N.J.; and New Tuscon, Arizona); the Del Webb Corporation; the Janss Corporation; Macco Realty; Ross Cortese; Gulf American Land Corporation; and Deltona Corporation. Other developer-builders such as Panitz, developers of Joppatowne, Maryland, and T. Jack Foster and Sons have had extensive experience in land development and construction.* Because of their previous experience in building as well as land development, these firms are more likely to engage in the construction phase of new town development more than other new town developers.

Large Land Owners

Large land owners may participate in new town development in various ways. Owners of large parcels of land (most of whom appear to be in the southwest, and particularly in California), may elect to become land-owner developers or set up land development corporations in which part of the land may be developed by the corporation or other portions sold to other land developers. Among these are: the Laguna Niguel Corporation; the Huntington Beach Company; and the

---

*Although many of these firms are listed as the "developers" of new towns, it should be remembered that they are often "backed" financially by large industries, insurance companies, and mortgage interests. In some cases, as will be discussed below, these firms are subsidiaries of companies which are not primarily in the business of community building.

Mission Viejo Company. The largest of the American new towns, Irvine Ranch, is to be developed by the Irvine Company, controlled by the original owner of the property. A 1,000 acre portion of the 93,000 acre site, to be called University City, will contain a large campus of the University of California.[9]

Non-Expansionists

Among the most closely observed and widely acclaimed new towns in the United States are those of the "non-expansionists," or developers who appear to be concentrating upon one particular project. Among these, Reston, Virginia, begun by real estate entrepreneur Robert Simon, has probably received the majority of attention.* Like Simon, whose initials are the basis for the name of Reston, mortgage banker James Rouse has almost become synonymous with Columbia, Maryland. Construction in Columbia is behind that in Reston, but the project has received much attention because of the consideration given to social as well as physical planning. Both Simon and Rouse have assumed the roles of spokesmen for the new town idea, and are sometimes regarded as the social visionaries of the private new town trend.†

Oil Companies

Because of their advantageous tax position and continual relationship with land, oil companies have become the

---

*Although Simon's experience in real estate might warrant his classification among the traditional builders and developers, that experience, which has been primarily in the management of Carnegie Hall and indirectly in shopping center development, is somewhat more specialized than that of other developer-builders. As will be discussed below, Simon has since lost control of the management of Reston's development, but he is referred to as the developer in most of this discussion because most of the planning and early phases of development were conducted during this period of control.

†Allen Lindsey, developer of El Dorado Hills, California, might also be classified among the non-expansionist group. Lindsey's major interests have been primarily in retail department stores.

dominant new investors in the new town idea, both as principal and financial backer. Gulf Oil has invested heavily in Reston and has since assumed management of the project,* and is also active in new towns in the San Francisco and Sacramento regions. Sunset International Petroleum (now Sunasco), having acquired a number of building companies, has progressed to the point where the vast majority of its earnings are derived from real estate. It is the developer of San Marin in Marin County, San Carlos in San Diego County, and Sunset City in Sacramento County. The California-based McCulloch Oil Company is the developer of Havasu City, Arizona; and Humble Oil, a subsidiary of Standard Oil of New Jersey, is the primary developer of Clear Lake City, outside of Houston.

Other Participants and Interests

In addition to the operations of oil companies, the involvement of a variety of other interests, both actual and potential, has given the primary impetus to increased enthusiasm and claims for the widespread significance of the private new town trend. In combination with other types of developers, the participation of these interests often results in bewildering corporate structures. The initial financing of Columbia, for example, involves a complex structure consisting of the Rouse Company, Community Research and Development (of which 30 percent of the stock is owned by the Rouse Company), and the Howard Research and Development Corporation (in which all 2,000 shares of stock are owned by Connecticut General).[10] Teachers Insurance Annuity Association of America and the Chase Manhattan Bank are also major backers of Columbia.

---

*Some oil companies have taken various positions with regard to their objectives in new towns. In addition to the profits from land development, for example, some companies have also formed monopolies on service stations in the new towns which they are developing or backing.

In return for title to all undeveloped land in Reston, John Hancock Insurance Company loaned Robert Simon $21 million for the early phase development of Reston.[11] In addition to John Hancock and Connecticut Mutual, the Metropolitan Life Insurance Company has been active in several retirement communities.[12]

Other investment interests and combinations of interests in new towns vary. In the Los Angeles region, one of the largest new towns, Vail Ranch (87,000 acres), is to be developed by Kaiser Industries, the Macco Realty Corporation, the Janss Corporation, and the Boston Mortgage House of Cabot, Cabot and Forbes. The latter is also a major interest in the new town of Laguna Niguel in Orange County, California. Goodyear Tire and Rubber Company is heavily involved in the development of Litchfield Park, Arizona (being developed on the Goodyear Farm landholdings).

The entry of several large national corporations into new town development, either directly or indirectly, appears to have been spurred by the potentials afforded by large-scale community development for diversification of investments and product testing and for sales stimulation, or for both. Also, "... financial analysts appear to upgrade the earnings multiple of real estate-oriented firms ..."[14] In a less direct manner, some corporations have indicated their interest in activities which may result in a general public benefit. As one article has reported, "General Electric, among others, feels that the new town could be both a stimulus and a proving ground for a new urban technology, comprising products and services that could make cities pleasanter, more efficient, more socially stable places to live."[13]

Some companies are already involved in projects. Westinghouse Electric Corporation, for example, is building an "experimental new town," Coral Springs, Florida, where it intends to test and improve its products with the assistance of a projected population of 60,000 persons.[15] General Electric has similar intentions and has announced plans for a community of 100,000 population (on a site to be selected). The community will be developed over a period of 15 to 20 years as a showpiece for technological innovation and other "breakthroughs."[16]

Another characteristic of the new interests in large-scale community development has been the increase in vertical integration and mergers of companies with products related to community development. Boise-Cascade, a lumber and timber company, for example, has absorbed several large homebuilding enterprises, including Perma-Built Enterprises (of California) and U.S. Land Corporation (developers of several resort communities in various parts of the country). Recently, Levitt and Sons, developers and builders for the forerunners of the current new towns, was purchased by International Telephone and Telegraph, and will embark on the creation of independent communities with sufficient business and industry to support populations up to 250,000 persons. Similarly, Macco Realty, developer of Porter Ranch and a holder of large areas of land in southern California, has been purchased by the Pennsylvania Railroad as a means of "diversification into areas clearly related to its basic endeavors."[17]

Aluminum companies also appear to have stepped up activity in new towns. Alcoa, which is already involved in community development, has been joined by Kaiser, which has recently formed a subsidiary land development corporation. Market creation is also one of the major objectives of American Cement, which is already involved in a resort community and Janss/Conejo. The company's president, James P. Giles, "talks about going beyond merely supplying materials to provide management and technical talent."[18] Lytton Industries is also reported to be seriously considering the potentials of new town development.

There are currently no new towns in the United States which are being developed under the sponsorship of a public-private consortium. However, the first stage of planning for a recently proposed experimental new town in Minnesota is being financed by $248,000 in grants from the Federal Departments of Housing and Urban Development, Health, Education and Welfare, and Commerce. The proposed new town would contain a population of 250,000 and will involve the operations of several Minnesota companies and the University of Minnesota. The purpose of the project is to establish a "self-contained" new town at least 100 miles from an existing metropolitan center.[19]

Operations of Private New Town Developers

As with the previously discussed new town developers, information for this section has been obtained from various sources. Some new towns have received more attention in the literature than others and more emphasis is placed on these developments. Other new towns are in such early stages of planning or development that only general information is available concerning them.

Since the number of new towns in the United States prohibits reference to all of them, an Appendix has been provided containing some of the characteristics of several new towns. The following discussion will be based in part on the data contained in the Appendix.

The actual operations of private new town developers may vary from developer to developer depending upon the basic objectives for the community, the type of developer, and the extent of financial commitment. The three major areas for profit appear to be: long-run returns from developed land (or simply re-zoned land in some cases); shorter-term income from sales of houses; and long-run returns from income properties such as office and retail space.[20] However, as was discussed above, the primary activity of most American new town developers appears to center on the infrastructural phase of community development. In this respect (as well as others) the role of the new town developer in the urban development process is somewhat distinct from that of the speculator, subdivider or builder. Land speculators seek

117

profits from the appreciation of land value, but do not perform an improvement function. Although the new town developer functions as a land subdivider, he performs the additional function of detailed planning. Developers may engage in the building of some "income property" in the new towns, such as recreation centers or shopping centers, but this is usually subordinate to their primary function of preparation of land for development.

Generally, the new town developer takes his profit from the sale of improved lots and parcels to residential, commercial, and industrial builders. However, he does have the potential to engage in any phases of community development beyond that of land development. Much depends upon the nature of the developer. Some development corporations which are composed of developer-builder combinations, for example, tend to be involved more extensively in community development. Large land holders or owners, on the other hand, tend to set up corporations for the land development and engage primarily in the sale of lots.

The above discussion focused in part upon one of the three major variables in private new town development—that of financing. However, the success of private new town development largely depends upon the interrelationship of financing with the two other major variables of the process—size and location.

Size

Perhaps the most distinguishing feature of many of the current new towns is their size, both in terms of the acreage which they encompass and their projected populations. Virtually all of the developments which have been referred to in the United States as new towns are over 2,500 acres. Population projection for most new towns ranges between 25 and 100 thousand persons.* However, densities will vary widely.

*Theoretical or ideal population sizes do not appear to have had much influence in the projected population sizes or acreages of American new towns. Target populations of most new towns are probably more a function of the developer's

For example, Laguna Niguel, at 7,100 acres, is projected for an ultimate population of 90,000. This is about double the density per acre of Westlake Village, which is projected for a population of 70,000 on 12,000 acres.

Generally, the new towns in the mid-Atlantic region are projected at higher densities than most new towns, and the southwestern new towns at lower densities than most. (Lake Havasa and Sun City, Arizona, at 3.7 persons per gross acre, are among the lowest.) However, the vast majority of new towns will contain multi-unit housing, and several are projected for high-rise development.

Sizes and projected populations of new towns are perhaps most striking relative to the prevalent scale of operations in community development. As Eichler and Kaplan point out,[21]

> Aside from a very few exceptions (such as Lakewood in Southern California, and the Levittowns), a large subdivider or merchant builder rarely works on a single parcel of more than 1,000 acres or 2,500 housing units. The largest merchant builders produce at most 700 to 1,000 housing units a year in any one location. A few may build a total of from 1,500 to 3,000 houses per year. Annual production of more than 200 houses (on about 70 acres) in any single location marks one as a large builder.[1]

By contrast, new towns appear to average out to around 10,000 acres, and range from 2,500 up to 90,000 acres.

Nearly all of the largest new towns are located in the southwestern area of the nation. California not only contains the largest number of new towns under way, but also the largest in scale. Notable among these are Irvine (93,000 acres), Vail Ranch (87,000 acres), Mission Viejo (55,000), and Valencia (a 44,000 acre portion of the Newhall Ranch). Another new town, as yet unnamed, is projected for the 88,000-acre Hearst properties south of Monterey.

The scale of new towns is probably the most influential factor with respect to the manner in which they are devel-

estimates of his investments program and capacity, and the areal size of his landholdings, and most important, the market and zoning characteristics of his area.

oped. As will be discussed below, the scale at which a developer decides to operate can influence the location of the town (although the opposite is true as well), and affects the development period, programming of development, land assembly techniques, the range of community facilities, and relations with local governments.

Location

From a national perspective, the locations of the majority of new towns reflect, for the most part, the fastest growing metropolitan regions in the nation. The largest number of new towns are being developed in California where the rapid rate of population growth and the availability of large parcels of undeveloped land in single ownerships have been the primary impetus to the founding of new towns. Other dominant regions include the remainder of southwest, the National Capital Region, and Florida.

However, within particular metropolitan regions a variety of factors may influence site selection. Most important are land price, site availability (including the factor of number of ownerships), access to the regional transportation network, and favorable zoning. There are various permutations among these factors which appear to influence the developer's decision. The size of the site itself is important if the prospective developer believes that a certain acreage is critical to achieving his objectives. Most developers are not original landowners and therefore must expend considerable sums for land acquisition, while retaining sufficient capital to enter into the development process. Generally, land prices are inversely related to the distance from existing centers of population.

Access to the transportation network is of particular importance because development focuses initially upon residential development. Although the majority of new towns in America are projected for some degree of self-containment and will attempt to attract industry to create sources of employment within their borders, their locations usually reflect a heavy dependence upon existing urban centers in the early stages of town building. One of the planners of Columbia states that:

> ... the site had to be located in the magnetic field of a growing metropolitan area. It could not be in an area set apart, because houses cannot be built without jobs nearby, and jobs need people. Therefore the site had to be where it was actually possible for people who would buy houses to commute to work.[22]

Favorable zoning is particularly critical in private new town development. In most of the areas in which new towns are located, the existing zoning is seldom fitted to accommodate large-scale, multi-purpose development. Therefore, developers must necessarily obtain zoning changes. The extent to which the zoning factor is critical to private new town success is illustrated by the case of one developer who was forced by local zoning officials to drastically revise his plan, which amounted to a reduction in his population projection from 31,000 to 20,000 persons.[23]

Most new town developers appear to have opted in favor of large sites under pre-existing single ownership. Consequently, most developers have had to locate beyond the established environs of metropolitan areas. For example, to find a site suited to his goals, Simon was forced to acquire land 18 miles west of the capital. Columbia may be better situated, since it will draw upon markets from both the Baltimore and Washington metropolitan areas. But it is located about the same distance from these centers as Reston is from Washington (15 miles from Baltimore and 25 miles from Washington).

A number of other large new towns are located several miles from their parent cities. Among them are: Litchfield Park, about 18 miles west of Phoenix; Valencia, about 30 miles north of Los Angeles; El Dorado Hills, 25 miles from Sacramento; Irvine, approximately midway between Los

Angeles and San Diego; and Clear Lake City, 25 miles from Houston.

Other developers (but fewer) have focused upon location adjacent or closer to existing cities. Redwood Shores, for example, is adjacent to Redwood City, California. However, most of the site was created by extensive land fill at the water's edge, a process which was also employed at Foster City, California.

In general, the locations of new towns indicate that they are primarily inspired by metropolitan expansion. With one notable exception—Havasu City, Arizona—all are located in the orbit of metropolitan areas.

Land Assembly and Development

It is sometimes difficult to distinguish with respect to the assembly of land for new towns the extent to which a developer's decision to operate at a certain scale influences the location of the town, or the extent to which the availability of land influences location. The difference may be in whether the developer owned the land prior to the decision to develop a new town. That is, some developers have owned large sites for several years and have waited for their ripening for urban development. Others, however, have purchased their land from single owners of large parcels. Still others, but apparently much fewer, have assembled parcels from several ownerships.[24]

Although the rapid growth of the southwest probably accounts for the large number of new towns being developed there, land ownership patterns also appear to influence both the number and size of these developments. Most of the large new towns in California, for example, are being constructed on lands (mostly ranches) which have been in single ownership or control for several decades—the Irvine property since 1864, Newhall Ranch since 1875, O'Neil Ranch (Mission Viejo) since 1906, and the Janss property since 1911.[25] Other large sites which were held in single ownership prior to the decision to develop new towns were Goodyear Farms (Litchfield Park, Arizona), and the Humble Oil property outside of Houston. The latter was purchased in 1938 for $300 per acre.[26] On the basis of existing prospects, it would appear that potential developers appear to prefer seeking out large parcels of land under single or corporate ownership, although the case is prejudiced somewhat by the fact that several original owners are themselves acting as developers. The reasons for this apparent preference may lie in the difficulties which attend attempts to assemble large parcels of land at reasonable prices from properties under different ownerships. When an area has a high development potential, such as Howard County, Maryland, where Columbia is to be built, the risks of rapidly rising land prices are considerable. Rouse, for example, found it necessary to acquire his land surreptitiously through dummy buyers and front organizations, in which many of the people whom he employed were unaware of the purposes of the operation.[27] As Eichler and Kaplan phrase it, "The story of Rouse's negotiations with land owners . . . reads like a James Bond novel; secret rooms, plot strategy, and dummy corporations characterized the process."[28] After six months and about 170 separate transactions, Rouse had managed to assemble 15,000 acres at an average of slightly less than $1,500 per acre. Rouse had originally considered building his new town in the corridor between New York and Boston, but found great difficulty in locating a suitable parcel for what he was willing to pay.

The site for Reston, Virginia was assembled with less difficulty, the majority of the town site being obtained from the ownership of a distillery. However, Simon had to pay $1,900 an acre for it. Rouse's land assembly technique brought some economies since the acquisition of Columbia's site averaged $400 less per acre than Reston's; however, the method employed in Columbia involved certain risks and waiting costs.[29]

More balkanized ownership patterns in the central and eastern portions of the country may account partially for the smaller new towns being developed in them. In the rapidly growing Baltimore-Washington region where nine developments over 2,000 acres have been announced to date, only Columbia is over 10,000 acres.

As was noted earlier, the primary function of most new town developers is infrastructural. Generally, this involves the improvement of land for lots, the implacement of utilities to service these lots (and, in some cases, community utility systems), streets, and the addition of certain amenities. Coupled with land acquisition and the size of new towns, this process results in considerably high "front-end" costs. If the developer does not own the land before his decision to develop a new town, land acquisition costs can be extensive. One article reports that a "typical" new town developer attempts to purchase land at about $1,500 an acre and may ". . . spend $4,500 to $5,500 on roads, utilities, and other improvements, raising the total cost of the land to between $6,000 and $7,000 an acre." Improved land is then sold for about $10,000 to $12,000 per acre.[30] However, another observer notes that simply obtaining favorable rezoning can increase raw land prices by $2,000 to $4,000 per acre, and improved land may sell for $25,000 to $50,000 per acre.[31] Thus, land acquisition costs for a 10,000-acre new town at what is considered a reasonable purchase price can result in an initial outlay of $15 million. If the developer programs one-tenth of the entire town as an initial phase he may approach an expenditure of over $20 million (with planning and engineering costs to be added) before land is ready for sale. Moreover, the new town developer usually adds to these pre-sale expenses in the implacement of special facilities which serve to promote the project. Both Reston and Columbia have artificial lakes and Foster City includes a system of canals. Several new towns will have marinas, and virtually all will have golf courses and recreation centers. Although these facilities are designed to produce income and/or enhance the sale value of land, they result in significant additions to front-end costs. Some indication of the extent of these costs is provided by Murray.

124

Such large-scale expenditure on facilities before housing sales start has now become a standard pattern for new town development. Most facilities include a championship golf course, and nothing but Olympic-size pools will do. Recreational facilities offered in various new towns include country clubs, restaurants, tennis courts, bowling greens, auditoriums, cafeterias, and theatres. Current leader in this all out approach is Ross Cortese, who spent $2.5 million on housing and facilities before starting to sell. His new 3,600 acre Laguna Hills community opened not only with the clubhouse . . . but with a completed Olympic pool and part of a big offices-and-stores center. Still to come: six smaller club buildings, a 1,800-seat auditorium, another $125,000 pool, a golf course, riding trails and stable, large hospital, and a 120-acre shopping center. Total value estimated when the project is complete: $500 million.[32]

Even after sales begin, development costs may continue to rise faster than revenues. The provision of community-wide infrastructure in new towns—roads, sewers, water, and community facilities such as police and fire departments—vary among new towns. From the variety of arrangements which have been made by developers with local governments it is difficult to generalize a given set of procedures. Most new towns, because of their remote location, are situated in areas where local governmental machinery is inadequate to accommodate large-scale development. Scott points out that

> . . . new local governmental arrangements have, in almost every case, proven to be essential for the development of large new communities. This has caused a great deal of casting about for methods of bridging the gap. Some of the experimentation has been guided by a moderate amount of thought and study, but much of it is opportunistic improvising.[33]

In practice, the method of provision of governmental services depends upon a number of variables including location, the character of the local government (most frequently a county), the type of developer, timing, and the laws of the state regarding formation of local governments.

Most new town developers have avoided incorporation, primarily because of the uncertainties involved in a new political entity and a change in zoning auspices. However, some (particularly those whose projects are near existing cities with favorable policies) have chosen to request annexation. Rancho Bernardo (which was annexed to San Diego), and Redwood Shores (adjacent to Redwood City), are two examples. However, the majority of new town developers do not have this option.*

Most new town developers have preferred unincorporated status and have provided services through annexation to existing special districts, the formation of new, owner-controlled special districts, or, where they have the financial capability or are forced to, they have provided the services themselves.[34]

To a certain extent, the prevailing practices of governmental formation in the states in which the new towns are located have been influential. In California and Florida, the primary method for financing basic services has been through the formation of special districts. The Advisory Commission on Intergovernmental Relations points out that

> In the Washington metropolitan area, where urban counties with very few independent incorporated municipalities surround the District of Columbia, governmental responsibilities have been rested with the county coupled with an emphasis on the use of special assessments and deed covenants as a source of finance and control. In Illinois, a tradition of incorporation of municipalities for providing services and planning and land use regulation is reflected in the new community developments.[35]

Scott, who has concentrated primarily upon California new towns, sums up the experience there to date as follows:

> ... a developer's view of how best to achieve his two basic goals—assurance that his plan will be accepted and carried out, and

---

*Rancho Bernardo is about 17 miles northeast of the center of San Diego. In the process of its annexation lands were added to the city which will include parts of another large southern California style new town, Rancho de los Penasquitos.

favorable financing—will depend in part on his evaluation of the existing and probable future land use policies and zoning processes of the county and any city to which annexation might be feasible. For example, a developer might annex to a city because it had weaker controls than the county, or because it had more imaginative and flexible policies, or more expeditiously exercised procedures. Or the situation may be reversed, causing the developer to shun annexation and prefer unincorporated status. Similar evaluations and comparisons will be made with respect to the possibility of financing public facilities.[36]

New Town Planning

Aside from the fact that a great deal of land has been assembled, most of the new towns in this country exist primarily on paper. Consequently, more attention appears to have been given to their planning than any other aspect of their development. Some of the procedural differences between new town planning and the more familiar master plan for existing cities were discussed in an earlier chapter. The following discussion will therefore concentrate primarily upon the substantive aspects of new town plans and their utility to the developer and residents of new towns.

Most physical planning literature reflects the influence of the Garden City idea and associated concepts such as the "neighborhood unit," "greenbelts," and "Radburn planning," but the land use patterns of existing cities have often made difficult their application. However, owing to the design freedom of new town planning, variations of these concepts appear in several new town plans. The pattern which appears to be most common in American new town plans employs a centrally located area of the town in which major commerical and administrative activities are situated. The road network of the town focuses upon the center and direct access is usually provided from regional linkages. In the most common scheme the central area is surrounded by a series of neighborhoods. In some cases these are referred to as villages. The particular nomenclature varies among new town plans, but in essence the hierarchy of uses is the same: a town center surrounded by sub-community units with their own subcenters.[37] In some cases there are slight deviations from this general scheme. The Litchfield Park plan, for example, will employ a linear rather than a nuclear town center.[38]

The general design scheme for some American new towns appears to have been influenced by British towns such as Cumbernauld and Hook (the latter town has not been constructed but the plan has been widely praised.) The Litchfield Park core plan, for example, borrows conceptually from the Hook central area and neighborhood layout.[39] The planners of Valencia, California state, "Based on the Garden City, Radburn Idea and the Neighborhood Unit, Valencia's heart will be a multi-decked civic center similar to that of Cumbernauld. . . ."[40] However, the majority of American new towns resemble the general configuration of the first series (Mark I) of new towns of the United Kingdom. On some exceptionally large sites such as Irvine Ranch, however, the entire development will likely resemble a series of smaller new towns.

The development of new towns according to neighborhoods or sub-committees may have more practical application for the new town developer than it has had in conventional city planning. One of the reasons the neighborhood unit concept may have found little application in the latter is that much of past urban development took place on a lot-by-lot basis. In a sense, the neighborhood unit concept was out of scale with traditional building practices. In new town and large subdivisions, developers are able to treat entire areas of the town as a planning and development unit. The primary utility of the concept probably derives from economic considerations in new development. With large areas of land, new town developers find it difficult and expensive to implace utilities and other improvements for the entire town early in the development process. Therefore, growth is usually staged into one or two neighborhoods or villages and these are allowed to reach a certain level of completion before others are opened for development. The neighborhood or village concept also appears to provide a convenient scheme for the developer to program housing in certain price ranges into separate areas of the town.[41]

Other Functions of the Plan

In addition to functioning as an outline and estimate of the developer's financial scheme and as a tentative program of community inputs, the plan also functions in several ways which are not characteristic of conventional city plans. For example, new town master plans have been employed as "political instruments" for gaining local acceptance of development proposals and relating development to local land use controls. The plan provides some indication to local officials of the type and appearance of the community to be built and may be employed to eliminate local apprehensions which delay local acceptance. Also, local officials may find a plan which proclaims the attributes of the area in which it is located and intends to accelerate local economic growth as a tool for political boosterism. Kaplan notes also that "preparation of a plan may become crucial if the developer comtemplates using any federal programs in a privately developed New Community, for attached to almost all federal programs is a comprehensive planning requirement.[42]

Probably the most important function of the new town master plan has been its use as a device for gaining local zoning approval. Eichler and Kaplan point out that subdividers and builders often experience considerable difficulty in getting their development proposals approved, but that

> For the community builder, the situation is markedly different. Some counties, such as Placer (Sunset/Sacramento) and El Dorado (El Dorado Hills), in confronting community builders have exhibited the traditional fears of a rural government suddenly faced with urbanization. Even here, however, the community builder ultimately is viewed with less alarm than are his traditional counterparts.
>
> In the more urbanized counties—Orange (Mission Viejo, Irvine Ranch, and Laguna Niguel), Ventura (Janss/Conejo and the

Albertson Ranch), San Mateo (Foster City), and Los Angeles (Ahmanson)—the community builder actually is seen by government as an asset. New planned-unit ordinances in several of these counties (Ventura and Orange), sponsored in part by specific community builders but applicable to other developments as well, have granted community builders almost all the freedom they want.[43]

Planned community (or "density zoning") ordinances play a particularly important role in the planning and development of new towns. Basically, these ordinances offer a procedure whereby land is rezoned on the petition of the developer and in which conventional zoning restriction on minimum lot sizes, setbacks, etc. are relaxed in return for agency rights of approval of a "detailed" plan of development. The area is then zoned according to the detailed plan. In essence, it is a quid pro quo arrangement whereby the developer is permitted greater freedom in his planning and where the local officials may judge the acceptability of the development on somewhat more subjective grounds. The new town, or parts of it, then becomes part of the zone-plan of the locality.[44]

In some cases, California developers have also taken the approach of submitting their land use plans for incorporation into the county master plan. Eichler and Kaplan have observed that "In almost every new community, the developer does what is regarded as *public planning* and then submits his plan to the County for approval. There is little evidence that County officials have raised any serious objections to these plans."[45] In some counties, developers have worked with local officials in the drafting of planned community ordinances and have even themselves submitted ordinances for local adoption.

However, the ability of new town developers to fit their plans to local planned development ordinances or convince local authorities to adopt such ordinances has not been the sole reason for local acceptance of project proposals. In fact, these are more likely only the effects of other factors in new town development which have helped (and, in some cases, hindered) developers to obtain local approval. The advantages (or disadvantages) which local officials may see in new town development probably vary among localities, but some of the apparent reasons for approval are related to the nature and scale of their operations. For example, since new town developers rely upon the appreciation of the value of their land for profits, they are less apt to engage in any activities which would lower property values in their area. Also, their development period is considerably longer than that of the subdivider and small builder; therefore, they must deliver on their proposals and promises to local authorities in order to sustain local approval. Furthermore, new town developers also employ staffs of consultants and provide (and sometimes manage) facilities and services which the locality would otherwise be responsible for.[46]

A third important function of the new town plan is as a device for marketing the new town. The master plan usually extols the virtues of the well-planned community such as safety for children, conveniently located schools and shopping areas, etc. New town plans almost invariably include a variety of recreational facilities, particularly golf courses, and several exploit the market advantages of natural or man-made bodies of water. In a study of planned communities which emphasized recreation and open space facilities in their plans, Carl Norcross found that 23.6 percent of the residents interviewed noted recreational facilities as one of the main reasons for their settlement in their communities. Norcross also determined that 93.3 percent of the respondents emphasized that their community was "well-planned."[47] Kaplan adds that "the plan offers an additional and useful means to assure (and insure) customers that their investment will be protected and that they will be able in time to 'trade up' on Equity—a very important factor attendant on the purchase of a home in a New Community."[48]

Problems and Potential Problems

Private new town development in the United States is a relatively new business. Although real-estate development in this country has received considerable study and analysis in the past, preliminary indications are that new towns raise some unique problems.

There are numerous problems which may and in some cases already have confronted private new town developers, many of which are directly related to the development processes and objectives which have been discussed above. In terms of the development process, the critical elements appear to revolve around the interrelationship of financing, location, size, and the rate of development. However, these elements are also affected by other factors such as the attempt to create socially balanced communities and multipurpose developments. These latter considerations will be touched upon in this discussion, but treated more extensively in a later chapter. The primary emphasis here will be upon the new town development process.

Since none of the recent American new towns is near completion, more is known of the front-end problems of new town development than of their success in the long-run. It will probably be several years, therefore, before a thorough examination of the financial success and failures of the idea can be undertaken. Nevertheless, there are some preliminary indications that there may be unique difficulties in private new town development in the United States concerning the conditions under which most developers are currently operating.

The scale of new towns appears to be one of the major variables in the problems which may be encountered in their development. One investigation of four large new towns states that size is at the root of the problems of large developments. It concluded that

> There are many projects of up to 3,000 or 4,000 acres that are doing well; so far, virtually none of the 50-odd projects of more

than 6,000 acres can, by any stretch of the imagination, be called successful. The logical conclusion: once a development grows beyond the 6,000-acre mark, its problems become too big—and too expensive—to be handled.[49]

The size of new towns contributes in one form or another to several other development problems in new towns. In most cases, in order to assemble large parcels of land at permissive prices, developers have had to go beyond the fringes of established areas. In the early phases of development, where it is likely that most or all of the working residents will be commuters, the more remote locations of new towns are at a competitive disadvantage with developments closer to central cities. Another disadvantage of more remote locations is that the pre-existence of facilities tends to diminish. Thus, developers may be forced to assume the costs of internalized sewage or improving or building access roads to the regional highway network. Reston, for example, will require $14 million in roads and sewer and water lines. At El Dorado Hills it cost the developers $1 million for a five-mile access road.[50] Some developers hope to recapture these additional costs by providing more open and recreational space and other facilities in the community to entice buyers. Still, the added costs may surpass these advantages.

The scale of new towns is also directly related to the fact that developers and investors must spend millions of dollars before actual sales and construction take place and returns are realized. The financial success of new town development hinges upon the ability of the developer to sustain the heavy front-end costs of the development until the project can become self-regenerating. It is this aspect of private new town development that accounts for its considerable risks, in contrast with less extensive real-estate ventures.

In the face of limited empirical basis upon which to evaluate the financial dangers of such large-scale development, there have been several attempts to construct financial models to determine critical points in the development process. Although it has been difficult to account for the number of variables which can affect the rate of return on large-scale developments, some models based on experiences to date show that rates of return are low relative to the risks involved.[51] The implications of these studies are that the high degree of risk may cause potential investors to avoid new town development, or that developers may have to sacrifice some control over development decisions in order to attract investors. One study points out that "More and more investors are realizing they can take the risk out of financing a new town if they can get control of the appreciating land."[52] As discussed above, both Rouse and Simon were forced to lessen their autonomy in order to acquire front money. Since that time, lagging sales and the financial burdens of the heavy carrying charges for front money have forced the management takeover of Reston by its major backer, the Gulf Oil Corporation.[53] The new corporation which will manage the community's future development, Gulf-Reston Inc., will have to pump substantial new capital in order to reduce its $45 million debt.

Reston's change of management has dampened some of the enthusiasm which the philosophy behind the community and its architectural merits served to stimulate. The community (or, more accurately, Lake Anne Village, the first of seven planned) received much of its acclaim for its village center, apartment building, town houses and other architectural features. However, the management takeover has since raised much doubt as to the relationship of its aesthetic achievements to sound marketing practice. Preliminary indications from Robert H. Ryan, Reston's new manager, are that greater attention will be paid to the more stable and time-honored segments of the suburban housing market.[54]

The implications of the extensive development period for new towns have yet to be fully determined, but there appear to be several potential pitfalls for developers. Since the new town developer relies heavily upon local political acceptance and favorable zoning, his protracted development period

134

increases the danger of a change in political climate. If the developer seeks approval of his plan in sections, or wishes to request a change in his original plan, he will need sustained local support. The length of the development period also increases the likelihood that residents of the new town may move to incorporate the development. In this case, the developer would have to contend with new auspices for local zoning.

Timing is also critical in other ways. Because of the massive initial capital outlay involved, new town developers must necessarily operate in a manner to effect the most rapid rate of sales. However, there are several decisions which affect the development process and are not directly controlled by the developer. The first, and one of the most critical, involves obtaining favorable zoning and other concessions of local governments necessary for development. Much hinges upon the speed at which local governments or special districts provide the necessary community facilities.[55] If there is too much delay, the developer may be forced to add to the front-money dilemma by providing some of these facilities himself. The protracted development period of new towns also increases the dangers of changes in the money market.[56]

In contrast with single land use developers and builders, new town developers and builders rely upon the reciprocal generation of the various land uses scheduled for the new town. Owing to the distance which many developers have chosen or have had to go from the established and rapidly suburbanizing environs of metropolitan areas, there may be difficulties in effecting this relationship. Individual and commercial land uses are valuable in terms of land profits and as an attraction to residential buyers and renters. However, the dilemma which may face new town developers is that these uses usually prefer areas where there already exists some population base. It has also been pointed out that the potential problems of establishing generation among various land uses may place the new town developers at a bargaining disadvantage for the potentially highly profitable industrial and commercial areas.[57] Moreover, some of the residential attraction created by the presence of employment opportunities may be siphoned off by competing residential developments outside the new town.

In the final analysis, it is evident from experience to date that the new town development process involves a great number of unknowns about the financial feasibility of large-scale, long-term, multi-use private development. For the most part, the process is a new one, and because of the number of critical variables involved, it is difficult to relate the successes or failures of one new town to another. But one thing appears to be coming into clearer focus—time (or more accurately, the rate of development and sales), can be of the essence in private new town development. For example, in discussing the role of local government in the pros and cons of planned community development, Masud Mehran, President of Sunset Development Company, stresses that "Time is the major concern with the developer and becoming lost in the maze of City Government can become a headache of major proportions."[58] A slow rate of development and sales is not simply a matter of waiting around until things pick up a little. Drachman points out that

> When developments of the scale of Reston, Va., and Litchfield, Ariz., are examined closely, the cost of carrying the land is frightening.
>
> The "new towns" of Reston, Va., with its some $60 million, and Columbia, Md., with its approximately $50 million investment, pose tremendously heavy loads to carry in their early stages of development. Interest alone at each of these new towns is roughly $10,000 per day![59]

From comparative research on current new towns there may emerge more predictable development strategics. Reston, for example, concentrated upon multiple-unit residences in its first phase of development, with limited success. Columbia's developers, however, will concentrate primarily upon single-family detached residences at low densities in the early phases in an attempt to stabilize the community before introducing other residential types.[60] Del Webb Corporation has employed another technique to help carry the costs of holding land. At Sun City, Arizona, the corporation has an arrangement with a farming company whereby the land is cultivated until the time for improvement. The farming company received equity in the development corporation and the farming operation takes care of land-holding costs.[61]

The extent to which the basic principles and assumptions of the new town concept are valid relative to the social, economic and political characteristics of American suburbanization is also as yet undetermined.* There are indications that multi-purpose development and socially balanced communities may be incompatible not only with prevailing attitudes and values, but also with the critical elements in the development process. Although new town developers may feel that industry is important to the success of the new town idea (both philosophically and economically), many home-buyers in the suburbs have moved to outlying areas, in part to escape industrial areas or the lower-income groups employed by some industries. Also, in trying to satisfy the most viable segments of the housing market, developers may, and have, placed such prohibitive requirements on the types of industrial uses which they will accept as to limit the potential for social balance. *House and Home* points out that

> . . . a new town must be selective about the types of industry it accepts, especially in the town's early stages. Some new towns have such stiff density requirements (number of employees per sq. ft. of building), they tend to ban anything but high-paying "think factories."
>
> At Reston, a few of Simon's aides frown on assembly plants because few workers could afford to buy houses in Reston's price range. Simon himself is more concerned with the town's appearance.[62]

---

*This line of questioning is taken up again in Chapters 7 and 8.

For the home-buyer and the industrial enterprise, then, there exists a potential conflict. Uncertainties on the part of both interests as to how the developer can resolve these conflicts and maximize the profit on his investment may give both groups second thoughts as to a new town location. Uncertainties are also raised as to the possibilities for economically balanced communities within the context of current development practices. But of more immediate and long-standing consequence to the developer—because timing is so critical—ambivalence can slow the rate of sales.

Several conflicts inherent in multi-purpose development may derive from the fact that the components of new towns mature in the market at different rates. The need for rapid returns forces developers to concentrate initially on the most mobile residential market. In so doing, however, they may tend to "build in" a set of attitudes which limit industrial attraction. That is, industries employing lower income groups may have second thoughts about locations in new towns which may not provide suitably priced housing for their workers.*

Developers may have to compromise on other aspects of the new town concept. For example, in opting for larger sites (or perhaps cheaper sites, or those under single ownership), developers have gone some distance from the urban fringe. Although this practice affords larger and lower-cost sites, it can result in substantial increases in other costs such as for labor and materials, off-site improvements to provide access, and marketing.[63] Also, venturing into areas where local government is unprepared for large-scale, multi-purpose development can result in costly delays while the necessary governmental machinery is created to accommodate the project.[64]

In general, there appear to be risks in new town building commensurate with the scale of their development. However,

_____

*The most often cited case of the consequences of unmatched housing and employment structures is the Canadian new town of Don Mills, from which a high percentage of residents commute to jobs in Toronto, and to which there is a high percentage of commuting to the town's industries from outside the community.

there is little empirical basis for very solid conclusions in either direction. Some projects are doing well, while others have grave difficulties breaking the front-end inertia.

James Rouse is convinced that " the market place is discovering that good environment pays,"[65] but it has yet to determine how much it will cost and how much it will pay over those costs. Many observers feel that public assistance is necessary to give the new town concept a fair hearing and that public support can enhance the furtherance of both public and private objectives in their development. The following chapter discusses various public approaches to new town development and focuses primarily on the initial public policy responses to the private new town trend in the United States.

Notes

1. Edward P. Eichler and Marshall Kaplan, *The Community Builders* (Berkeley: University of California Press, 1967), Chapter 4.

2. Marshall Kaplan, "The Roles of the Planner and Developer in the New Community," *Washington University Law Quarterly,* MCMLXV, No. 1 (February 1965), p. 89.

3. *Architectural Record*, CIX, No. 5 (May 1951), 197. In addition to these, American Community Builders saw several other potential profitable enterprises in connection with new town development, including the sale of water and the operation of a community bus line.

4. Eichler and Kaplan, op. cit., pp. 91 and 133-34.

5. Kaplan, op. cit., p. 90.

6. Victor Gruen Associates, *Valencia,* Proposed Land Use Plan, California Land Co., (n.d.).

7. "Master Builder With a New Concept," *Business Week,* No. 1929 (August 20, 1966), 106.

8. Kaplan, op. cit., pp. 90-91.

9. See Alberto F. Trevino, "The New University and Community Development on the Irvine Ranch, California," *Urban Land* XVII, No. 9 (September 1966), pp. 1, 3-7. In contrast to the projects of large builder-developers and large land owners is the new town of Columbine, outside Denver, which is the venture of a group of small builders. See Gordon Edwards, "New Town Planning in Rapid Growth Areas," text of an address by the Chief of the Planning Branch, Office of Metropolitan

Development, HHFA, before the Fairfax County Federation of Citizens Associates, Annandale, Virginia (January 16, 1964), p. 6.

10. The evaluation of Columbia's financial and administrative structure is discussed in detail in Eichler and Kaplan, op. cit., pp. 57-61.

11. "New Towns: Are They Just Oversized Subdivisions—With Oversized Problems?" *House and Home,* XXIX, No. 6 (June 1966), 94.

12. James Ridgeway, "New Cities Are Big Business," *New Republic,* October 1, 1966, pp. 15-17.

13. "Where City Planners Come Down to Earth," *Business Week,* No. 1929 (August 20, 1966), 102. Although industry is exhibiting an interest in direct community development it has had experience in the past. Several of the early planned communities in the United States were founded by industries. However, their objectives at that time differed from current interests, particularly in the fact that most of the planned company towns were directly connected to the primary operations of the founding industry and their locations were often related to primary productive operations such as extraction of raw materials or early stage refinement of them. Some of these towns are discussed in U.S. National Resources Committee, *Urban Planning and Land Policies,* II of the Supplementary Report of the Urbanism Committee to the National Resources Committee (Washington, D.C.: U.S. Government Printing Office, 1939).

14. Donald R. Riehl, "Caveats for Corporate Real Estate Development," *Urban Land,* April 1970, p. 4.

15. "New Town News," *American Society of Planning Officials Newsletter,* XXXIII, No. 5 (June 1967), 71.

16. ACIR, *Urban and Rural America: Policies for Future Growth,* Report A-32 (Washington, D.C.: U.S. Government Printing Office, 1968), p. 80.

17. Ibid., pp. 80-81. See also, *House and Home,* XXXIII, No. 2 (February 1968), 18.

18. "Where City Planners Come Down to Earth," *Business Week,* p. 102.

19. *Architectural Forum,* CXXIV, No. 6 (June 1966), 28. See also *HUD News,* U.S. Department of Housing and Urban Development, April 13, 1967.

20. Muriel I. Allen, ed., *New Communities: Challenge for Today* American Institute of Planners Background Paper No. 2 (Washington, D.C.: American Institute of Planners, 1968), 17-18.

21. Eichler and Kaplan, op. cit., p. 38.

140

22. W. E. Finley, "New Towns of the Future," *Building Research*, III, No. 1 (January/February 1966), 24.

23. *House and Home*, XXVIII, No. 4 (October 1965), 12. As will be discussed below, most new town developers appear to have been able to obtain favorable zoning in their areas, although it is difficult to determine the extent to which other sites were eliminated from consideration because zoning could not be obtained.

24. Eichler and Kaplan point out that the difference between the "historical land owner" and the recent purchaser of land for new town development has income tax implications. They observed that under the current rulings for capital gains tax eligibility it is less likely that a historical owner would be classified as a "dealer" in real estate. Land owners will often establish elaborate corporate structures and package sales procedures to developers in order to retain capital gains tax advantages. Some of the complexities of the owners' and developers' tax positions are discussed in *The Community Builders*, pp. 130-139.

25. Eichler and Kaplan, op. cit., p. 41.

26. "On a Texas Prairie—Space City for 200,000," *U.S. News and World Report*, LIV, No. 7 (February 18, 1963), 68. Humble had originally intended the land for industrial development because it was thought to be unsuitably located for residential development; however, the establishment of the Houston Space Center and the demand which it fostered enhanced its potential for residential and commercial development as well.

27. Anthony Baily, "Through the Great City—III," *The New Yorker*, August 5, 1967, p. 52.

28. Eichler and Kaplan, op. cit., p. 61.

29. Fifteen hundred dollars appears to be the average price which new town developers are paying, although the reported prices per acre in one survey of eight new towns ranged from $641 to $5,000/acre. (ACIR, op. cit., p. 87).

30. "New Towns—Answer to Urban Sprawl?" *U.S. News and World Report*, LX, No. 7 (February 14, 1966), 116. Another report states that, "As a rule of thumb, new town developers do not like to spend more than $1,500 an acre." *House and Home*, XXIX, No. 6 (June 1966), p. 94.

31. Allen, op. cit., p. 18.

32. Robert W. Murray, Jr., "New Towns for America," p. 128.

33. Stanley Scott, "Local Government and the Large New Communities," *Public Affairs Report*, Bulletin of the Institute of Govern-

mental Studies, University of California, Berkeley, VI, No. 3 (June 1965), 3.

34. However, this statement may reflect the dominance of California in new town development, where the provision of governmental services in outlying areas has been characteristically through special districts. See, Richard Nolen et. al., *Local Government and Pre-planned Communities in San Diego County* (San Diego: San Diego State College, Public Affairs Research Institute, 1968), p. 10.

35. Advisory Commission on Intergovernmental Relations, *Urbanization and New Community Development* (n.d.) p. 4-44. This report was the draft version of ACIR's final report, *Urban and Rural America.* The author expresses his thanks to Page Ingrahm of ACIR for loan of the draft.

36. Scott, op. cit., pp. 3-4. Formation of owner-controlled special districts for the financing of services has raised some concern. In some cases it is argued that their formation has been permitted to enhance the profit motive of private developers. Concern has also been voiced as to the stability of bonds issued for thinly populated and developed districts, and the dangers of default injuring the credit of sound districts and neighboring cities. See, for example, Norman C. Miller, "Land Developers Form Public Districts With Right to Sell Bonds," *The Wall Street Journal* March 14, 1962, pp. 1, 22.

37. See, for example, Robert Tannenbaum, "Planning Determinants for Columbia," *Urban Land*, XXIV, No. 4 (April 1965), 2-6; *Reston, Virginia,* a brochure published by Simon Enterprises, Fairfax, Virginia (unpaged); "El Dorado Hills: New Model for Tomorrow's Satellite Cities," *House and Home* XXIII, No. 3 (March 1963), 107-115.

38. "Litchfield Park Properties," *A New Kind of City,* Litchfield Park, Arizona, n.d.

39. Ibid. See also London County Council, *The Planning of a New Town* (London: London County Council, 1961).

40. Victor Gruen Associates, "Valencia, A Planned City," *Arts and Architecture,* XXXVIII, No. 10 (November 1966), 18.

41. See testimony of James Rouse in *Demonstration Cities. Housing and Urban Development, and Urban Mass Transit.* Hearings before the Subcommittee on Banking and Currency, 89th Cong., 2nd Sess. (Washington, D.C.: U.S. Government Printing Office, 1966), p. 1055.

42. Kaplan, op. cit., p. 95.

43. Eichler and Kaplan, op. cit., p. 44.

44. Under some planned development ordinances, the developer may have the option to submit parts of the community plan for sepa-

142

rate approval. This may also be required by the locality as a means for insuring satisfaction of prior plan submissions. The importance of planned development ordinances to new town development are discussed in Robert E. Simon, "Modern Zoning for Reston," *American County Government*, XXXII, No. 5 (May 1967), 17-20; and Thomas G. Harris, Jr., "Howard County Plans Its Future: Columbia," *American County Government*, XXXII, No. 5 (May 1967), 20-23. Examples of planned development ordinances are provided by William H. Whyte, Jr., *Cluster Development* (New York: American Conservation Association, 1964); and Jan Krasnowiecki, *Legal Aspects of Planned Unit Residential Development*, Technical Bulletin No. 52 (Washington, D.C.: Urban Land Institute, 1965).

45. Eichler and Kaplan, op. cit., p. 95.

46. Ibid., pp. 99-100.

47. Carl Norcross, *Open Space Communities in the Market Place . . . A Survey of Public Acceptance*, Bulletin No. 57 (Washington, D.C.: Urban Land Institute, 1966), p. 21. See also "Land Planning: New Way to Attract Tenants," *House and Home*, XXV, No. 5 (May 1964), 90-98. The role which planning plays in attracting buyers to new towns is evaluated in Carl Werthman et al., *Planning and the Purchase Decision: Why People Buy in Planned Communities*, Preprint No. 10 of the Community Development Project, Institute of Urban and Regional Development, Center for Planning and Development Research (Berkeley: University of California, 1965). The implications of this study are discussed in a later section.

48. Kaplan, op. cit., p. 94. Related to this use of the plan is its function as a mechanism to attract potential investors and nonresidential land uses to the community.

49. "New Towns . . . Oversized Problems," *House and Home* p. 93.

50. Ibid., p. 94.

51. See, for example, Eichler and Kaplan, op. cit., p. 151-54; and Paul F. Wendt, "Large-Scale Community Development," *Journal of Finance*, XXII, No. 2 (May 1967), 220-239. Research on community development processes is also being undertaken by corporations currently active in new town development. For example, Sunset International Petroleum and the Irvine Company are approaching the economics and management of new towns through computerized models of development in order to assess the implications of alternative development decisions. See, for example, Ted Dienstfrey, "A Note on the Economics of Community Building," *Journal of the American Institute of Planners*, XXXIII, No. 2 (March 1967), 120-123. See also

R. Bruce Ricks, "A Tool for Managerial Analysis in Land Development," *Journal of the American Institute of Planners*, XXXIII, No. 2 (March 1967), 117-20.

52. "New Towns . . . Oversized Problems?" *House and Home*, p. 94.

53. See "Can 'New Towns' Meet a Budget?" *Business Week*, (November 18, 1967), p. 103 ff; Robert B. Semple, Jr., "Major Changes Due at 'New Town' of Reston, Va.," *The New York Times* (October 13, 1967), p. 42; and "Thistles in the New Towns," *Time Magazine* (September 29, 1967), pp. 87-88.

54. Semple, loc. cit.

55. This point is given considerable emphasis by Bruce R. Ricks, "New Town Development and the Theory of Location," *Land Economics*, XLVI (1970), pp. 5-11.

56. See testimony of Anthony Downs in U.S. Congress, Senate, *Federal Role in Urban Affairs*, Hearings Before the Subcommittee on Executive Reorganization of the Committee on Government Operations, 89th Cong., 2nd Sess., and 90th Cong., lst Sess. (Washington, D.C.: U.S. Government Printing Office, 1966, 1967), Part 17, pp. 3497-3498.

57. "New Towns . . . Oversized Problems?" *House and Home*, p. 95. See also Lloyd Rodwin, "Economic Problems in the Development of New and Expanded Towns," *Round Table Conference on the Planning and Development of New Towns*, Background Paper No. 4 (New York: United Nations, 1964), p. 21.

58. Masud Mehran, "The Pros and Cons of a Planned Community," *Current Municipal Problems*, V (November 1963), 101.

59. Roy Drachman, "The High Cost of Holding Land," *Urban Land*, (October 1968), p. 11.

60. Chester Rapkin, "New Towns for America: From Picture to Process," *The Journal of Finance*, XXII, No. 2 (May 1967), pp. 212-13.

61. Drachman, op. cit., p. 12. Goodyear has a similar arrangement at Litchfield Park, Arizona.

62. "New Towns . . . Oversized Subdivisions?", *House and Home*, p. 95.

63. Ricks, "New Town Development," pp. 9-10.

64. Ibid., p. 7. See also ACIR, op. cit., p. 104.

65. U.S., Congress, House, *Demonstration Cities*, p. 1095.

6 Some Operational Considerations for New Towns Policy

The translation of a concept into a public program involves a number of complex legal, administrative, and political variables. Thus far, the discussion has been concerned with the new town concept itself, its goals, the problems which it seeks to overcome, and current applications. These have been seen to be composed of lines of reasoning ranging from judgments as to the spatial configuration of urban forms upon social behavior to the implications of urban forms for national defense. However, the underlying principles have generally been uniform: that development should take place in wholes and multi-purpose units; that it take place under some form of unified ownership or control; that it be pre-planned; and that it be considered in a regional context. Generally, any endorsement of the new town concept in America today involves the endorsement of these principles.

The purpose of this chapter is to discuss legal and operational considerations in the translations of the new town concept into public policy, or what might be considered to be the program machinery and procedure for a new towns program in the United States. It is necessary to point out that this consideration will not delve into the detailed mechanics, but will focus upon the program procedure and the level of public involvement. Its primary purpose is to discuss basically three alternative types of programs, the implications which they have for the realization of some of the major objectives of the new town concept, and their feasibility implications for translation into public policy.

In any type of new town development program, despite the auspices, certain procedural steps of the development would be basically the same. These steps would generally include: site designation or selection, site acquisition, internal planning, land development (implacement of infrastructure), land disposition, and construction. Some of these steps would be combined under certain types of programs, but for the purposes of this discussion they are initially considered as separate stages in new town building.

The auspices under which each of these steps are undertaken—public, private, or a combination of both—have significant implications for the nature of the new town, its impact upon the metropolitan region, and the incorporation of public objectives in the development process. The following discussion will therefore treat each of these steps under alternative sponsorship in an attempt to point up these implications. Basically, the discussion will be concerned with the performance of these phases of development under alternative levels of public involvement.

Since the United States does not have a tested new towns program, and no new towns have been constructed under the experimental new community development program, much of this discussion is necessarily speculative. The analysis will draw generally upon three types of established programs: the new towns policy of Great Britain; the American Experimental New Communities Program and New Communities Act; and the U.S. urban renewal program. Emphasis will be upon the procedural operations of each type of program.

Optimum Governmental Involvement: Government as Principal

The British New Towns Policy

Of the national programs for the construction of new towns, the British new towns policy has probably been the most closely observed and widely influential. However, of the various schemes which have been considered as a basis for an American program, it has probably also been the most promptly dismissed by policy-makers. At the outset of a consideration of the nature of the British program, the differences in governmental structure, political philosophy, and traditional attitudes toward land and property appear to overwhelm any possibility of wholesale extrapolation of the program to the United States.[1] The following discussion is not intended to suggest that such a possibility exists. However, an investigation of the broad machinery employed in the British program can be instructive for several reasons. First, the problems with which the British new towns policy generally seeks to deal are not dissimilar to those which proponents in the United States envision as the rationale for a new towns program, although the stated objectives differ. Second, the program "On the whole . . . represents Howard's ideas translated into a national policy."[2] Third, the program is based upon highly centralized machinery, and provides some indication of the limitations and potentials of optimum governmental involvement.

Major Elements of the British New Towns Policy

The British new towns policy was formally established with the passage by Parliament of the New Towns Act of 1946.[3] The program is administered by the national government through its Ministry of Housing and Local Government in which is vested the primary responsibility for national planning in England. Mandelker points out that the program

"probably incorporates the maximum amount of governmental direction acceptable in any society that avoids direct
limitations on population movement."[4]

Initiative

The New Towns Act empowered the Ministry to create ad
hoc development corporations to undertake the actual
development of new towns. No limit was set on the number
of development corporations which it could create, and
hence the number of new towns which could be established.
A synopsis of the powers and functions of the development
corporations is provided by Osborn and Whittick:

> Subject to the approval of the Ministry, the corporations were
> given ample powers to acquire sites sufficient for complete new
> towns, to undertake all the necessary kinds of development, in-
> cluding provision of houses, factories and commercial buildings,
> and where necessary to provide public services, to appoint and
> employ full-time officers and construction workers—in fact to
> have all the necessary powers that an ordinary large-scale develop-
> ing landowner would possess, plus one or two ancillary powers
> usually exercised by local authorities.[5]

The Ministry and its appointed development corporations
therefore possess the entire range of powers to not only
initiate, but also to develop new towns to be financed by the
national government.

Site Selection and Designation

Initiative for the selection of a new town site may come from
the Ministry or from local authorities (in the latter case, from
local planning surveys). Approval of a suggested site, however, is vested entirely with the Ministry, and site proposals
are evaluated on the basis of criteria established by the Ministry. These criteria appear to be based heavily upon the capabilities of the site for infrastructural functions, particularly

water supply, power, transport, and sewage disposal. Also, McFarland notes that "land may be selected irrespective of its unsuitability for development if it will preserve for agricultural purposes other more suitable land."[6]

The powers of the Ministry in designating new town sites are extensive. Although provisions are made for review of a "designation order" at a local public inquiry, "the Minister need only be satisfied . . . that [a new town] is expedient in the national interest,"[7] in order to overrule local objections. The designation order must also be subjected to consultation with local authorities, but it has been pointed out that "even this limitation is slight since [the minister] is to decide which local authorities must be consulted."[8]

Site Acquisition

The acquisition of new town land is undertaken by the development corporation which is established after the designation order has become final, although the acquisition procedure itself is subject to the approval of the Ministry. Acquisition may be accomplished by voluntary or compulsory purchase. In most cases, land is acquired by agreement; but where Compulsory Purchase orders must be issued, the "market value" of the land must be determined by the "Lands Tribunal."[9] Although the designation order sets the site for a new town, the development corporation is not required to acquire all of the new town land before development can proceed. The corporation can only be forced by law to acquire all of the designated land after seven years from the issuance of the designation order have elapsed.[10]

Planning

Master plans for British new towns depict the general land use composition of the town, the circulation system, and development stages. They are developed by the development corporation, often with the assistance of planning consultants. Hearings are held on the plans, but Mandelker notes that "...no official Ministry approval is given, so that the plan does not have official sanction and does not automatically control the character of development within the new town."[11] Actual development is controlled through specific development proposals (called Section 3[1] proposals), each of which must be submitted for the Minister's approval. These proposals usually cover smaller areas of the town, such as a neighborhood or town center. Although the Minister is required to consult with local planning authorities before approval of a 3(1) proposal, local planning authority approval is not required. In effect, then, the powers of local planning authorities are superseded by those of the national government even at the most detailed planning levels.[12]

Land Development

Although new town development corporations are empowered to carry on any business necessary for the development of a new town, local authorities remain responsible for the provision of public facilities such as public buildings, amenities, roads, and sewage facilities. The corporation has authority to make contributions to the costs of needed improvements, and may carry out some of the actual construction work. However, if suitable cooperative arrangements cannot be made with local authorities for the provision of sewerage and disposal facilities, "... the development corporation may be authorized by the Minister to exercise the powers of a local authority in constructing sewers and sewage disposal works or in making agreements for their acquisition and use."[13] Similarly, development corporations are not delegated authority to construct public utilities, such as electric power or gas supply, except where "statutory undertakers" are unwilling or unable to provide their services.[14]

Construction

The building of housing, commercial and industrial structures

150

is undertaken by the development corporation. Construction is financed by long-term loans advanced by the national treasury (corporations are not permitted to borrow money from outside sources). Outside contractors are usually employed to undertake actual construction.[15]

Although the development corporation is normally the principal builder of the British new town, private builders are also permitted to participate. However, permission for private builders is contingent upon acceptance of the development proposal by local planning authorities as well as the development corporation.[16] In effect, then, the British new town development corporation actually functions more as town-builder than land developer (as the term land development is generally employed in the United States). The primary responsibility for construction is vested in the development corporation, subject to the controls of the Ministry and the Treasury.[17]

This brief discussion of the mechanics of the British new towns policy shows that policy to be highly centralized in terms of the major authority for development, with virtually all the major decisions in town development exercised directly by the Ministry of Housing and Local Government, or indirectly through its control over the actions of the development corporation. Local authorities and planning bodies are provided with a major role only in the land development phase, but with little threat to the autonomy of the Ministry and the powers of the development corporation.[18] The process is clearly one in which the national government designates, builds, controls, and operates the new town.

Minimum Public Involvement:
Government As Assistant

In contrast to the level of governmental participation of the British new towns policy is the U.S. "Experimental New Communities Program" which was enacted by Congress under Title IV of the *Demonstration Cities and Metropolitan*

Development Act of 1966, and the "New Communities Act of 1968" which was enacted under Title IV of the *Housing and Urban Development Act of 1968* (See Appendix B).[19]

Purpose of Title X

Part of the rationale behind proposals for Federal legislation for new town development was treated in the previous chapter. However, the reasoning which more clearly describes the intent of the Title X legislation and its relation to private new town development is outlined as follows:

> Without benefit of mortgage insurance, private enterprise has already undertaken the development of a large number of extensive new communities. Many of them have been planned with imagination and boldness characteristic of private enterprise at its best.
>
> But the scale of these projects is such that only large developers can find an adequate volume of favorable financing for site preparation. Even for them, financing is often inadequate for efficiently scheduled land development operations, or else the cost of it is out of line with the financing charges that the market demands for smaller scale development, or for actual housing construction.
>
> This bill would provide needed credit assistance to facilitate broader participation in these efforts. It will encourage adequate financing at reasonable cost for large-scale preparation of sites in well-planned communities. The sites produced with FHA mortgage insurance aid will be made available to a cross section of private builders, especially small builders. They will thus be able to participate more fully in this increasingly important segment of the housing market. If this segment of the market is lost to our small- and medium-sized builders, our new communities will lose the enormous vitality that a diversified home-building industry is uniquely capable of producing.[20]

Site Selection and Acquisition

Under the provisions of Title X, the selection and acquisition of sites for new towns would be undertaken by private developers. The act requires that the approval of such sites for mortgage insurance would be contingent upon the satisfaction of two requirements governing accessibility which would be evaluated by the Secretary:

> . . . maximum accessibility from new residential sites to industrial and other employment centers and commercial, recreational, and cultural facilities in or near the community; and maximum accessibility to any major central city in the area.[21]

In the judgment of the Secretary, the development proposal would also have to create ". . . substantial economies, made possible through large-scale development, in the provision of improved residential sites," and the development would be required to include ". . . adequate housing . . . for those who would be employed in the community or the surrounding area. . . ."[22]

However, the Secretary's judgment as to the acceptability of the development proposal is not, under the provision of the act, unilateral. A further requirement governing eligibility of a development proposal stipulates that

> No development shall be approved as a new community . . . unless the construction of such development has been approved by the local governing body or bodies of the locality or localities in which it will be located and by the Governor of the State in which such locality or localities are situated: Provided that if such locality or localities have been delegated general powers of local self-government by State law or State constitution, as determined by the Secretary, the approval of the Governor shall not be required.[23]

Planning

Nowhere in the language of Title X is it stated explicitly that a new community must be planned in any manner in order to be eligible for mortgage insurance. Although it is implicit that the developer would need to submit materials which would indicate the nature and form of the development to be undertaken as part of the general requirements of approval (discussed above), all planning requirements for the development are treated as part of the administrative procedures which have been designed for the program.

It is curious that the act contains no mention of planning requirements in view of the fact that the several planning requirements which have been developed under the administrative procedures constitute significant approval power. One prerequisite states, for example, that "the land development must be consistent with a comprehensive plan which covers, or with comprehensive planning being carried on for, the area in which the land is situated."[24] The requirement states that comprehensive planning for the area in which the new town is situated "may be carried out by a city, county, a metropolitan planning agency or other public body." However, it does not indicate which plan would take precedence, stating only that:

> To be eligible under Title X, the land to be developed must be located in a political jurisdiction which has placed comprehensive planning responsibility in an officially established body and must be consistent with the plan, or planning, being carried on by such a body.[25]

In addition to evidence that a new community would be in conformance with local comprehensive land use plans, the new community developer would also be required under the administrative procedures of Title X to submit what is termed a "General Community Plan" for the development. The purpose of this level of planning appears to be to set the general land use pattern of the community.[26] This plan would be subject to the review of FHA and the local planning authorities. However, approval of the development would be contingent upon acceptance of more detailed plans termed "General Neighborhood Plans," which would be the site plans (as opposed to general land use plans) for specific areas of the new town.[27]

The General Community Plan and the General Neighborhood Plan would be prepared by the developer's planning staff or planning consultants. Both plans would be reviewed by FHA and then by local planning authorities, and the General Community Plan would also be reviewed by the planning branch of the program coordination and services division of the HUD regional office, and appropriate metropolitan and regional planning agencies.[28]

However, the requirement for a comprehensive plan by the jurisdiction within which the development is to be located appears to be a controlling criterion as to whether a new town would be eligible. For example, the administrative procedures state that:

> If a 701 grant plan has been completed but no action of any kind has been taken or is being taken by the responsible governing body to put the plan into effect, and there is no other planning activity, the 701 grant plan under those circumstances would not be sufficient to meet the requirements of subsection 1003 (b) (3) [of the Housing and Urban Development Act of 1965] and the development would be ineligible.[29]

In order to encourage local planning bodies to bring their planning activities into compliance with these requirements, Section 701 (a) (4) of the Housing Act of 1954 has been amended by Title IV to extend local planning assistance to ". . . areas where rapid urbanization is expected to result on land developed or expected to be developed as a new community approved under [Title X] ."[30]

Land Development

The improvement of land for building construction is the primary phase of new town development at which the Title X legislation is aimed. The administrative procedures of the title state the following requirements for development improvements:

> Subdivisions must be served with electricity, telephone, and whenever available, gas service. All utilities must be provided by

underground distribution except where such distribution is not economically feasible.

Street pavement is required. Pavement widths and sidewalk provision must meet the specific needs of the development plan. Trees must be preserved wherever possible and tree planning must be specified where trees are lacking at the completion of land development construction.

The site after development must be served by public systems of water supply and sewerage, or by an adequate privately or cooperatively-owned system regulated in a manner acceptable to FHA.

Construction of all buildings which will be part of the land development must meet or exceed FHA minimum property standards. All other improvements must meet or exceed applicable FHA standards.[31]

With respect to sewage disposal systems, later requirements stipulate that, although privately or cooperatively owned systems are permissible, where public systems can not be provided, the Secretary must "receive assurance satisfactory to him of eventual public ownership and operation of the sewer system, and of satisfactory terms and conditions relative to any sale or transfer."[32] In order to encourage the establishment of public systems, a conforming amendment under Title IV provides for the extension of public facility loans regardless of population limits, to "be provided in connection with the establishment of a new community under Section 1004 . . ."[33]

Disposition and Construction

Disposition of new town land and the construction of buildings under Title X would be similar to that of unassisted development. Improved sites would be purchased from the developer by builders, and the developer would also be allowed to participate as builder. However, Title X would also require that "FHA encourage the maintenance of a diversified local home-building industry, broad participation by builders, and the inclusion of proper balance of housing in the community for families of moderate or low income."[34]

Public-Private Partnership

In the housing bills of 1965 the administration introduced as a companion provision to its proposal for mortgage insurance for new communities a proposal which would have made loans or the purchase of securities available to state land development agencies, "In order to encourage and assist in the timely acquisition of open or predominantly undeveloped land to be utilized in connection with the development of well-planned residential neighborhoods, subdivisions, and communities. . . ."[35] The language of the proposed legislation specifies the following conditions for the eligibility of developments under the auspices of such agencies:

> The Administrator shall not extend any financial assistance . . . unless he determines that (A) the financial assistance applied for is not otherwise available in reasonable terms, (B) the development of a well-planned residential neighborhood, subdivision, or community on such land would be consistent with a comprehensive plan or comprehensive planning, meeting criteria established by the Administrator, for the area in which the land is located, and (C) a preliminary development plan for the use of the land meets criteria established by the Administrator for such preliminary development plans.
> Land . . . shall be disposed of for development in accordance with a current development plan for the land which has been approved by the Administrator and shall not be sold or otherwise disposed of for less than its fair value for uses in accordance with such development plan. Such plan shall wherever feasible in the light of current conditions, encourage the provision of sites providing a proper balance of types of housing to serve families having a broad range of incomes.[36]

Although not included in the language of the proposed legislation, publicly acquired new town land would also be available for development by private developers under the Title X program. The legislation would also make available urban planning assistance grants and public facility loans to localities in which such development were situated.[37]

Proposals for public development agencies were not enacted in 1965. Virtually the same proposal was resubmitted in 1966, which was also not enacted. In 1967, Senator Ribicoff reintroduced the public land development agency proposal under the title of the "New Towns Development Act of 1967" (S. 2680).[38] Basically, the operation of the New Towns Development Act follows the same general procedure as the two prior bills for public land development agencies.* However, the act would also introduce some apparently significant changes. Although the 1965 and 1966 proposals contained provisions for the extension of public facility loans to localities in which publicly sponsored new towns would be situated, the New Towns Development Act would extend loans or provide for government purchase of securities for "the construction of necessary improvements." The act would therefore encourage the public development agencies themselves to undertake some of the land development phases of new town development; whereas prior proposals extended loans only for land acquisition, leaving the land development option to private developers or localities.

A second difference between the proposals involves the matter of local approval. The 1965 and 1966 proposals appear to have disregarded formal local approval as a prerequisite to FHA approval of a development proposal, stating only that such development would have to be in conformance with comprehensive plans for the area in which the town is to be developed. The New Towns Development Act does not specify the nature of local approval, but states that as a requirement for eligibility that a development proposal must have ". . . received all governmental approvals required by State or local law. . . ."[39]

---

*Unlike the legislation for privately developed new communities, for which detailed administrative procedures have been established, the proposals for public land development agencies can only be compared and evaluated on the basis of the legislation itself and any testimony which elucidates its provisions.

158

The Ribicoff bill also contains slightly stronger language to require varied income housing in new towns, stating that development plans for the proposed community must demonstrate that "The proposed community *will* contain adequate housing to meet the needs of families of varying income levels, and maximum opportunities in the choice of housing accommodations will be accorded to all citizens."[40] The 1965 and 1966 public agencies legislation would "encourage" provision for varied income housing ". . . where feasible in light of existing conditions. . . ."[41]

However, common to each of these proposals is a basic format which imitates the process and division of responsibilities employed in the urban renewal process. The potential significance and implications of this approach are treated in the following discussion.

Some Implications of Alternative Schemes

The three types of programs which have been outlined in general terms in the foregoing discussion have varying implications for the infusion and satisfaction of public goals in new town development. The level of involvement also has implications for the extent to which alternative programs would be politically or constitutionally acceptable in the American governmental system and the division of responsibilities between the public and private sectors. The following discussion treats some of these broad implications in a comparison of the above discussed alternative types of programs. Greater emphasis will be placed upon those programs which have been enacted or proposed in legislation in the United States.

Maximum Public Involvement

It may be axiomatic that the greater the level of public involvement in a new town development program the greater the potential for the realization of the publicly established objectives which have been ascribed to it. The British new

Table 1
New Town Development Program Alternatives

Development Phase	Total Public Involvement	Minimum Public Involvement	Partnership
Initiative	Public	Private	Public
Site Designation and Acquisition	Public	Private	Public
Planning	Public	Private	Public
Land Development	Public (local and/or national)	Private (and/or local public)	Public or Private
Disposition	Public	Private	Public or Private (or local)
Construction	Public	Private	Private

These development schemes correspond generally to the types of legislation which are discussed in the narrative. Optional responsibilities are explained more fully in the text.

town program obviously maximizes the level of public involvement under a program in which the national government either directly or indirectly performs (or is empowered to perform) all of the major functions of the development process. The considerations of local governments, land owners, utilities, and other entities which would be concerned with the impact and effects of new town development in a given locality appear generally to have little effect upon the initiation of development. National goals for new town development override those of local or regional planning authorities and governments.

It is doubtful that a direct role for the Federal government in the land development and particularly the construction phases of new town development is politically feasible in the United States. The vigor with which the Federal policymakers have attempted to dissociate proposed new towns policies from the British style program provides some indication of the opinion that any confusion with the latter program would be detrimental to public and Congressional acceptance. Such a level of public involvement would also be inconsistent with some of the aspects of the case for the Title X program, particularly the role and capabilities of the private sector. However, differences in political and governmental tradition would be the overriding factors. In effect, through ownership of new towns, the Federal government would be intruding into the time-honored domains of state and local governments and the private sector and would clash with some of the basic principles of the Federal system of government.

The direct role of the Federal government in community development appears to have ended rather decisively with the Greenbelt Towns of the 1930's, and even the government's role during that period of high direct government action in private affairs was subject to considerable constitutional controversy. McFarland suggests that it may have been only the absence of judicial challenges which enabled completion of the three towns that eventually got under way.[42] The Federal government will probably be more directly involved in the location and construction of specialized new towns such as the defense communities, but there are indications that even in these instances, private resources will be employed to the maximum extent possible.[43]

Minimum Involvement

In the absence of any tests of the operations of Title X, any assessment of its operational procedures must necessarily conjecture upon the character of the legislation and its objectives. The following discussion treats the major features of this legislation in terms of some potential operational limitations.*

*As of late October 1967, only four applications have been submitted to FHA for new communities. Two other applications were submitted but were withdrawn. Letter from Richard H. Heiderman, Acting Director, Land Development Division, Federal Housing Administration, October 25, 1967.

The major implication which emerges from the nature of the Title X program (as well as Title IV) revolves around the matter of initiative. As an "enticement" program, Title X bears the burden of offering sufficient machinery to attract private resources. The strength of the program relies upon the nature of the quid pro quo arrangement which would be effected between the Federal government and the developers. But the immediate implication of this system of approach is that its optional nature provides no means by which the Federal government or any other government can initiate new town development.

This system contrasts sharply with the British policy, in which direct action is taken by the national government to create the development machinery for new town development whenever it is deemed in the national interest. Furthermore, the initiation of new town development is not only (under the language of the legislation) a matter of agreement between the Federal government and the prospective new community developer. The requirements that a new town proposal have the approval of the local governmental unit in which it will be located (or the approval of the Governor of the State where there are not powers of local self-government), vests veto power with the local government concerned.

Thus, two basic conditions must be met before the program can begin to operate: the assistance offered by the program must provide a sufficient enticement to the prospective new town developer to foster his consideration of application; and the local government, or Governor (state authorities under Title IV), must ratify his proposal. The Federal role is therefore indirect, and does not become involved until the basic decision regarding the community's location is determined by the developer. Since the cost of the money over the protracted period of new town development is a significant factor in the return which the developer receives on his investment, insured mortgages would certainly assist the developer in obtaining more favorable financing terms.* As Eichler and Kaplan point out, such long-term low interest loans would enable "many firms to undertake a new community for which sufficient funds might not otherwise be available, from any source at any cost."[44] However, the potential developer's decision will also be influenced by the manner in which the eligibility requirements which he would have to meet would otherwise limit the profitability of his operation.

Site Designation and Acquisition Under Title X

The site designation and acquisition phase in new town development is also related to the matter of initiative and contrasts with those employed in the British program. The major difference is again in terms of auspices, which under Title X lie with the developer, and with the Ministry under the New Towns Act. The British procedure virtually suspends local planning and governmental powers and individual land ownership rights, and sites are designated according to criteria set by the national government. Title X contains no designation phase, and land acquisition is undertaken by the prospective developer within the supply and price constraints of the land market.* Paralleling the matter of initiative, the effectiveness of the American program is left to the developer's ability not only to assemble sites of sufficient size to undertake new town development, but also to his ability to assemble a site in a location which satisfies the proposal evaluation requirements of the Secretary and FHA.

*The New Community provisions of Title X allow FHA to insure loans valued up to 50 percent of the cost of the land and 90 percent of the cost of the improvements, but not exceeding 75 percent of the Commissioner's estimate of the value of the improved land. The interest rate on such loans may not exceed 6 percent, and the maximum mortgage amount is $25 million. Loans insured under Title X are also eligible for purchase by the Federal National Mortgage Association. The maturity period is unspecified.

*Although, of course, the availability of a site and the size of a site can be affected by the amount of credit a developer has at his disposal.

Mandelker emphasizes that "Site selection is the initial and perhaps the most critical decision in the development of a new town community. . . ."[45] As was pointed out in Chapter 4, location is probably the most influential variable affecting the economic feasibility of a new town development. If developers are forced to continue to seek out sufficient sites in locations distant from the central city, they could conceivably encounter difficulty meeting the risk criteria of FHA.

Furthermore, the site selection procedures which would operate under Title X raise serious implications as to the efficacy of the program as a device for guiding or directing metropolitan area growth. Title X provides no direct means by which the federal government or any other level of government can directly influence the supply of land for new town development in desired locations.* Since the legislation would in effect call for a continuation of site selection and acquisition procedures currently employed by unassisted developers, the primary criterion will continue to be the availability of sizeable parcels at prices which developers can meet rather than any determinations which may be made by the Federal government or regional planning authorities as to the "best" or desirable locations for new towns.

The assumed continuance of new town development trends upon which the justifying language of the legislation is currently based may have been misleading. With the notable exception of Columbia, Maryland, virtually all of the new towns currently under construction are being developed on sites which have been acquired from what were previously large open land holdings. As a result of further suburbanization, the supply of sites will decrease and the land ownership patterns will tend to become more balkanized. As was also indicated in Chapter 4, rapid growth areas contain the major-

---

*With an increase in money available for new town development, more developers could become involved. However, the increased demand raises the spectre of inflationary prices. This matter will be discussed in the following chapter.

ity of new town enterprises, but the availability of large parcels under single ownership also appears to be significant in determining the size and location of projects. The majority of California new towns are being constructed on large ranches. In the National Capital area, which also has a large number of new developments under way, the majority of new towns are far below the average size of those in the far west. Consequently, one effect of the differences in land availability patterns may be that enticement programs will be less workable in some areas of the country, or that the potential for new towns of sufficient size to render the "economies" of large-scale development which underscores the purpose of the legislation may be exaggerated.

Planning

As noted above, the absence of a planning requirement in the legislation itself is surprising in view of the manner in which the program was promoted, more so because the planning requirements which have been developed for the administration of the program constitute a significant factor in its feasibility. For example, even if a locality is receptive to a developer's proposal, it would have to have an operating comprehensive plan in order to be eligible as the site for a new community. The availability of 701 assistance would make it easier for local governments to comply with the requirement, but it could also cause serious delays which could affect land availability and land prices.* Also, Feiss is of the opinion that "it is difficult to conceive of the local one-third share being publicly provided for the planning work of private developers."[46] Moreover, the requirement places communities which have completed planning programs in a

---

*The normal time for the completion of a 701 program is two years, excluding the time which is absorbed by the application and review process, which is often several months. Although it may not be considered necessary for a locality to have completed the program in order for a new community to be eligible, the time factor can be extremely important.

priority position as the locale for new town development, irrespective of the possibility that communities without local plans may be better or more desirable locations for new towns in terms of relationship to central cities, market characteristics, and the availability of land for new town development.

Also, since new towns are usually of necessity (because of their size) located further out from the established portions of the metropolitan area, there is greater likelihood that the governmental jurisdictions in which they are located will not have comprehensive plans. Areas which have greater supplies of land open for development are also likely to have less existing population. Since existing population has been one of the requirements for local planning assistance, there is a greater possibility that areas in which new towns development is contemplated will not have been previously eligible for 701 assistance.*

The manner in which the local comprehensive planning requirements have been established for new communities may also function to limit the feasibility of the program in other ways. For example, there is a likelihood that local comprehensive plans which have been established and otherwise meet Federal requirements may not be geared to accepting new town development. That is, in order to be receptive to new town development, pre-existing comprehensive plans would have to have allocated substantial areas of open land for urban development, and in a manner and location roughly

---

*The validity of this question would vary from state to state because some states do not have townships and political jurisdictions with sizeable areas of undeveloped land would be counties. In these states, it appears initially that there would be less of a problem in finding areas without local comprehensive plans. However, in states in which there are townships, the likelihood of a township not having a completed comprehensive plan could be greater. Furthermore, there is greater chance that a new town proposal would overlap local jurisdictions, and, therefore, compound the planning and local government approval requirements. In this respect, the program may also be biased to some areas of the country.

*The development of a local comprehensive plan normally pays greater attention to existing land use rather than land ownership patterns. Although both are

166

consistent with the new community proposal.* Furthermore, the various elements of the local comprehensive plans (the capital improvements program, circulation plan and particularly zoning ordinances, etc.), would probably have to be amended in most cases in order to bring a new town development proposal into conformance. These changes make questionable the requirements that developers' proposals be in conformance with local plans. An equally significant effect may be that the requirements will provide the locality with an additional veto power over assisted new town development.

In view of the Metropolitan Development legislation which accompanied the new communities program in the 1966 legislation, requirements for participation by area-wide planning authorities are conspicuously weak.* It does not appear that such planning bodies are provided with an influential role in the program as to the location of new towns or the facilities which are provided in them. The assumption is made that local community plans are "normally coordinated with metropolitan planning for the wider areas," but review by area-wide planning authorities of the General Community Plan is scheduled late in the application process.[47] The entire matter of coordination itself is open to wide interpretation, since the more general the area-wide plan, the greater the apparent lack of conflict.

Planning requirements which must be met by the developer may also function to limit the acceptability of the program. For example, a developer may be unwilling to commit

important in terms of new community development, land ownership is usually the controlling factor for new town development because the developer will seek out parcels of land which he can obtain as a whole and in the shortest period of time. That local comprehensive planning has not taken sufficient account of the local land ownership pattern and the local real estate market increases the possibility that local plans would not contain provisions for new town development.

*There are no such requirements on the language of Title X and the requirements for conformance with "comprehensive" plans in Title IV is unspecific as to the relationship between new town and metropolitan or regional plans.

himself to a particular plan for the community and may wish to retain sufficient flexibility to accommodate changes in the market. He would be able to do this more easily under local zoning alone than with the added necessity of amendment procedures with the Federal government.

In general, the planning procedures designed for the administration of Title X contrast significantly with those employed in the British program. The provisions of the New Towns Act virtually suspend local planning powers and confer the primary responsibility for the development of plans upon the development corporation. Although the plans of local authorities may function to initiate new town development in Britain, it does not appear that they are frequently employed to effectively veto such development. In contrast, the American programs provide the local community with a veto power over new town development, and place the prospective developer in a two-sided bargaining position in which he must gain the approval of the local government and its planning officials and attempt to bring the results of the arrangement into conformance with the requirements of Title X and Title IV in order to be eligible for assistance.

Land Development

In general, the land development phase under Title X would probably not differ significantly from the procedures which new town developers are currently following. However, the timing and procedure involved would be subjected to Federal approval and standards. Problems of timing could be created where local governments and service districts would have the primary responsibility for implacement of sewer and water facilities for the development; but the availability of public facility loans to local governments (supplemental grants in the case of Title IV) should encourage local governments to cooperate with developers. This arrangement would not differ greatly from the British procedure, which recognizes provision of basic facilities as primarily a function of local government, and allows development corporation administration of these functions only where local governments are unwilling or unable to comply with or accommodate new town development.

Disposition and Construction

The final phases of new town development in the United States are distinctly different from those employed in the construction of the British new towns. Disposition of lands for development under Title X would take place in a fashion similar to unassisted new town development. Improved lots would be marketed to private builders (preferably small builders under the objectives of the program), although the program also allows the developer to function as a builder. However, developers would be required to allocate sites to include ". . . a proper balance of housing in the community for families of moderate and low income."[48]

The extent to which small builders would be able to participate in the program can only be determined after the program has been tested in actual development. But there is some question of whether this requirement would come into conflict with the objective of FHA and the new town developer. For example, it would seem that the greater the number of builders involved in the new town's construction, the greater the likelihood of conflict and coordination problems of various builders in achieving their objectives. Builders of higher priced housing, for example, may wish to have their areas of the town relatively isolated from areas where lower priced housing is being constructed, since both builders and bankers are aware that lower priced housing can have a depressing effect upon the market for and value of higher priced housing.[49] Choice sites in the new town may be distributed to higher priced builders, which may limit the willingness of smaller builders to participate in the program.

Part of the rationale for the new communities program is to obviate the necessity for new town developers to make commitments on sites to large homebuilders in order to obtain financial backing or advance assurances from them,[50] but it is still questionable whether other differences between small and large builders will override these considerations. The new town, for example, cannot only function as a semi-monopolistic situation for the land developer, but where the large residential builder is involved, competition with other builders is also lessened. The more builders involved in the construction phase of the new town, the greater will be the uncertainty of each builder as to the current and future operations of other builders, and the greater the competition. Fewer builders would facilitate coordination of operations and division of the local housing market into non-competitive price ranges. Since developers would be allowed to participate as builders, there is also greater likelihood that choice locations and types of land uses will be reserved for the developer or large builders. If the developers wish to engage in the construction of certain types of "income property" such as shopping centers or recreation facilities, builders of such facilities may be forced out of consideration for participation in the new town.

It would also seem that the involvement of many builders in the construction phase could complicate land disposition. With large builders, large areas of the town site could be more rapidly disposed, and the review operations by local governments, FHA, and HUD would be minimized. Since the carrying costs of money are one of the most significant factors in financing new town development, it would be in the interests of the developer, the mortgagers, and FHA if new town land turned over as rapidly as possible. The lower-rate, longer-term loans under Title X would probably permit greater participation by small builders, but they may nevertheless not be "preferred" builders because of the uncertainty which they would create and timing considerations.[51] It seems reasonable to assume that developers will move to lessen such risks and increase their profit margin.

Other Relationships between Goals and Operating Procedures

With respect to the feasibility of the program in terms of its goals and procedures, it is conceivable that the requirements for local governmental approval and planning conformance could serve to limit the acceptance of the program both by private developers and local communities. For example, one of the objectives of the program will be to encourage the development of housing for lower income groups in new communities. However, if a suburban locality is disposed to avoid the in-migration of such income groups, this objective may be sufficient to bring local disapproval of a developer's proposal. Or, the community may prefer to have unassisted development rather than suffer the risk of a developer who would be under pressure from the Federal government to implace low income housing in his project. Furthermore, the local comprehensive plan, an additional factor in Federal approval, may be drawn in such a fashion as to prohibit the development of low income housing in the community, or perhaps industry.

If it could be implemented, the low-income housing objective could also function to strain the relationship between developers and builders. For the most part, new town developers have attracted builders of middle- and high-income housing. If these builders are of the opinion that low-income housing and low-income groups would be detrimental to the sale of higher-priced housing, the economically critical early building stages of the project could be seriously affected. Much would depend upon timing; but if the dominant early settlement is in middle- and upper-income groups, the developer is also likely to encounter stronger resistance in later phases of development.*

It may be fitting at this point to raise the question of the appropriateness of FHA's administration of the Title X program. Perhaps one of the ironies of the manner in which the

*These considerations are discussed in more detail from a sociological perspective in the following chapter.

Federal government has initially considered assistance for new town development is that it has vested the primary authority for the program's administration with a Federal agency whose operations are often cited as a contributor to the conditions which the new town concept seeks to overcome. Mayer has observed, for example, that

> The new towns effort, its purposes and implications, represent a philosophy and conception of living and work relationships which is too drastically different from our present slipshod laissez faire attitudes, methods, and their physical embodiment to be attained by a mild and painless adaption of the present set-up. Placing it under FHA, the most custom-bound and developer-bound of all the agencies, perhaps epitomizes this under-estimation of the real magnitude and nature of the issues.[52]

Also referring to the new communities program, Feiss remarks that

> ... the Federal Housing Administration ... is notoriously lax in its planning standards and requirements at the regional and local levels. It operates largely under the strong hand of insurance underwriters who have little knowledge or interest in sound planning.[53]

In view of the weakness of the regional planning requirements in the administrative procedures for Title X, Feiss's apprehensions appear to be corroborated, although in the light of the weaknesses of the legislation itself FHA might not be entirely to blame.

With respect to the low-income housing goals of the new community program, FHA administration may also be cause for some concern. Some housing experts and Federal legislators, for example, appear to doubt that the nature of FHA's function is attuned to the need for low-income housing since the agency is deeply risk-conscious and committed to the "economic soundness" of the projects which it insures.[54] Furthermore, the nature of FHA's operations may also function as a limitation on the initial functioning of the Title X program. As was pointed out in Chapter 5, land development is considered to be a high-risk venture in real-estate investment, and new town development appears to magnify the element of risk.[55]

Many of these operational questions will not be answered until the program has been tested in actual development. However, it appears from the general mechanics of the program that some of its objectives and requirements may be unrealistic in terms of the operations of the land market, the objectives of private developers, and the types of requirements necessary for project approval.

The New Communities Act of 1968

The Title X program having cleared away some of the philosophical, semantic and legislative obstacles to Federal support for private new town development, the New Communities Act of 1968 received less opposition.[56] The basic relationship between government and the new town developer and the basic operations of Title IV closely resemble those of the Title X program. Like Title X, the New Communities Act is aimed at the financing of land acquisition and development of private projects. However, where Title X provides for mortgage insurance guarantees on loans to private new town developers, Title IV authorizes the Secretary of Housing and Urban Development ". . . to guarantee, and enter into commitments to guarantee, the bonds, debentures, notes, and other obligations issued by new town developers . . ."[57] Although the major function of the act is to guarantee financing for land acquisition and development, the general purposes of the act include ". . . the general betterment of living conditions through the improved quality of community development . . . , [to] contribute to the sound economic growth of the areas in which they are located . . . , [increase] the general housing supply . . . , provide opportunities for innovation in housing and community development . . . , encourage the maintenance and growth of a diversified local homebuilding industry . . . , [and employ] to the greatest extent feasible . . . new and improved housing technology . . ."[58]

In return for the full faith and credit of the United States Government, developers will be required to demonstrate to the satisfaction of the Secretary of Housing and Urban Development that:

(1) the proposed new community (A) will be economically feasible in terms of economic base or potential for growth, and (B) will contribute to the orderly growth and development of the areas of which it is a part;

(2) there is a practicable plan (including appropriate time schedules) for financing the land acquisition and development costs of the proposed new community and for improving and marketing the land which, giving due consideration to the purposes of this title and the special problems involved in the financing of new communities, represents an acceptable risk to the United States;

(3) there is a sound internal development plan for the new community which (A) has received all governmental approvals required by State or local law or by the Secretary; and (B) is acceptable to the Secretary as providing reasonable assurance that the development will contribute to good living conditions in the areas being developed, will be characterized by sound land use patterns, will include a proper balance of housing for families of low and moderate income, and will include or be served by such shopping, school, recreational, transportation, and other facilities as the Secretary deems satisfactory; and

(4) the internal development plan is consistent with a comprehensive plan which covers, or with comprehensive planning being carried on for, the area in which the land is situated, and which will meet criteria established by the Secretary for such comprehensive plans or planning.[59]

Thus, where the eligibility requirements of Title X are concerned principally with economic feasibility and contribution to orderly growth, the New Communities Act places much stronger emphasis upon planning, scheduling, and the land use character of development. As under Title X, the development proposal must receive State and local approval, and the plan must be consistent with local comprehensive plans or planning. However, Title IV includes stronger (but still very vague) language requiring housing for low and moderate income families. The other major addition of the New Communities Act is the authorization for "supplemental grants" of up to 20 percent of the required local costs of Federal grant programs to states and localities for assisting new communities with basic water and sewer and open space land projects. (But the grants may not exceed 80 percent of total facility costs.) However, this provision is tied directly to the Secretary's satisfaction ". . . that a substantial number of housing units for low and moderate income persons is to be made available . . ."[60]

The New Communities Act is also similar to Title X in that the principal obligation which may be guaranteed for any single project may not exceed $50 million, and the total outstanding guarantee fund for the act may not exceed $250 million.[61]

With respect to the basic stages of new town construction used for comparative purposes in this analysis, the operations of the New Communities Act resemble those of Title X. Like Title X, it is a "carrot" program which offers a quid pro quo arrangement to prospective developers in return for expanding their credit and lowering their risk.[62] The initiative for the project must come from the developer. Therefore, as with Title X, the government cannot directly institute the development of a new town. Site designation would also be the responsibility of the developer, although presumably the availability of Federally guaranteed obligations would expand his options.* But the developer would have to assemble the site without benefit of public powers of compulsory acquisition.

Planning for the new town would also be undertaken by

*However, there is somewhat of a "chicken-and-egg" dilemma in this case, since the act implies that the developer must have a site upon which he bases his application. Still, if this is the intention of the act, a developer might use the provisions of the act to expand his project.

the developer, but the "internal development plan" would be subject to the scrutiny of the Secretary of HUD and would also have to satisfy any required state or local reviews. In addition, the planning of the community must also be consistent with prevailing comprehensive plans for the area in which it is located.

Land development would be the principal obligation of the developer. However, aspects of the land development phase may be assisted by state and local agencies through Federal programs for community facilities and supplementary grants.* The final phase, disposition and construction, would be similar to that under Title X or unassisted new town development. Lots and subdivisions would be marketed to builders, and the developer would have the option of participating.

There is little question that the New Communities Act can function to expand the credit and lower the risks for private new town developers. As Keegan and Rutzick see it: "Without the government guarantee, most new community developers would either have to pay very high interest rates or give the lender substantial equity participation. Despite the speculative nature of the new community project, the addition of the government guarantee should produce an interest rate and yield comparable to good corporate bonds."[63] However, the act does pose many of the same potential conflicts among provisions and intentions of the legislation. One such problem, which is discussed more extensively below, concerns the stronger language regarding housing for low- and moderate-income groups, and the relationship of this requirement to the developer's eligibility for other provisions of the act.* Such provisions, coupled with required approvals on plans by state and local officials and planning bodies, may in them-

*This appears to be a considerable advantage over the provisions of Title X, which offer only loans for public facilities.
*The language itself—". . . a proper balance of housing for families of low and moderate income . . ."—poses a number of difficulties in interpretation. This question is taken up in greater detail in the following chapter.

selves begin to cause delays and other problems which erode some of the financial advantage of the legislation.

It should be noted that Title IV will be administered by the Assistant Secretary for Metropolitan Development, Community Resources Development Administration. Although those critics of FHA administration of Title X are probably pleased by this, only time and the development of a number of projects assisted under each program will provide a basis for comparison.

Public Land Development Agencies

In the absence of administrative procedures for the proposals for new town development through public land development agencies, the advantages and disadvantages of this type of program are difficult to assess. However, in general, this type of program appears to possess significantly different implications than the minimum involvement of the mortgage insurance program.

From an operational point of view, the major advantages contained in a program in which public initiative and control are directly involved in the early phases of new town development contrast significantly with the Title X and Title IV programs. First, the program provides a means by which states or localities could directly initiate new town development of a type and location consistent with publicly established goals for the community. This type of program would place the vital phases of initiation, planning, and disposition under the auspices of a public agency, which would mark a significant departure from the traditional measures for the control of suburban development, which separates regulation from execution.

Some proponents of a program of direct public involvement contend that such a program would be in keeping with the broader legislative intent of the Housing Act of 1949, for which procedures for the administration of the urban renewal program stated that

In the administration of this title, the Administrator shall encourage the operations of such local public agencies as are established on a State, or regional (within a State), or unified metropolitan basis as permits such agencies to contribute effectively toward the solution of *community development* or redevelopment problems on a State, or regional (within a State), or unified metropolitan basis.[63]

It has also been noted that the unused "open land" provisions of Title I (of the Housing Act of 1949) could be construed as a means by which the urban renewal program itself could be employed for publicly initiated new town development.[65]

There is also much evidence that several new town advocates who have considered the merits of alternative operational schemes are of the opinion that a positive participation by government in the process of urban development is both necessary and justifiable. In hearings on the 1964 new communities proposal, Nathaniel Keith of the National Housing Conference stated that

We support the provisions in the administration bill with regard to the new communities as important first steps toward the development of these needed programs. However, we believe that the complete answer to this problem will require much broader public action than would be involved in the present proposals. In particular, we feel that it is essential that Federal assistance be available to local public bodies for the assembly of land reserves which would be planned and improved and then disposed of by sale or lease for private or public development, including recreation. We call the attention of the subcommittee to the fact that a readymade instrument for this approach already exists, subject to minor amendments, in the open-land provisions of Title I of the Housing Act of 1949, which have been inactive since enactment.[66]

Basically, this approach centers around the matter of public land acquisition and temporary public ownership. Reps, for example, affirms that

> ... effective implementation of urban plans in the United States requires large-scale public land acquisition. I suggest that virtually all land to be urbanized should come into public ownership and then be made available for development as needed, where required, and under conditions that will assure building only in conformity with public development plans. ... I assert that such a system is in our own tradition of fashioning empirical solutions to problems of this magnitude without regard for doctrinaire dogma, and that it is wholly compatible with our fundamental political beliefs and economic system which puts heavy emphasis on private initiative and profit.[67]

Although Reps states that his proposal is a "far more radical" approach than traditional approaches to planning and land use control in the United States,[68] its basic principles (as will be discussed below) do not appear to have been too "radical" to be put forth in proposed Federal legislation. The proposed legislation for public land development agencies appears to conform most closely to a variety of practical proposals by persons concerned with the new town concept and generally with the control of urban expansion. Some of the impetus for the Federal proposal, for example, was provided by recommendations which evolved from a study of housing in California in 1963, which recommended at that time that "The Housing and Home Finance Agency should make long-term loans and grants to states for land acquisition of open spaces to be developed under rational planning principles much as redevelopment operates in urban areas.[69] The report also recommended adoption by the state of a program in which

> Loans can be made to cities or counties to enable them to buy land in outlying areas for resale to private developers as is being done in slum areas under the urban renewal program. The main difference is that the new program is designed for slum prevention rather than slum clearance, and for expanding the housing supply and making it available to all who need it. In some unincorporated areas the state might assume the function of pur-

chasing the land directly, but in any case, the land would be disposed to private developers after schools and utilities are planned as proper sound development.[70]

The land development agency proposal is also related to several other theoretical proposals for direct governmental participation in urban development. One such proposal is Clawson's "Suburban Development District," which takes the concept of the special district into the realm of performing operations of general government, with additional power for land acquisition. Basically, Clawson envisions the suburban development district as a new form of local governmental unit which would cross existing municipal boundaries and would be governed by representatives of various governmental and private interest groups in the district. The major activities of the district would be to plan its growth, acquire "control over land area, by purchase or option, to the extent necessary," contract with developers for actual development, and contract with local governmental units for the necessary services.[71]

The concept of public land development agencies also appears to be aligned with proposals to enable central cities to employ the new town concept both internally and externally. Matthewson, for example, proposes a "skip" annexation approach coordinating renewal and new town development which "would call for the enlargement of the inner city through the annexation of a new and large piece of non-contiguous unimproved land." He allows that the approach would require changes in the annexation laws of most states, but contends that "there are no basic principles of constitutionality involved . . . ."[72] Internally, the concept of public land development agencies compliments Perloff's notion of the "new town intown," which proposes that the redevelopment of large inner city areas be undertaken on the basis of sub-communities and staged in a manner similar to that of suburban new town development.[73]

Some of the operational implications of a program styled along the mechanics of the urban renewal program parallel

180

the implications of the urban renewal process. Although the general goals of the program would be set by the Federal government, the initiative and operation of the program would still rest with different auspices (in this case, state and/or local governments). The utility of the program would rely upon permissive legislation by the various state governments since the powers of eminent domain would be involved in the process. This condition would apply if state development corporations were employed or local corporations chartered by the state. The extent to which Federal goals such as, for example, low-income housing in publicly sponsored new towns are enforced could have significant implications for the acceptability of such a program and for relations between state and local governments. In effect, the program would shift some of the political burdens arising from the operations and goals of the program from the Federal government to state governments. Like urban renewal, some of the Federal goals of the program could be blunted by the purposes for which the program is employed by state and local governments.

Initially, the feasibility of a new town program based upon the use of public development agencies may be largely a constitutional issue. Although such a program would emulate a division of public and private responsibility which has become established, opinion is mixed as to whether the "public purposes" which would be attached to the rationale for public acquisition of land for new town development would be acceptable. Slums and blight are existing, urgent, and tangible problems which have been difficult to resolve without public intervention in the operations of the private development market. However, a new towns program would be based upon the argument that orderly and efficient development would be preventative rather than curative. Rapkin observes that

> Authorization and use of eminent domain for new towns would give rise to a round of constitutional challenges, comparable to the one that grew out of urban renewal legislation. These challenges, however, would not have to delay purchases from willing

sellers. And, although the result in the courts is far from clear, there is basis for at least limited optimism. For example, the same courts that found a "public use" in urban renewal because it eliminated blight might also find a "public use" in new town programs designed to prevent blight from occurring in the future.[74]

Gladstone points out that some states already permit the state government and special types of development and municipal corporations to engage in development operations which would appear to be compatible with the public development agency concept.[75] Schulman appears convinced that judicial interpretation of "public use" has broadened to the extent to which new approaches to direct public involvement in urban development could be constitutionally justified. He observes that

> Public use has become public purpose and is now being broadly expressed by the phrase public benefit. There is no clear indication of the ultimate extent to which eminent domain may be used by the municipalities in their capacities as developers or as aids to private developers so long as the concept of public benefit is being even more broadly interpreted and applied. There seems to be no limit now to the authority of government to acquire any lands, whatever their characteristics may be, in order to undertake direct public development or in order to assemble such land for subsequent development by private individuals, for whatever purpose.[76]

Still, the questions surrounding the justification of the use of eminent domain for new town purposes are necessarily academic. Much would depend upon the kinds of relationships established between public agencies and the private sector. For example, it is conceivable that localities could set up local agencies to acquire land which would be to the benefit of certain land developers or builders. Collusion between local agencies and developers would raise the questions as to the balance between the public interest being served by the new town and the extent to which it was functioning as a windfall to private interests. Other public interests, such as the provision of low-income housing, would also likely be employed in an assessment of the extent to which the public interest would be served by a particular development.

It is unclear from all of the legislative proposals reviewed in this study exactly what type of public land development agency would undertake the land acquisition and possibly the land development functions of new towns. However, a wide range of possibilities exists, each of which might have different political implications and administrative consequences.[77] If development agencies were created directly by the state for new town development, they would function somewhat in the fashion of the British development corporations because it would involve a direct intrusion into the affairs of local governments and would complicate the matter of control over local land use. Wheaton suggests that this procedure raises the question of "whether in any state the state government would act over local opposition."[78] However, the political considerations would appear to be different if a special type of corporation similar to Clawson's suggestion were voluntarily established by several units of government, or if the development were established by a municipality within its corporate boundaries. Even in this case much would depend upon the size of the development, its fiscal impact, the area in which it is located, and its composition.

One of the curious aspects of the proposal for state land development agencies was its introduction (with the proposals for public assistance) of proposals for private land development operations, since in some respects they are potentially competitive. As was discussed in Chapter 5, the major objective of private land development corporations is to acquire large parcels of land which are improved to appreciate the price of lots for resale to private builders. In effect, then, public land development agencies could usurp this function and would be competitive with the objectives of the developers which the mortgage insurance provisions were designed to aid.

State land development agencies with the powers of compulsory acquisition would also pose a serious threat to other private land developers since they would possess the ability to acquire more choice parcels of land. Private new town developers must acquire land through the normal land price systems, and are often forced to seek land further from the central city in order to assemble sizeable sites. If land acquired by public agencies was also developed by those agencies it is conceivable that public agencies could be in a better competitive position to attract builders by offering locations closer to the central city at controlled prices.

Conceivably, such agencies might restrict themselves only to the acquisition of land (although the Ribicoff bill would encourage public land development), which would then be resold to private developers, but the operations of private developers would probably be subject to limitations imposed in land pricing requirements in the legislation. Whichever type of corporation performed the land development function, land pricing problems could emerge. Current proposals do not treat the matter of land disposition, under either public or private auspices. However, there are some foreseeable difficulties generated by the fact that new town land will tend to appreciate in value as construction takes place. If public agencies act as new town developers, the land pricing mechanisms will initially involve a decision as to whether prices should be controlled according to their original level or not. The use of original land prices would provide later land purchasers with a subsidy. On the other hand, land could be subject to continual re-evaluation. If private developers were employed, some controls would probably be necessary to prevent developers from speculating in new town land, which in itself might discourage some developers from participating in this type of program.[79]

Other problems might result from the encouragement of low-income housing in the new town. As was noted under the discussions of Title X and Title IV, builders of higher-priced housing might be discouraged from participating in publicly sponsored new town development because of its uncertainty with respect to the depressing effects of lower-priced housing, or purchasers might be wary of the effects which lower-priced housing may have upon their equity.

As the least structured and most flexible of the three types of programs reviewed in this discussion, the use of public development corporations leaves many questions unanswered as to the impact which such a program would have upon constitutional and political issues. Much would depend upon the particular manner in which the program is employed, each of which might have different consequences. In a broad sense, some of the problems which might emerge would be similar to those of urban renewal; that is, the extent to which the program is utilized in a manner which is consistent with goals formulated at the Federal level, the extent to which fiscal considerations might predominate where the program is employed by individual local governments, and local attitudes toward racial and low-income groups.

It would be difficult at this stage to simulate the various permutations of issues and problems which might emerge from the very general framework which has been outlined by current legislative proposals. If such a program were to be enacted, complex administrative procedures would govern its actual operation. Like urban renewal, these provisions would change with the feedback of information gained from actual tests of the program. Public development corporations might be required to submit surveys and analyses such as those of the Workable Program for Community Improvement; or, the Community Renewal Program could be broadened to embrace the notion of an assessment of new town needs, locations, and priority sites throughout the metropolitan region. Coordination and hierarchical relationships with other Federal and state programs affecting the pattern of urban development in the region would be another factor which would affect the utility of such a program. These factors could also complicate the administration and, hence, the operation of the program.

Backers of the public development corporations proposals[80] will undoubtedly follow closely the progress of the state development corporation created by the New York State legislature in 1968.[81] The Urban Development was created as a "... complex interlocking corporate structure which included a governmental development corporation, a quasi-public development and research corporation, and a quasi-public guarantee fund."[82] The state legislation granted the corporation, which is under the direction of former New Haven and Boston renewer Edward Logue, substantial legal and financial powers.

> The Corporation is authorized by law to move into any community in the state, take whatever property it wants by condemnation, raze any structures on the site, and replace them with homes, factories, schools, or office buildings, as it sees fit—all without paying attention to local zoning laws and building codes. It could put up a vast Negro housing project in the middle of Scarsdale, the richest white suburb in the state. It could build entirely new cities in the open countryside (and, in fact, already has three of them on the drawing boards). Furthermore, it has a lot of money; well over a billion dollars at its own command, and possibly another five billion in private investment to be spent under its direction.[83]

UDC is already involved in the development of two new towns in upstate New York—northeast of Buffalo and northwest of Syracuse. Both projects are within the suburban environs, and the Buffalo community will be tied in with the development of a 1,000-acre campus of the State University of New York.[84] With these projects, and others in Utica, Binghamton, Ithaca, and Welfare Island, Logue hopes "... to help the poor and the black escape from the decaying core cities to the suburbs, as the white middle class has been doing for generations."[85]

On the basis of its legal and financial powers, the Urban Development Corporation would appear to be an ideal model of the proposal for state-sponsored public development corporations. A few other states are already considering following New York's lead. However, they will also be interested to determine the degree to which the corporation can provide political insulation and cope with the resistances by cities to threats of their cherished powers of home rule, and by suburbs to their assumed rights to exclude low-income and racial groups.

Some Observations on the Legislative History of Title X and Other New Town Proposals

This discussion focuses upon the Title X program because its history is more relevant with respect to the initial consideration of a Federally assisted new towns program. In many ways, Title X paved the way for passage of the New Communities Act of 1968.

Although the Title X program has been enacted by Congress, there are several questions which remain as to the role of the Federal government in the development of new towns. It is difficult to evaluate the fact that it took three years for the administration to muster sufficient support and understanding of the bill before it was passed.* One of the major reasons for the demise of the bill in committee appears to have been the novelty of the new community concept (although the actual support mechanisms were not novel). Several of the witnesses who testified on the bill made it clear that they had doubts as to the significance and impact which the provisions might have as to the role of the government in private development and the relationship between support for essentially suburban development and the government's

---

*The original new communities bill, which was introduced as Title II of the *Housing and Community Development Legislation of 1964*, contained substantially the same provisions as successive bills. The major exception was that the maximum mortgage amount under the 1964 bill was $50 million. In 1965, this amount was reduced to $10 million, and in 1966 it was raised to $25 million.

commitment to the problems of the central cities. Mayors tended to stress this point.

The doubt raised concerning the possible consequences of the bill for the cities as well as other interests can be attributed in part to the administration's strategy in the introduction of the bill. An analysis of the bill by *House and Home* offered that one of the primary reasons for its generally cool reception by witnesses and subsequently by the committee was that it was secretly drafted by HHFA with no outside consultation from private groups in the home building industry. Both witnesses and committee members were therefore largely unprepared to comment and evaluate its provisions.[87] Strong opposition from such groups as the National Association of Home Builders and the National Association of Real Estate Boards reflected lack of prior consultation with the home-building industry.[88] In August of 1964, the House Subcommittee reported on both the new towns and new subdivisions proposals ... "that their complexity and far-reaching nature required further study. Testimony during the hearings made it clear that some public and private housing groups had not had time to consider some of these new and complex proposals ...."[89] In general, testimony on the new community bill disclosed that supporters of the bill had a greater tendency to support it on the basis of the general principles of new town development, with some reservations about the effects of the bill as to land price inflation, and the effects of some procedural requirements.*

It is also interesting that among those who testified on the bill there were none of the traditional proponents of the new town concept. It appears that some of those, particularly planners, who have campaigned for new towns legislation,

---

*Some of the points of contention raised by some of the opposing witnesses were that FHA purchase authorization might result in the placement of large areas of land under the direct control of the Federal government, and that the Davis-Bacon prevailing wage requirements which were attached to the provisions of the bill would have made the program unworkable.

188

were of the opinion that the bills would not have been adequate to create "genuine" new towns. Feiss remarked, for example, that "Some of us who had hoped and worked for adequate 'new towns' or 'new communities' legislation, regretted that we could not support this one."[90]

With respect to mortgage insurance provisions, the 1965 version of the new communities bill was substantially the same as that of 1964 with the exception that the maximum allowable mortgage was reduced from $50 million to $10 million. Basically, the same objections and doubts concerning the provisions of the bill were voiced, although witnesses appeared more familiar with the provisions. However, sufficient doubt remained as to the effect which the program might have upon the problems of the central cities and as to the necessity for the program (in view of the ostensible ease with which many developers had been able to acquire large parcels of land and favorable zoning). With respect to the position of the cities, Mayor Cavanaugh of Detroit testified that

> ... both the National League of Cities and the U.S. Conference of Mayors have not moved to endorse ... the new towns proposal. This is a position consistent with the position they held last year. They have not formally adopted a resolution in opposition, but I think it would be safe to say that ... it is essentially a negative position towards this proposal. ... there is a self-interest involved here, because there is a great feeling that these public facilities, as important as they are in suburban areas, are just as important in older urban areas, and the same treatment would be received.
>
> I think it is more a question of fear of competition.[91]

It appears that the question of the uncertain effects of the program coupled with the continued strong opposition of homebuilding interests convinced the subcommittee that the new communities proposal should undergo still further study.[92] Only provisions for "new subdivisions" were enacted.

The enactment of the 1966 bill for mortgage insurance for

new communities was not the result of any significant "watering-down" of the bill. In fact, the allowable maximum mortgage amount was increased from $10 million in 1965 to $25 million in 1966. However, hearings upon the bill indicated some softening of the positions of those groups which had opposed prior submissions. The cities groups and the National Association of Housing and Redevelopment Officials, for example, stressed caution as to the application of the program and its possible ill-effects upon existing cities, but NAHRO endorsed the provisions, and the cities groups in effect took no position.[93] Homebuilding interests continued their general opposition to the mortgage insurance program, but their strongest disfavor had shifted to the provisions for public land development corporations, a concern which they shared with lending institutions.[94] Furthermore, the administration assembled favorable testimony for several developers engaged in the construction of new towns.[95] The developers concentrated upon the particulars of the bill as well as its general intent. A fourth factor which may have made the bill more acceptable in 1966 was the fact that it was finally introduced as an "experimental" program. The House subcommittee reported out that it was "persuaded that the new communities provisions . . . would be instrumental in encouraging well-planned developments on the scale necessary to move toward orderly metropolitan growth."[96]

One of the major reasons for the initial uncertainty about the new communities bill on the part of both the witnesses and the subcommittee appears to have resulted from a confusion as to what was meant by "new communities." Testimony on the bill corroborates the contention of Chapter 3 of this study, that the new town concept is not viewed in any widely accepted terms. Witnesses, for example, referred to new communities, new towns, new cities, and planned communities with little distinction in discussion of the bill. The mortgage insurance provisions were recognized by the cities as being primarily a new form of suburban aid, but their major misgivings appeared to result not so much from the amount of aid involved as from what effects the actual development of new towns would have upon the future of central cities. Homebuilders' groups viewed the bill as primarily assistance to large developers, and in addition, had philosophical objections with respect to the expansion of government further into the operations of the private sector.

Further examination of the provisions of the bill may have disclosed to some of these opponents that the bill was not as revolutionary as it was originally thought to be. It may have been recognized that, as an optional program in which the role of the Federal government in private land development was limited to the confluence of the interests of developers and local officials, they provided no direct means by which the government could initiate new town development. An additional factor may have been that the provisions for loans to public land development agencies functioned as a red herring with respect to the objections of homebuilders' groups. The lack of serious objection by the cities and favorable testimony by several developers engaged in new towns appeared to amount to sufficient support for passage.

Public Land Development Agencies

In hearings on the new community proposals in 1965 and 1966, relatively little attention was accorded to the proposal relative to the mortgage insurance provisions for public land development agencies. Cities groups appeared to be more concerned with the competitive effects of the provisions for private land developments than with the potentials of the public agency proposal for purposes that might be beneficial to the city.* However, homebuilding groups appeared to have recognized the implications of the proposal and generally

---

*In 1966, this may have been partially attributable to the fact that the Demonstration Cities proposal was the primary element of the administration's bills and received greater attention by the cities groups. However, it may also have been a result of the fact that these groups did not appear to have examined in

stood vehemently opposed to it on the grounds of governmental intrusion into the affairs of the private sector. Perry Willits, of the National Association of Home Builders, stated in 1965 that

> We are flatly and unalterably opposed to this section . . . . This raises the fundamental questions of the philosophy of government in relation to private business. The homebuilding industry is firmly dedicated to the proposition that Government should never do what industry can do as well or better for itself. . . .
>
> No serious abuses of land development now exist sufficient to require in the public interest that Government supplant regulated private enterprise in the development of residential land.[97]

Moreover, of the developers of new towns who testified in 1966, only Rouse referred to the need for a program enabling public agencies to acquire land for new town development, and even this reference was brief and somewhat vague.[98] The primary concern of the developers appeared to be with the mortgage insurance provisions, and if any fear of competition was felt it was not evident in their testimony. On the other hand, the large developers may have deliberately intended to dissociate their support for the Title X provisions from those for public land development agencies to avoid the interpretation of a blanket endorsement of all the new town provisions.

Claims of Opponents to New Towns Assistance

In the absence of any real tests, there is no way yet of determining whether those interests which are skeptical or opposed to government assistance to new town developers are correct in their assessment of it. The more rapid passage of Title IV might be interpreted as a change of mind on the part of these interests. On the other hand, with the very slow acceptance by developers of the Title X program, they may

---

depth the implications of the new community proposals, and that there was some apparent confusion between the two types of programs. Also, in a broad sense, the public land agency proposal bore some similarity to that for demonstration cities.

have adjudged that governmental assistance is a minor factor at this time.

Nevertheless, though still somewhat hypothetical, the concerns of small builders, mortgage lenders, and large city mayors appear reasonably well founded. For the most part, as Rouse has pointed out, the building industry is largely composed of small-scale enterprises. Homebuilder associations represent the collective interests of the predominantly small-scale homebuilding industry.[99] The prospect of large developments which may be highly competitive in land acquisition, and more competitive in terms of the scale-economies and amenities which they may be able to achieve, can predictably be seen to elicit negative views on the part of small builders. These builders also compete among themselves, but generally are limited by the scale of the developments and financial constraints in the extent to which they can create significant product diversification. The large land developer poses the threat of the capture of large areas of land where demand is likely to emerge for new housing and commercial facilities, and in effect can function in the monopolistic fashion of a land speculator. Arrangements between large developers and local governments may also threaten the position of smaller developers and builders. Large developers are able to secure substantial areas of land beyond the fringes of developing areas, and, by advancing into sparsely developed areas, may be able to secure large portions of favorable zoning of such areas. As Eichler and Kaplan have pointed out, some California counties have shown ready acceptance of proposals for new towns because of the advantages of long-term relationships with the developer. In securing favorable zoning for new town development, the developer poses a threat to the small builder by capturing zoning for industrial parks and commercial areas. Smaller developers of these later-maturing enterprises must normally act responsively to pre-existing development; however, the large developer is better equipped financially to secure these areas in advance of development.

Whether or not subsidies for land development will result

193

in increased opportunity for small builders is open to some question. There has been a tendency for new town developers to seek out or act in concert with large-scale homebuilders because these larger commitments assure the movement of lots at a faster rate. Furthermore, as indicated earlier, coordination of several builders within a community may result in coordination problems for the developer. Although the developer is a monopolist in terms of his control over new town land, builders are in more of a competitive position. The more remote locations of new towns may also prejudice new town sites in favor of large builders since mass housing builders will be better able to realize scale economies in construction and possibly reduce friction costs for labor and materials.

The resistance of homebuilders' interests to land subsidies may also result from differences between the operations of builders and developers with respect to land. Homebuilding interests are much concerned about the rising price of land in metropolitan areas and the effects of price increases upon the price of their product. This concern is well documented in articles in some building trade magazines which have strongly urged for changes in tax policies to eliminate some of the incentives to speculation in land.[100] Builders are fearful that assistance programs which inject additional money into the market for land may function to aggravate the land price problem. As one critic of the land development legislation has affirmed, "experience and pretty much everything else has shown that making a purchase easier to finance usually makes it more expensive."[101]

The counter to this argument is that the net effects of land subsidies are potentially deflationary. In 1965, testimony on the bill stated that in contrast to high land prices (from $5,000 to $10,000) on the fringes of developed areas,

> ... those who have begun to develop new communities have been buying thousands of acres at less than $2,000 per acre for residential and other urban use development. They can buy this land at such comparatively low prices because they will go 10 to 15 miles

beyond the developed areas in order to obtain the large acreage required for a new community. The further from the central city that a developer goes, the more land is available and probably more undeveloped land. Thus, within a metropolitan area in the circular belt that lies between a 5-mile and a 10-mile circle from the center there will be 235 square miles; in a belt between 10 and 15 miles from the center there will be 393 square miles; in a belt between 20- to 25-mile circle there will be 707 square miles.

As those new communities develop and provide dwelling units, they will absorb some of the demand pressures for homebuilding sites within the metropolitan areas. There will be less tendency than heretofor for the price of closer in land to rise. The average price of homesites being utilized in the entire metropolitan area would decline.[102]

Still, homebuilding interests are doubtful of the validity of attempts to curb the land price problem by increasing supply by bringing more land under development at remote locations. Testimony submitted in recent Federal hearings stated, for example, that

It is often said that there is insufficient land for growth in many of our urban areas. It is the Sub-Panel's belief that this widely held notion is incorrect. Rather, it is more accurately said that there is insufficient land readily available at a reasonable cost for residential development in urban areas, particularly within the country's large metropolitan areas.[103]

Homebuilding interests may, therefore, be less interested in the hoped-for long-term deflationary effects than they are concerned about the greater immediate possibilities of inflation.[104] Coupled with the fact that land subsidies may be initially inflationary, the deflationary argument necessarily implies that such sites will be competitive with areas in which smaller builders are already operating and may have already acquired land, and therefore will effect the demand for housing in these areas. Ultimately, much depends upon the degree to which more remote sites would compete with those within and at the fringe of developing areas; but this uncertainty could be sufficient to sustain the resistance of small builders.

For related reasons, savings and loan associations and mortgage lending interests are likely to take a negative view of land subsidies which appear to favor large developers and builders. Although not as localized as builders themselves, such lending institutions are closely tied to the predominantly small-scale building industry. Consequently, they may be inclined to be apprehensive of subsidies for developments which are competitive with the small builder. Large-scale developments are more likely to produce greater fluctuations in local markets for housing and threaten to change development patterns significantly. Furthermore, traditional home-lending institutions may also foresee a greater threat to their interests in the local housing market where large insurance companies, oil companies, and other large corporations often associated with new towns enter into the home building business.

Most of the claims made as to the advantages new towns legislation would create for central cities are shallow, defensive, and almost always indirect. As noted above, few mayors voiced mistrust of the provisions, perhaps because of the very vague and palliative manner in which the case was phrased. Robert Weaver offered the following:

> Thus, Federal support for new communities is not an anti-central-city proposal. Rather, it is an indispensible element to an area-wide approach to land utilization and urban development. Such an approach must, if it is to succeed, coordinate and reconcile the needs and functions of all elements which constitute the urban complex. New communities, planned in the context of area-wide considerations, can make a significant contribution to rational expansion of urban development. This expansion, in turn, will strengthen the central city and delineate more clearly its role in urban America.[105]

Although the new town proposal might not be considered by some as an "anti-central—city" proposal, it is, by the same token, not a pro-central-city proposal. Moreover, the benefits claimed for the central city are unclear and unconvincing. In terms of priorities, the new town proposal compares unfavorably with programs aimed at specific central city problems.

In a more general sense, there are several inconsistencies between the vague claims of benefits to the cities and the objectives of the new town concept. Although on the one hand it is claimed that new towns would and should be related to the central city and the metropolitan area as a whole, the legislation encourages relatively self-contained urban settlements in the suburbs with local sources of employment. Thus, the legislation would encourage the relocation into large suburban developments of economic activities vital to the declining tax bases of central cities. In addition, new communities legislation would also promote the utilization of "raw land in areas somewhat *removed* from existing centers of population,"[106] presumably out of the reach of core city workers.

Summary and Other Observations

This chapter has attempted to analyze some of the operational considerations of alternative new town programs and to indicate some of the political considerations which may impinge upon their feasibility. It is clear that there are problems of comparative analysis where one type of program has become relatively well-established, another is in its formative stages and untested, and the third has been outlined only in broad operational terms. Moreover, there exists no empirical basis for analysis of the latter two.

Some indications of the views of different interests groups which would be affected by alternative new town policies have been provided in the hearings which were conducted on the new communities bills; however, these have limited utility in view of the fact that there was little common understanding by many of those who testified both for and against them as to what was meant by the new town concept, and considerable uncertainty as to what the effects of the different programs would be. This analysis has therefore relied upon a speculative consideration of some of the potential problems of alternative policies from both operational and political perspectives. In this sense, it suffers from the same uncertainty which surrounded the legislative history of the new communities bills.

The operational feasibility of alternative types of programs appears to hinge on the manner in which each would relate to several interrelated factors: the role and objectives of the new town's locality; the fixed factor of land supply; and social and economic factors which are not directly controllable by the policy. Underlying these factors is the extent to which different forms of aid or direct participation or control by government are politically and constitutionally acceptable. Although some of these interrelationships have been discussed, there are vast permutations which would apply under each of the alternative types of programs.

In general, it appears that the greater the level of governmental involvement and control, the more matters of political and legal acceptability impinge upon the initial acceptance of a program. With programs involving a minimum of public participation and control, legal and broad political factors tend to become of lesser concern, while the major consideration becomes the extent to which lack of initiative, control, and enticement erode the utility of the program for direct public guidance of growth. Most observers, for example, have written off the possibilities of a British-style program on political, constitutional and traditional grounds. On the other hand, the Title X and Title IV programs would not provide sufficient basis for governmental control to influence the initiative for and locations of new towns. An urban renewal style program has caused some observers to doubt whether the necessary powers of eminent domain could be justifiably employed to create new towns, even though such a program would imitate what has generally become an accepted division of responsibility between government and the private sector.

One of the most important factors in alternative types of programs would be that of initiative. Each program has different implications. A British-style program would place both the initiative and powers of follow-up development in the hands of the national government. The Title X program leaves the matter of initiative to the developer, but it would also be shared with the locality in which the proposed new town would be located. Public development corporations would place initiative with the state, or with a local governmental unit which would apply to the state for powers to undertake new town development. In the first case it appears as a remote possibility that a program would be devised in which the Federal government would directly initiate new town development. In the case of Title X, it appears that the type of assistance offered would make possible the participation of more developers, but some of the factors which might offset the amount of increased activity could be the necessity for local approval and requirements built into the program which could create local objection or inability to comply on the part of both the developers and the locality.

However, the major limitation of the Title X program appears to be that the locations of new towns could be left to similar circumstances which confront unassisted developers. The goals which the Federal government has set for the program—the encouragement of a private new town development, sound land use planning, varied income housing, conformance with local plans, and maximum accessibility to major cities—are, in many cases, likely to be blunted by the desires of local governments, the objectives of private developers, and available land supplies. Moreover, the program could be stalled by either the lack of acceptance or the inability to comply with the requirements on the part of local governments.

The public development corporation program would provide, in terms of the machinery it would create, a means of overcoming the major weaknesses of the Title X and Title IV programs, but it is difficult to judge the extent of initiative that states might be willing or allowed to take, or what the effects of constitutional challenges might be. Furthermore, it is not entirely in keeping with the operations of most of the private developers who are engaged in new towns; that is, the development corporation would usurp the control over new town land.

It is also difficult to speculate upon the extent to which the program based upon the use of public development corporations would be received by the cities' groups. Their reactions may depend upon the extent to which the program could be employed by the cities themselves. Some indication that the administration might have tried to make the program more acceptable to the cities is indicated by the change in the types of auspices envisioned for what appeared to be purely "state" agencies in 1965 to the inclusion of municipalities in 1966. However, the utility of the program for the cities may, in the final analysis, be a limited one, since cities are less likely to have large areas of open land sufficient for the development of what are termed "new towns intown." Coordination with redevelopment would make the process even more complicated. In terms of the space needs for new town development and the market for new development, the program may still constitute a predominantly suburban aid.[107]

Furthermore, the strength of traditional conceptions of the new town should not be disregarded in attempting to foresee the manner in which representatives of the cities' interests may view proposals for new towns programs. Where, for example, the Federal government has been responsible in many of its programs (such as those of FHA and the highway program) in assisting in the suburban exodus, these forms of assistance do not appear to be directed toward any particular concept of urban growth and form. (This is also a criticism leveled at Federal aid programs which is employed in the case for new towns.) However, the new town concept is still viewed by many as an anti-city or alternative-to-existing-cities concept. The Federal highway program has abetted the movement of industry and commercial uses to the suburbs, but its benefits to the central cities have also been emphasized. Aside from the possibility that the cities may themselves participate in a new town program, it would appear to be more difficult to demonstrate how new towns would be of benefit to the central cities, and to disabuse city officials of the numerous ill effects which they are more likely to foresee.

To a large extent, the effects of such a program upon the operations of private developers will depend upon the manner in which the program is employed by localities. It would operate differently in relatively unsettled areas than within city boundaries, where much of the infrastructure for development may be already implaced. In the latter case, there may be a more limited role for participation by the private land developer. Other questions arise concerning the effects of Federal requirements for low-income housing, which if observed may limit the attraction of the new town site to builders of higher-income housing.

Many of these problems would have to be treated by administrative procedures attached to such a program. Like urban renewal, it could become an exceedingly complex arrangement between the Federal government, the state, the locality, and the private developer. It remains to be seen how much pressure could be exerted by private builders to bring about changes in the original plan of the community and what kinds of controls would be built into the program to prevent land speculation or building delays by builders who are unable to complete their agreements with the public agency.*

From the point of view of the new town concept, one of the basic weaknesses of the new communities proposals reviewed here is the lack of concern for the locations of new towns. It may be a factor which is considered given by those

---

*Other side effects of urban renewal style new towns program will likely emerge. New towns will involve substantial areas of land which will be removed from the tax rolls during the development period, which may be a critical factor with regard to the "new towns intown" approach.

who have proposed the use of public development corporations; but in general, the emphasis appears to be placed upon machinery and review procedures which are directed to the internal aspects of new town development. The Title X and Title IV programs, for example, provide no significant role for metropolitan or state planning bodies, except where the decisions of these bodies might be reflected in local decisions concerning new town development. Although administrative procedures are not available for the public land development programs which have been proposed, it appears that the initial emphasis is upon encouraging the construction of new towns, rather than directing the location of new urban development.

However, it appears more likely that a more concerted arrangement would be effected between state and metropolitan planning bodies where new town development would be initiated by a public corporation. Some observers appear to be of the opinion that this type of program offers more potential for improved coordination of publicly sponsored new town development with state highway programs, highway interchange development, and other state investments such as the locations of state colleges.[108]

Another factor related to metropolitan and regional planning which the current proposals for new towns programs have accorded little attention is that of control over peripheral new town land. A new town with industrial, commercial, and other facilities will not only affect the lands which are held by the private developer or the public development corporation, but also lands in its vicinity. Since the success of privately developed new towns depends ultimately upon their capture of large parts of the local housing market, they could be adversely affected by nearby residential and commercial facilities. To some extent, public or private developers may be able to effect local zoning agreements which would prohibit the development of competitive uses; or stronger control could be exercised through the purchase of development rights to surrounding land. Both types of control have their advantages and disadvantages. Reliance on peripheral control through zoning alone creates the risk that zoning policies might change in the future—a risk which a new town developer would have to run for a far longer period of time than the small subdivision or shopping center developer. The latter approach involves a greater expenditure in the early phases of new town development. Neither approach, however, would provide complete protection from nearby competition.

Many of the apparent shortcomings and uncertainties of the Title X and Title IV programs are to be expected in attempting to translate an idealized concept into an administrative format. The factors which appear to prohibit further consideration of a maximum level of public involvement further emphasize the many complexities of American urbanism which a new towns policy would have to deal with. The immediately significant fact is that publicly assisted new towns programs are being seriously considered in the United States, even though they appear to be characterized by what Feiss refers to as "a faltering step in the right direction."[109] It would be folly to expect that initial attempts to design a program for new town development will immediately result in an operational framework and division of responsibilities between the public and private sector which would result in the satisfaction of all the inherent public and private goals. Experience with the urban renewal program should be sufficient evidence to dispose of that misconception. Any type of policy would be initially an experimental one. Even though the Title X and Title IV programs have been enacted, they are based largely upon a relatively few years of private sector experience with the new town concept. As the successes and failures (and their causes) of these enterprises are tallied and analyzed, there will emerge a stronger empirical base for policy changes.

Much will also depend upon the manner in which the administrative procedures and legislative requirements of the various Federal proposals are interpreted in the evaluation of development applications and administration of projects.

Some of the language of the legislative proposals leaves considerable latitude for interpretation, and in some cases raises serious doubts as to whether accurate interpretation is possible. Such terminology as "maximum accessibility," "substantial economics," "adequate housing," and "a proper balance of types of housing," etc., is difficult to define and evaluate, and raises the question of priorities.[110]

In some ways, new towns legislation may be premature. First, few of the facts are in on the private developments which are currently under way. Preliminary indications are that these new towns possess serious obstacles to financial success, but for the most part must be considered to be in the early stages of development. If these developments are unsuccessful, there may be greater cause for public assistance. On the other hand, if privately developed new towns are successful, the indications are that they will have significant impact upon the areas in which they are located, and therefore may become more of a matter to be contended with than simply voluntarily subsidized. At present, it appears that there is no direct way in which the Federal government can control private new towns or infuse public objectives into their development. For the most part, relations between private developers and government are primarily at the local level, and, where the formation of special districts is involved, the state level.

In the case of Title X and Title IV, many of the factors which would limit the effectiveness of the program and which would blunt the Federal objectives for it have not been fully considered. In the case of the proposals for public land development agencies, the significance of this approach as a new means of land use direction at the regional level does not appear to have been fully explored, nor do the apparent legal and administrative complexities which would result from this approach appear to have been recognized by some supporters.

Finally, as the hearings on the new communities bills demonstrate, the political aspects of policy formation cannot be ignored. The "best" or most desirable types of programs are often not the most politically feasible. In discussing some of the faults of the Title X program, one of its authors, Marshall Kaplan, emphasizes that "the Bill was the best we could get within a political context."[111]

This chapter has focused primarily on the general operational considerations for alternative new towns policies, primarily from the point of view of public control over the various aspects of new town development. However, it is evident that these factors cannot be considered in an isolated context; each alternative has its political and administrative consequences in addition to its level of control. Moreover, it has been by no means an exhaustive consideration of the numerous questions which surround the matter of public assistance and control of new town development. What it has attempted to point out is that, particularly in the case of Title X, there are several operational problems which would impinge upon the effectiveness of a new private new town development. Still, a full appreciation of private new town development mechanics and its problems and potentials is some years off.

This discussion has also touched upon some of the broader considerations which would effect the implementation of a new towns policy and the satisfaction of its goals. The following chapter will attempt to view the new town concept and new town policies in light of some relevant characteristics of metropolitanism.

Notes

1. Weaver's assessment of national differences, coupled with his less traditional notion of the new town concept, lend some "official" recognition to those differences. See *Dilemmas of Urban America*, (Cambridge: Harvard University Press, 1965), pp. 14-16. See also, Bowery Savings Bank, *The English New Town* (New York, 1953).

2. Lloyd Rodwin, *The British New Towns Policy*, (Cambridge: Harvard University Press, 1956), p. 57.

3. 9 and 10 Geo. 6, C68 (1946).

4. Daniel Mandelker, "A Legal Strategy for Urban Development," *Planning For a Nation of Cities,* ed. Sam Boss Warner, Jr. (Cambridge: MIT Press, 1966), p. 217.

5. F. J. Osborn and A. Whittick, *The New Towns,* (New York: McGraw-Hill, 1963), p. 88. "Local Authorities" as defined in Section 6 of the New Towns Act appear to refer to the type of general government in the area in which the new town is being developed, ". . . the council of a county, county borough, metropolitan borough, or county district. . . ." or single function authorities such as highway districts.

6. John R. McFarland, "Administration of the English New Towns Program," *Washington University Law Quarterly* MCMLXV, No. 1 (February 1965), 21.

7. New Towns Act of 1964, Section 16.

8. Unresolved differences at this stage must be considered by Parliament. McFarland, op. cit., pp. 22-26.

9. For a more detailed description of the compulsory acquisition process see McFarland, op. cit., pp. 34-44.

10. Daniel Mandelker, "Some Policy Considerations in the Drafting of New Towns Legislation," *Washington University Law Quarterly,* MCMLXV, No. 1 (February 1965), 80 and appropriate footnotes.

11. Ibid., p. 82.

12. Rodwin, op. cit., p. 42.

13. McFarland, op. cit., p. 31.

14. "Statutory Undertakers" correspond to public utilities in the U.S., such as power corporations or other quasi-public corporations which are granted certain competitive privileges in return for their public service obligations and control (Rodwin, loc. cit.). Development corporations are empowered to acquire necessary lands for such utilities and to contribute to the cost of their development.

15. Loans are advanced by the Treasury only after the Minister and the Treasury concur that a Section 3(1) proposal is likely to guarantee "a reasonable return in relation to the costs of the undertaking." New Towns Act, 1946, Section 12(7).

16. In practice, private builders have played a minor role in the construction of British New Towns. Of the 142,000 dwellings which have been constructed in the new towns, private builders have contributed less than 8 percent. See K. W. Bland, "Private-Enterprise Housing in New Towns," *Town and Country Planning,* XXXVI, Nos. 1 and 2 (January/February 1968), 101-102. The development corporation must

also be consulted on any development proposal by other builders within one mile of the designated area of the new town, but local planning authorities retain the right to approve or disapprove such proposals, McFarland, op. cit., p. 28.

17. However, the development corporation is not technically the property owner of structures in the new town. In 1959, the national government decided to separate the roles of land owner and builder, and, in 1961, the Commission for the New Towns was established "to take over the assets and liabilities of each development corporation as it completes its work (Osborn and Whittick, op. cit., p. 105). The Commission may also receive loans from the Treasury to make improvements in the new town which will enhance the value of the enterprise.

18. One of the forms of control which local authorities had been able to exercise over the construction operations of the development corporations was in the administration of local building codes. However, McFarland explains that this authority may also be lost to local authorities if proposed legislation for nationally developed regulations is adopted. These regulations would more uniform and flexible; but more importantly, they would remove review power from local authorities and vest it with the Ministry of Public Buildings and Works (McFarland, op. cit., p. 29). This is not to say that the national government will always necessarily act over strong local opposition. Construction of the already planned new town of Hook has been forestalled indefinitely as a result of the local controversy which the proposal engendered. Stevenage, which was the first town constructed under the New Towns Act of 1946, was also the source of considerable political friction. The point here is to simply contrast the pervasive powers of the British program with American legislative proposals and traditional attitudes toward public ownership and control of land.

19. Public Law 89-754 and Public Law 90-488, respectively. Title IV of the 1966 act amends Title X of the National Housing Act and is usually referred to as the Title X Program, as it will be in the following discussion. The New Communities Act of 1968 will also be referred to as the Title IV program.

Most of the following discussion will focus upon the history and provision of the Title X program, since most of the research and analysis for this study was conducted during the development and passage of that legislation and prior to the enactment of the New Communities Act of 1968. However, as will be discussed below, for the purposes of this discussion, most references to Title X will apply equally to the

Title IV program, since the basic operations of the programs as compared to other types of new towns programs are the same. Differences between Title X and Title IV in eligibility and other administrative requirements are treated later in this chapter.

20. Statement of Robert C. Weaver, *Demonstration Cities. Housing and Urban Development, and Urban Mass Transit,* Hearings before the Subcommittee on Housing of the Committee on Banking and Currency, 89th Cong., 2nd Sess. (Washington, D.C.: U.S. Government Printing Office, 1966), I, 39.

21. Ibid., Sec. 1004(b) (3&4), p. 17.

22. Ibid., Sec. 1004(b) (1&2), p. 17.

23. Ibid., Sec. 1004(c), p. 18.

24. Department of Housing and Urban Development, Federal Housing Administration, *Land Development Handbook for Title X Mortgage Insurance,* FHA, No. 3560 (Washington, D.C., 1966), Section IX, Part C, p. 6. This requirement for new communities is the same as that for new subdivisions development for which similar assistance was made available in the 1965 Housing Act.

25. Ibid.

26. *Land Development Handbook,* Addendum II, pp. 22, 23. There do not appear to be any Federal requirements that would dictate that the General Community Plan be adopted as part of the comprehensive plan of the local community. This has been the procedure with the development of some unassisted new towns; but since local community plans are usually not legally adopted documents it is questionable what utility such a requirement would have.

27. *Land Development Handbook,* Addendum II, p. 23.

28. Ibid.

29. *Land Development Handbook,* Addendum I, p. 26. This requirement has been carried over from the administrative procedures under the Title X provisions for new subdivisions.

30. *Demonstration Cities,* Sec. 406, p. 19.

31. *Land Development Handbook,* pp. 7-8.

32. *Land Development Handbook,* Addendum II, p. 2.

33. *Demonstration Cities,* Sec. 407, p. 19.

34. *Land Development Handbook,* p. 8.

35. U.S., Congress, House, *Housing and Urban Development Act of 1965, Hearings Before the Subcommittee on Housing of the Committee on Banking and Currency,* 88th Cong., lst Sess. (Washington, D.C.: U.S. Government Printing Office, 1965) Part 1, p. 8.

36. Ibid., p. 8.

37. Ibid., p. 195.

38. S. 2680 is described in the *Congressional Record,* CXIII, No. 190 (November 21, 1967).

39. *New Towns Development Act,* Section 3 (c) (3).

40. Ibid., Section 4 (6).

41. *Housing and Urban Development Act of 1965,* p. 8, and *Demonstration Cities,* p. 9. The New Towns Development Act would also establish a new town "advisory committee" to advise the Secretary of Housing and Urban Development on matters pertaining to the administration of the act [Section 6 (a)].

42. See, for example, John R. McFarland, "Administration of the New Deal Greenbelt Towns," *Journal of the American Institute of Planners,* XXXII, No. 4 (July 1966), p. 218.

43. U.S., Congress, Joint Committee on Atomic Energy, *Nevada Test Site Community,* Hearings on H. 8003 and S. 2030, 88th Cong., 1st Sess., p. 95.

44. Edward P. Eichler and Marshall Kaplan, *The Community Builders,* Berkeley: University of California Press, 1967), p. 165. One new town developer states that "Conventional financing for land development is usually for a term of three years or less, while the development of a true new community will take from ten to twenty years to complete," *Demonstration Cities,* p. 423.

45. Daniel Mandelker, "Some Policy Considerations in the Drafting of New Towns Legislation," *Washington University Law Quarterly,* MCMLXV, No. 1 (February 1965), p. 71.

46. Carl Feiss, "U.S.A.: New Communities—Or Their Simulacrum," *Town and Country Planning,* XXXV, No. 1 (January 1967), 35. The delay of a local planning assistance program introduces a number of uncertainties, including the possibility that the program itself might function to change local sentiment towards new town development.

47. *Land Development Handbook,* p. 8. In general, there appears to be some confusion as to the role of area-wide planning in the new community development process. Contrast, for example, the administrative procedures with Secretary Weaver's remarks in Department of Housing and Urban Development, *Questions and Answers On the Urban Development Bill* (Washington, D.C.: U.S. Government Printing Office, April 8, 1966), p. 17.

48. *Land Development Handbook,* p. 8.

49. Cf. Rouse's testimony on this point in *Demonstration Cities,*

p. 1055. It follows that this is also a matter of concern for the home-buyer who buys for prestige purposes or is interested in protecting his equity. This matter is discussed in the following chapter.

50. *Demonstration Cities,* p. 56.

51. Paul F. Wendt has observed that "Profits are high in land and community development when rates of absorption are high, land prices are rising, holding periods are relatively short and when long-term commitments can be secured at favorable terms." "Large-Scale Community Development," *Journal of Finance,* XXII, No. 2 (May 1967), p. 238.

52. Albert Mayer, "Ingredients of an Effective Program for New Towns," *Proceedings of the 1964 Annual Conference,* (Washington, D.C.: American Institute of Planners, 1964), p. 190.

53. Feiss, op. cit., p. 35.

54. "Can FHA Switch for Slum Housing Problem," *Business Week* (December 9, 1967), pp. 146-47.

55. See also Wendt, op. cit., p. 238.

56. Title IV of the *Housing and Urban Development Act of 1968.* Public Law 90-488, 90th Cong., 2nd Sess. See Appendix B.

57. *New Communities Act of 1968,* Sec. 403.

58. Ibid., Sec. 402.

59. Ibid., Sec. 404.

60. Ibid., Sec. 412.

61. Ibid., Sec 405 (b) and Sec. 407 (d).

62. John E. Keegan and William Rutzick, "Private Developers and the New Communities Act of 1968," *The Georgetown Journal of Law* LVII (June 1969), p. 1134.

63. Ibid., p. 1142.

64. Office of the Administrator, Housing and Home Finance Agency, *Urban Renewal Provisions of the Housing Act of 1949, as Amended Through August, 1955, and Excerpts from Other Federal Laws Authorizing Federal Assistance to Slum Clearance and Urban Redevelopment and Urban Renewal* (Washington, D.C.: U.S. Government Printing Office, n.d.), p. 4; McDade alludes to this dual purpose of the urban renewal legislation in "Considerations of a Federal Program for New Community Development," *Proceedings of the 1964 Conference of the American Institute of Planners* (Washington, D.C.: American Institute of Planners, 1964), p. 194.

65. Letter from William L. C. Wheaton of March 4, 1964. The "open land" provisions of the title permit open areas to be developed as urban renewal projects where it can be evidenced that "the proposed

development of land is an adjunct to or necessary part of an overall program of the community for the elimination and prevention of the spread of slums and blight." U.S. Housing and Home Finance Agency, Urban Renewal Administration, *Urban Renewal Manual*, I (Washington, D.C.: U.S. Government Printing Office, n.d.), 5-6. See also, A. A. Foard and H. Fefferman, "Federal Urban Renewal Legislation," *Law and Contemporary Problems*, XXV, No. 4 (Autumn 1960), 668.

66. U.S. Congress, Senate, *Housing Legislation of 1964*, Hearings Before a Subcommittee of the Committee on Banking and Currency, 88th Cong., 2nd Sess. on S. 2468 and other bills to amend the Federal Housing Laws (Washington, D.C.: U.S. Government Printing Office, 1964), p. 801.

67. John Reps, "The Future of American Planning: Requiem or Renascence?" *Planning 1967* (Chicago: American Society of Planning Officials, 1967), p. 59.

68. Ibid., p. 49.

69. Governor's Advisory Commission on Housing Problems, n.d., *Housing in California* (Summary), p. 15.

70. *Housing in California*, p. 17. The program was not acted upon. See also Charles Abrams, "A Land Development Program for California," *Taming Megalopolis*, ed. H. W. Eldredge, (New York: Praeger, 1967), pp. 848-854.

71. Marion Clawson, "Suburban Development District," *Journal of the American Institute of Planners*, XXVI, No. 2 (May 1960), p. 77.

72. Kent Mathewson, "Skip Annexation," *Nation's Cities*, V, No. 10 (October 1967), 42, 43.

73. Harvey S. Perloff, "New Towns Intown," Journal of the American Institute of Planners, XXXII, No. 3 (May 1966), 155. A practical demonstration of Perloff's ideas may be in the offing in the nation's capital, where 335 acres of Federally owned land was deeded to the city for the development of a mixed income community of 25,000 persons. *Architectural Forum*, CXXVII, No. 3 (October 1967), p. 28.

74. Chester Rapkin, "New Towns for America: From Picture to Process," *The Journal of Finance*, XXII, No. 2 (May 1967), 218.

75. Robert M. Gladstone, "Planned New Communities and Regional Development," Proceedings: 1965 Government Relations and Planning Policy Conference (Washington, D.C.: American Institute of Planners, 1965), p. 50.

76. S. J. Schulman, "The Public's Response: Planning For and Against Development," *Land Use Controls*, I, No. 2 (1967), 21-22.

77. In the 1965 bill the reference to a "state land development agency" appears to mean a corporation created directly by the state for the purpose of new town development. *Housing and Urban Development Act of 1965*, p. 8. In 1966, the reference was only to "land development agencies" and the meaning was specifically broadened to mean "Public corporations, including municipalities," authorized by state law to carry out the development of new towns. *Demostration Cities*, p. 9. The Ribicoff bill again uses the term "state land development agencies" which "means any political subdivision of State or other governmental entity or public corporation or body . . ." designated by state law for the purpose of developing new towns. *Congressional Record*, CXIII, No. 190 (Washington, D.C.: November 21, 1967), p. 2.

78. William L. C. Wheaton, letter to the author dated March 4, 1964.

79. See Mandelker, "A Legal Strategy," p. 223.

80. As of 1969, the list of supporters of such proposals added the Advisory Commission on Intergovernmental Relations and the Council of State Governments, both of which have adopted model legislation for "State Land Development Agencies" in their suggested state legislation programs. This model legislation is based in part upon the act which created the New York State Urban Development Corporation. ACIR also has created model state legislation for "Conditional Property Tax Deferment for New Community Development." Advisory Commission On Intergovernmental Relations, *State Legislative Program: New Proposals for 1969*, Report M-39 (Washington, D.C.: U.S. Government Printing Office, 1968), pp. 507 and 511.

81. N.Y. Sess. Laws 1968, Ch. 173-175. See also: New York State Urban Development Corporation, *New York State Urban Development Acts of 1968* (Albany: Urban Development Corporation, 1968).

82. Robert S. Amdursky, "A Public-Private Partnership for Urban Progress," *The Journal of Urban Law*, XLVI, 207.

83. John Fischer, "Notes from the Underground," *Harper's* (February 1970). p. 22.

84. Peter Khiss, "State Starts Plans for 2 'New Towns'" *New York Times* (August 4, 1969), pp. 1 & 26.

85. Fischer, loc. cit.

86. See, for example, the testimony of Mayor John F. Collins of Boston in *Housing and Community Development Legislations of 1964* (Hearings), p. 408; and the testimony of Mayor Henry Maier of Mil-

waukee in *Housing Legislation of 1964,* Hearings Before a Subcommittee of the Committee on Banking and Currency, p. 561.

87. *House and Home,* "Land Loans: Congress is Cool," XXV, No. 4 (April 1964), 6.

88. Confer the testimony of their representative in *Housing and Community Development Legislation 1964,* op. cit., pp. 358-59, 633-34.

89. *Housing Act of 1964,* Report No. 1703, 88th Cong., 2nd Sess. (Washington, D.C.: U.S. Government Printing Office, August 1964), p. 2.

90. Feiss op. cit., p. 35.

91. *Housing and Urban Development Act of 1965, Hearings,* Part I, pp. 523-24. See also, the opinions of representatives of some life insurance companies, Part II, pp. 617-18.

92. *Housing and Urban Development Act of 1965,* Report No. 365 of the Committee on Banking and Currency, 89th Cong., 1st Sess. (Washington, D.C.: U.S. Government Printing Office, 1965), p. 17. The provision for public land development corporations were also introduced with the mortgage insurance provisions for new community development in 1965, and, although the subcommittee's report does not make reference to the unacceptability of this proposal or the need for further study, the proposal was not enacted. Some implications of these considerations are discussed below.

93. *Demonstration Cities,* Part I, pp. 199-200, 430.

94. Ibid., pp. 505, 600.

95. Developers were absent for the most part at hearings on the previous two submissions of the new communities bill. However, at the 1966 hearings favorable testimony was received from James Rouse of Columbia, MD., Frederick Simpich of Oceanic Properties, Harlan Geldermann of Gelco Developments, Fred Kramer, of Draper and Kramer, Inc. (concerned with Park Forest and other large-scale developments in the Chicago area), and Victor Palmiere of Janss Investment Corporation, in *Demonstration Cities,* pp. 194 ff, 421 ff, 1007 ff, and 1088, respectively.

96. *Demonstration Cities and Metropolitan Development Act of 1966,* Report No. 1931 of the House of Representatives, 89th Cong., 2nd Sess. (Washington, D.C.: U.S. Government Printing Office, 1966), p. 26.

97. *Housing and Urban Development Act of 1965,* pp. 550-551. See also the testimony of the National Association of Real Estate Boards,

pp. 878-879. Both NAHB and NARB took similar positions in 1966; See *Demonstration Cities,* pp. 508, 595.

98. *Demonstration Cities,* p. 1052.

99. Testimony submitted in Federal hearings in 1967 stated that: "Housing is a highly local and fragmented activity. Of the 1.28 million units built in 1960, for example, no single builder or home manufacturer accounted for more than 5,000 units—and most erected fewer than 20. It has been estimated that there are some 125,000 building contractors, most of whom operate within a given metropolitan area and many of whom operate within a single suburb. The same lack of large units exists among the professions, the manufacturers, and the suppliers, and to some extent, even among those who provide financial backing." Sub-panel on Housing, Office of Science and Technology, "Better Housing for the Future," *Federal Role in Urban Affairs* (Washington, D.C.: U.S. Government Printing Office, 1966, 1967), p. 3316.

100. See, for example, *House and Home* (August 1960), pp. 98 ff; and *House and Home* (September 1964), p. 41. The Department of Housing and Urban Development cites that in the period from 1951 to 1965 the site costs for homes insured under FHA increased 205 percent, and the "site costs of the average house from 12 percent of its total value to 20 percent." *Federal Role in Urban Affairs,* Appendix to Part I, p. 85.

101. "Land Legislation: Inflationary Time Bomb?" *House and Home,* XXV, No. 4 (April 1964), p. 105.

102. *Housing and Urban Development Act of 1965,* p. 240. See also *Federal Role in Urban Affairs,* Appendix to Part 1, p. 86.

103. "Better Housing for the Future," *Federal Role in Urban Affairs,* p. 3317. See also *House and Home* (August 1960), pp. 106-14.

104. Secretary Weaver, although he held to the conviction that land subsidies will ultimately be deflationary, conceded that the initial effects might "result in added inflationary pressures on land for a few years": *Urbanization in the Middle and Late 1960's,* text of the Lorado Taft Lecture delivered . . . at the University of Illinois, March 18, 1964 (Washington, D.C.: Housing and Home Finance Agency, 1964), p. 8.

105. *Dilemmas of Urban America,* pp. 36-37.

106. *Federal Role in Urban Affairs,* Appendix to Part I, p. 86.

107. There is also some question of the willingness or ability of cities to undertake projects involving only open land. For example, of the 1,180 urban renewal projects which had been authorized as of December 1965, only 12 were classified as "open land" projects. Half

of these were under 100 acres, and only the unusual 2,506 acre East-wick project would probably be considered of new town size. Department of Housing and Urban Development, *Urban Renewal Project Characteristics*, (December 31, 1965), Table 4.

108. See, for example, the testimony of Harold Wise on behalf of the American Institute of Planners in *Demonstration Cities*, I, 410, 411; and generally, Reps, op. cit., pp. 47-65.

109. Feiss, op. cit., p. 34.

110. Some indication of the ambiguous interpretation of these legislative intentions are contained in the administrative procedures of the Title X developments. See, for example, *Land Development Handbook*, pp. 22-23.

111. Marshall Kaplan, Comment made in the *Proceedings of the 1964 Annual Conference of the American Institute of Planners*, Newark, (Washington, D.C.: American Institute of Planners, 1964), p. 198.

7 The Relevance and Feasibility of the New Town Concept

The preceding chapter was primarily concerned with the translation of the new town concept into a public program in the United States—or, as some may prefer to say, the first faltering step in that process. The analysis focused mainly upon the operational aspects of current programs (Title X and Title IV), and the relationship between this type of program and concerns and operations of developers, local governments, and prospective residents. The objective, therefore, was to determine (and speculate about), with virtually no emperical base, whether the current manifestation of our American new town program could satisfy the goals which were explicit in the legislation which created it.

The purpose of this chapter is to ask and attempt to answer related but broader questions. Basically, the following discussion attempts to determine whether the goals and objectives generally associated with or considered achievable by implementing the new town concept are relevant to and/or feasible for the processes and characteristics of metropolitan growth, composition, and change in America.

It is clear by now that there are a large number of goals and objectives of new towns. This discussion cannot treat each of these or give most of them separate consideration. The analysis is therefore selective, but generally described as the major themes in the case for new towns in the United States.[1]

The chapter draws upon a wide variety of social science data concerning urbanization and social processes in general and specific aspects of metropolitanism which call into question some of the assumptions of the new town concept. The objective is not to present a comprehensive case which counters the argument for new towns on a point-for-point basis. Rather, it is to point up some of the inconsistencies and conflicts in the goals of the new town concept, its tenuous relevance to the social aspects of metropolitanism and its ignorance of the limitations upon our capabilities to shape that process according to a predetermined urban form and social structure.

Urban Sprawl

Undoubtedly the dominant spacial theme in the case for new towns revolves around the phenomenon of suburban sprawl. Depending upon the point at which one takes up the issue of urban sprawl, its causes can be identified at a variety of different levels. However, it seems that, initially, the root cause of sprawl (or, more accurately, the phenomenon which makes sprawl a potential form of development), is population growth and its effects upon the demand for space. Technological advancements have obviously played the dominant permissive role in the process: the automobile shrinks the distances between various urban activities, and communications advances have lessened the necessity for many of these linkages to take place on a face-to-face basis. More than being a cause of sprawl, these advancements permit various urban functions to operate over more extensive distances.

The conditions which produce the sprawl phenomenon are numerous. One of the institutional causes of sprawl is the monopolistic nature of land ownership, in which owners operate independently in decisions as to the use of their land. Individual land owners respond differently to increased demand for development: some release land for urban development, others maintain land in an undeveloped state, speculating upon future value expectations. The speculative causes of sprawl may be further refined to include tax policies which abet speculation in land. Eichler observes, for example, that "By making property taxes and interests deductible from ordinary income tax and profit on the sale of raw land taxable only at capital gains rates, the Federal Government has invited speculation."[2] Local property tax policies have also been identified as a cause of discontinuous development when such policies tax subdivided land at higher values and therefore encourage development on a lot-by-lot basis.[3]

A variety of other factors can also be identified as causes of or contributors to sprawl. Highway programs have obviously facilitated the movements of people and activities to outlying areas. Dominant attitudes towards housing, particularly that toward single-family home ownership, have been accompanied by lending and mortgage insurance policies which permit and create a more spread pattern of development.[4] The physical character of land may also force land developers to avoid terrain which requires expensive modification.

These conditions appear to result in three basic forms of suburban sprawl. One consists of relatively contiguous low density development, which, although it tends to absorb large quantities of land, appears from the point of view of the efficiency of some urban functions to be the least offensive form. A second form is characterized by the spreading of development along transportation axes, or ribbon development. The third form is the patchwork or "leapfrog" form of sprawl which is characterized by discontinuous subdivisions separated by areas of un-urbanized land. Much of the disfavor with sprawl on the basis of inefficiency of urban functions is concentrated upon this third form, although indictments of sprawl often do not refer to these distinctions and are aimed at suburban development in general. Still, these definitions of sprawl are not entirely clear, and furthermore, a given area may be characterized by all these forms.

For all the talk about sprawl, however, it does not appear to have received much study and analysis. Perhaps this is because assessments of the costs and benefits of alternative configurations raise several problems, not the least of which would be the determination of which costs and benefits should be measured, whether to include non-monetary costs and benefits (and how to weight them), and whether adjustments should be made for the incidence of costs (which groups bear them), and the relative importance of costs and benefits on different interests and groups.

One such study which attempted to make comparisons between the effects of two idealized urban configurations upon selected urban economic activities reported that a meaningful systems approach is "well beyond the reach of current theory and empirical knowledge."[5] Various configurations based upon the new town concept would appear to reduce the vast number of alternative spatial arrangements for metropolitan regions; but even in this case the numerous permutations among sizes and locations, distribution and composition, renders comparison extremely difficult.[6]

The dilemma which plagues studies comparing idealized urban forms with existing metropolitan forms is that, even if the idealized form is ascertained to be more economical, efficient, or better in terms of whatever is being measured, it is virtually impossible to calculate the costs to be incurred in switching from one form to another. This no doubt accounts for the dearth of such studies. What is usually discovered eventually is that even the most minor attempts to induce changes in the status quo encounter resistance (which can be proxies for real or imagined costs resulting from the change). This should not be interpreted to mean that it is futile or unnecessary to attempt to make change; rather it is meant to raise the question of whether urban policy should emanate from idealized and inadequately tested models.*

*To those who claim we have tests of these models in Britain and Scandinavia, the principal reply is that these new town policies are only relevant to those particular nations and their governmental structures. There is some reference to aspects of these policies below.

Community Development Efficiency

In one particular respect the new town concept, or, more accurately, the new town development process, appears to offer significant potential for more efficient intra-community development. This potential appears to derive primarily from the key element in the development of new towns, that of pre-planning and of single ownership of land.

As noted earlier, the land use objectives of conventional community land use plans are often frustrated by the caprices of individual decisions regarding the use and transfer of land. The scattered and uncoordinated fashion in which these land use decisions take place are partly responsible for the random development of urban uses. Neither the conventional community land use plan nor the zone plan are equipped to effectively direct the sequence or timing of the conversion of land into urban use. The community zone plan functions as a constraint upon market decisions by designating areas for particular uses, but it does not directly influence the location of development decisions within the boundaries of a particular zone. The unpredictability of growth can therefore result in utility systems which are unmatched to current densities, and which, if further development does not occur, could remain so (or additional development could conceivably bring about a situation where systems are underdesigned for densities).[7]

Often, the provision of water supply and sewage disposal systems in suburbanizing areas involves two stages: a reliance upon septic tanks and ground water supplies in early phases; and a conversion to sewerage systems and community water supply systems as densities increase. In general, the use of septic tanks and ground water supplies are considered to be undesirable systems for several reasons. When employed together the systems are potentially uncomplimentary because leaching fields may pollute ground water supplies. This type of system also introduces constraints into the density of development because certain soil types are unsuitable (although some developers have ignored this consideration). Furthermore, since these systems necessitate large lot development, they have been considered to be a cause of sprawling residential development. In addition, conversion of individual systems to community systems has been found to be both difficult and extremely expensive.[8]

These problems do not necessarily lead to the necessity for new town development, but the pre-planning and staged development control associated with the new town concept would seem to offer opportunities for more efficient utility implacement.[9] The new town development process provides the opportunity to direct development into the desired areas while holding other areas out of development. It possesses the potential of forcing development into certain pre-determined and artificially accelerating the rate of growth within a particular area. This phasing of development permits better coordination of streets, water, sewer lines, and facilities with actual development, and facilitates the most rapid rate of development toward the full utilization of these systems. Secondly, it permits more efficient balances between projected population for given areas of the town or the entire town to be determined in advance of development.

Although the scarcity of research in this area and the need for replication dictates caution in drawing conclusions about the relationship between new towns and community development efficiency, a study of three growth models by Howard County, Maryland planners claims that ". . . when the costs of all functions are totaled, the disparities between models became a conclusive indication of the economic savings that can be realized through more intensive planning."[10] The study compared cost data based on agricultural land and providing basic urban services for a "trend" model, a second model in which Columbia was the only new town in the county, and a third model in which all new development took place by new towns. Cost savings increased with the degree of new town development.

However, it should be kept in mind that residents' costs for services, which are somewhat responsive to densities (streets and utilities), may not be as heavy relative to the total tax burden as other public expenditures. For example, new towns do not appear to offer any particular advantages for savings in education expenditures. Also many proponents of new towns have probably inaccurately assumed that new town development would necessarily result in higher densities and cost savings in suburban development. In practice, it appears that most new towns, because of zoning or marketing requirements, are being developed at average densities comparable to other suburban areas, or about 3 to 3.5 dwelling units per acre.[11] Even if such densities were not a reflection of the market, new town developers in many areas would probably be unable to arbitrarily raise densities. As was discussed in an earlier chapter, most new towns are being developed under the provisions of "planned community" or variations of the "density zoning" provisions in zoning ordinances. Density zoning provisions permit more flexible land use arrangments in new towns, but developers must usually keep within the average densities which would obtain under conventional zoning (which may be low). Furthermore, although it is commonly argued that density zoning permits the retention of more open space, generous open spaces within the new town will tend to spread developed areas and offset the advantages of compaction.[12]

The marketing complexities of new town development may also tend to dilute some of the advantages claimed by new town proponents. As will be discussed below, marketing problems which attend attempts to integrate different styles and price ranges of housing may force developers to undertake the implacement of utilities in different areas of the community. If the developer intends to sell to builders of various forms and prices of housing simultaneously, he may be forced to implace roads, utilities and other improvements in several areas of the town as opposed to a single area.[13] In addition, many proponents of new towns appear to have ignored the fact that the more remote locations of new towns may create higher utility costs or make tie-ins to existing community systems infeasible.[14]

It would be extremely difficult to calculate the net effects of these varied considerations; but in general they appear

223

sufficient to discredit the assumption on the part of some new town enthusiasts that new towns necessarily mean more efficient community development in suburban areas. The many variables involved—the rate of development, location, composition of land uses, and existing zoning—suggest that such generalizations are dubious and as yet emperically unverified.[15] As discussed above, the new town development process appears to possess the potential for more efficient development; however, this potential could be considerably offset by other factors, particularly by pre-existing low density zoning, the multiple market for housing, and remote locations.

Internal efficiencies must also be viewed from another perspective—the region. Would the conditions necessary to create internal efficiency necessarily result in a more efficient development pattern for the total urban region?

Proponents of new towns and the new community legislation itself also appear to have ignored the significance of the locations of new towns. As noted above, one of the purposes of new communities legislation advanced by the administration is to permit more developers to seek out large parcels of land beyond the established areas and fringes of the metropolitan area. Such a policy not only raises the question of whether new towns would function to prevent sprawl in other areas of the region, but also whether the development of more remote new towns might not function to encourage "leapfrog" sprawl on a large scale. It would appear that, initially, such a policy might replace private savings in terms of land prices with increased public costs for regional infrastructure necessary to link new towns with other parts of the metropolitan area.

None of these criticisms of new town proponents' claims should be taken as an endorsement of sprawl development or of all forms of contemporary suburban development. They are intended to point out that some of the "efficiency" assertions of new town enthusiasts are really assumptions; some are incorrect, and where there are efficiencies to be realized from different development configurations, they will probably not result in significant reductions in total public service costs, since the heaviest part of the tax burden for suburbanites is in services such as education rather than in water and sewer charges.[16]

New Towns and Metropolitan Planning

As discussed earlier, one of the most appealing characteristics of the new town concept is that it offers a rather simplified and organic spatial form or process for the growth and organization of metropolitan regions. Spokesmen of the utility of new towns to regional planning frequently contrast the advantages of "poly-nucleated" or "multi-centered" metropolitan regions to the existing amorphous pattern.

Although the new towns concept is employed in a variety of forms in a number of plans for metropolitan regions, the basic elements of the new towns concept are probably most faithfully reproduced in *The National Capital Plan for the Year 2000* and *The Wedges and Corridors Plan.*[17] A brief evaluation of the principles and objectives employed in these plans serves to illustrate some of the basic issues of regional planning for new towns.*

Basically, *The National Capital Plan* employs forms of the dominant regional elements of the new towns concept. Future growth is to be channeled into six "corridors" of new towns radiating from the District of Columbia into Maryland and Virginia. Corridors are to be separated by wide green "wedges" and individual towns surrounded by low density

---

*The Wedges and Corridors Plan, which encompasses two Maryland counties (Montgomery and Prince George), is an extension of the National Capital Plan and has adopted its basic principles. In terms of their objectives and spatial principles, therefore, these are considered as one plan. They are selected as a means of illustrating some of the problems confronting regional planning for new towns because of their adoption of several of the elements of traditional new town thought. It is not suggested that they, or even any single plans, are illustrative of regional plans based upon new town development. The purpose here is to evaluate the relevance of the elements of the new town concept to contemporary suburban development and to examine the internal consistency of the objectives of the concept as translated into a regional plan.

development greenbelts. Towns within each corridor are to be interconnected by high-speed highways and mass transportation systems. The plan was derived from a consideration and rejection of different proposed "alternatives" for metropolitan spatial organization, including "planned sprawl," "new independent cities," and the restriction of suburban growth.

There are several objectives of *The National Capital Plan* which illustrate some of the basic issues which will impinge upon other regional plans employing the new towns concept as the principal form for organizing metropolitan expansion. One such issue revolves around the internal consistency of the planning objectives which are the foundation of the plan. For example, although one objective of the plan is to direct growth into corridor towns, a second is to encourage "already urbanized areas . . . to develop to their fullest capacity."[18] The new towns of the conforming *Wedges and Corridors Plan* are proposed to provide ". . . the fullest range of commerical services, employment, [and] cultural opportunities . . ." while an efficient rapid transit system is proposed between new towns and the central city to "meet a major part of the critical rush-hour need."[19] *The National Capital Plan* will attempt to create new towns with a "high degree of local self-sufficiency," but also will provide for a highly efficient and diversified mass transit and highway system linking the new towns and the central city. Although it is claimed that the radial pattern would provide ready access to "every part of the region," the plan provides for no direct linkages between new towns in different corridors.[20] A similar inconsistency is evident in that the plan specifies a joint system of efficient highway and mass transit systems within each radial corridor but contends that "most automobile users will be converted to the public system only after congestion on the highways reaches intolerable levels."[21]

Both plans purport to provide a "wide variety of living environments" while simultaneously directing urban growth almost solely into new towns. The assumption is made that choice of living environments exists in terms of the types of housing which are offered, but no consideration is accorded to location.

The planned withdrawal of large areas of the region for green spaces is also questionable. In effect, the withdrawal of large areas of open space could function to make private new town development more difficult, not only by removing large portions of undeveloped land from the reach of private developers,* but also by placing a premium upon those areas designated for urban development. The result of an aggressive open space acquisition policy might be a rise in land prices (which new communities legislation seeks indirectly to avoid), or the forcing of private new town development into more remote locations, thereby aggravating the spread of development.[22]

The emphasis upon green spaces is also questionable in terms of the relevance of large green areas to American suburbanization. The association of the new town concept with policies for the preservation of open areas owes much to their common British antecedents. However, the English reverence for open countryside may be more of a cultural peculiarity "based on the power of generally accepted values" than is to be found in the United States.[23] Lower density suburban development, less traditional concern for immediately accessible countryside, greater land availability, and more wide-spread use of the automobile in the United States may serve to make large areas of open space surrounding urban areas both less necessary and less desirable. A good deal of recreation in American suburbia takes place on larger single-family lots, and specialized recreation areas usually require an automobile trip.

In practice, most private new town developers appear to concentrate upon internal open spaces, either in terms of

*Presumably, areas of largely undeveloped land would be selected for open spaces. The reciprocal effects of greenbelt and new town policies do not appear to have to be assessed in depth. It is assumed that the acquisition of large open spaces would function to force private development into selected areas; however, such a policy could also serve to limit the locational alternatives for private development.

single-family lots or community or home association controlled interior green areas. In fact, these areas may have greater utility for recreation and other leisure activities than large open space areas such as greenbelts or wedges. As one study of open space use has pointed out, the most intensively used open space appears at the edges of open space rather than more distant parts,[24] suggesting that narrower interior open spaces would provide for greater accessibility and use.

Besides the internal inconsistencies in the features of *The National Capital Plan* (as well as its questionable relevance to private new town development practices), there are serious questions of the feasibility of such plans in terms of the governmental structure and process in metropolitan regions.

First, there are doubts as to the utility and validity of metropolitan plans based upon a predetermined, static future state of the metropolitan region. Current metropolitanism is sufficient evidence of the effects of technological change upon the structure of urban growth, as witnessed particularly by the effects of widespread acceptance of the private automobile. Although the septic tank has its limitations, development of highly efficient and sanitary individual home sewage treatment and disposal systems could drastically affect one of the basic urban systems and its relationship to urban form and finance. Water re-use systems currently being developed and tested in aerospace technology have similar implications. The relationships between rapid technological and social change and urban structure and life styles, and the concomitant difficulties in forecasting, seriously question the validity of regional plans based upon future physical forms as far in advance as 10, 12, or in the case of The National Capital Plan, nearly 40 years. The unitary direction of metropolitan plans based upon one selected alternative form for future urban development would be less able to accommodate social and technological change than less rigid spatial schemes. For example, less than a decade after it was published, *The National Capital Plan* has been declared outdated by the Metropolitan Washington Council of Government. The Capital area's population is increasing at a much faster rate than the plan had anticipated and the open spaces which were to be the green wedges of the plan are being diminished by private development. Washington's subway, which was to be part of the high density corridors, is barely under way, and probably will not reach suburban areas until the late 1970's. As one spokesman summed up the reassessment of the Year 2000 plan,

> Before we ever come out again with anything called a plan with a capital P . . . we're going to want to know a whole lot more about the region. We don't want to play games. We want to be real, and being real requires a whole lot more than drawing a map on a piece of paper.[26]

Another serious problem is the lack of common goals in the metropolitan region. The metropolitan area is composed of a variety of "publics" with different needs, life styles, incomes, and aspirations. Although there may be some broad consensus on values and aspirations within metropolitan areas, it is currently doubtful whether planners can discover a set of "public purposes" which can be translated into a desired spatial framework for the metropolitan region.[27] Such an attempt by the New York Regional Plan Association, which surveyed the opinions of 5,600 of the New York Region's residents, is instructive. The study's general conclusions state, for example, that "the Goals responses indicated a strong support for more urbanity, more public open space, more public transportation, more beauty and greenery . . . ," adding that respondents ". . . hoped they could get the region they want even while living on much larger lots (on the average) than they do now."[28] It seems doubtful that better public transportation could be devised, or more "urbanity" achieved, while the majority of residents prefer larger lots. Even if these general aspirations could be translated into compatible goals, there remains the planner's task of deciding how much more, where, in what spatial arrangement, and according to what priorities—factors which, once presented in a spatial scheme or map, would undoubtedly affect responses significantly. Some suburbanites may nod approvingly to the proposition of decent and safe housing for all residents of the region, but they may also react negatively to a more specific proposal for a county-wide housing authority which would threaten to bring the occupants of public housing into their neighborhood or school district.

Public administrator Lyle Fitch claims that the formulation of goals is primarily the job of experts, but that "marketing goals is the job of community leadership."[29] However, Fitch's assertion raises perhaps the most serious impediment to the satisfaction of metropolitan plans. The decentralized governmental structure and consequently the decision-making structure of metropolitan areas is largely incompatible with the aims of metropolitan plans. As Banfield has pointed out, "This is the American democratic way, of course, but it often leads to stalemate or compromise, both of which are the antithesis of comprehensive planning."[30]

Urban planning has been traditionally oriented to individual units of government; whereas metropolitan areas are by definition multi-jurisdictional in composition. Although in many ways metropolitan areas function as an interrelated unit, a unified market for housing, jobs, etc., the physical expansion of the metropolis has been characterized by a proliferation and fragmentation of the number of governments which comprise them. The salient consequence for metropolitan planning has been, then, that in the process of metropolitanization, there has evolved no area-wide governmental jurisdiction to which the comprehensive planning of metropolitan areas may be attached. As a result, the metropolitan planning function has been forced to adjust to the multi-jurisdictional framework of metropolitan areas in a manner which has severely limited its effectiveness.

Although it is difficult to generalize upon the activities of the varied types of metropolitan planning agencies, it appears that their multi-jurisdictional purposes have relegated them primarily to coordinative, hortative, and advisory roles. The advisory Commission on Intergovernmental Relations reports that

A common activity of the metropolitan planning agency is to prepare a comprehensive plan for the area and to coordinate plans of local units within its geographical boundaries. . . . Usually coordination of local plans consists only of the metropolitan agency's effort to keep itself informed of local plans and projects and to inform localities of instances where local plans do not conform with the metropolitan agency's comprehensive plan. Few have the authority of mandatory review of local plans. Other responsibilities of metropolitan planning agencies are, for example, development of cooperative techniques among local governments for solution of metropolitan problems; preparation for local governments of standards for zoning, building, and subdivision control ordinances and other planning regulation; and contracting with other governments to provide specialized planning services.[31]

Consequently, the effectiveness of most metropolitan planning agencies depends heavily upon the degree of voluntary cooperation which can be elicited from the units of government within their purview.

Part of the metropolitan planning problem also derives, as noted above, from apparent conflicts between local and area-wide planning programs. Although recognition of the need for area-wide planning has increased in recent years, planning, and particularly legislation to effect zoning, are primarily oriented to individual units of local government. The Urban Planning Assistance (701) Program has strengthened this orientation at the same time it has provided for metropolitan planning.

Some of the problems which confront metropolitan planning also derive from the more general problem created by the planning function's somewhat remote relation to political and decision-making processes. With many of its roots extending from the period of governmental reform the planning function today is still strongly affected by the early philosophy that it should operate outside of political processes. Consequently, the function has been, in most cases, responsible to semi-autonomous commissions or boards. The effects of this positioning of the planning function may vary from place to place, but there has been increasing concern as to whether planning can be influential where it is insulated from political processes. As Banfield and Wilson have pointed out,

> Many semi-independent planning commissions are authorized by law to prepare and publish master plans and to pass upon all public works and zoning changes. In a few instances their decisions can be overridden by a two-thirds or three-quarters vote of the city council. The effect of these arrangements has almost always been to render the planning agency ineffective. Those who could win elections, i.e., "politicians," have never had any trouble finding ways to bypass independent planning commissions when they wanted to, as they usually have.[32]

On the other hand, mere movement of the planning function closer to political processes may not obviate these difficulties. The idea of long-range planning, for example, may be out of step with the time periods on which most political decisions are based. Executives and legislators, being faced with re-election every few years, are most likely to be strongly influenced by considerations of their political popularity at these crucial times. Consequently, they may be unsympathetic to planning proposals which, although they may appear acceptable in the long run, may have short-run political consequences.

Furthermore, the implementation measures employed by planners may be out of scale with the operations of the private sector. O'Harrow states:

> A basic weakness of present land use control techniques is an inadequacy to handle development at the modern scale. Subdivision regulations were conceived to regulate the layout of individual lots, upon each one of which an owner would build his unique house. Zoning ordinances were designed to control the use of each single lot that the subdivider laid out. These two types of regulations have been carried foreward with a minimum of change from the days of little construction—the days before tract housing, shopping centers, and industrial parks. The zoning and subdivision ordinances themselves are out of scale, their administration is out of scale, even picayunish when they try to cope with today's construction methods.[33]

Although efforts are being made to make metropolitan planning more effective and the need for area-wide planning is consistently reiterated, most planners and other students of the subject would probably agree that metropolitan governmental structure and the absence of area-wide land use controls seriously hamper genuinely effective comprehensive planning at the metropolitan level. An American Institute of Planners National Policy Committee on Metropolitan Planning has explicitly admitted that metropolitan government is a precondition to effective comprehensive planning.

> In general the highest levels of coordinated metropolitan planning will be able to occur only after some form of metropolitan government has been established; for only in the context of unified governmental structure can there be achieved the fullest collaboration among public and private agencies and a regular and responsible resolution of many conflicting interests leading to effective action.[34]

This is not to say that metropolitan planning is necessarily an unproductive pursuit; however, it appears that current metropolitan planning implementation powers are inadequate to implement effectively metropolitan plans based upon spatial patterns which attempt to reorder drastically the current form and process of metropolitan expansion. A recent study designed to assess the feasibility of an idealized spatial configuration resembling a constellation of new towns offers the following assessment of its feasibility:

> . . . it is apparent that change in urban form and land use patterns of the magnitude envisioned cannot be effected by reliance on fragmented governmental control extant in most urban areas. Planning on the scale required to implement a decentralized metropolitan configuration will call for a much higher degree of area-wide coordination than that likely to be achieved by voluntary cooperation of scores—and in many areas, hundreds—of local jurisdictions. In the opinion of the authors, the most desirable arrangement for metropolitan planning designed to implement an ordered sprawl urban pattern will be one in which the responsible agency is an integral part of metropolitan government.[35]

Generally, existing patterns of development have not engendered a sufficient crisis among the residents of metropolitan areas to bring about metropolitan government. Whatever advantages planners and proponents of metropolitan government have claimed and promoted for area-wide planning and administration of metropolitan areas has been insufficient to muster effective support for large-scale reform.

If new towns are to be employed in the planning of development at the regional level, it is doubtful that metropolitan plans based upon new towns are relevant to the political and government realities of metropolitanism and perhaps even the objectives of private new town developers. It is highly unlikely that rigid design schemes which hope to create some optimum pattern of regional land use development will of themselves bring about a desired future state in the absence of substantial increases in public authority over private development and the establishment of metropolitan government.

Even under these conditions, long-range static planning by tight conceptualizations is a questionable approach. In many ways, the "totally designed community" is out of keeping with the increasing awareness and acceptance on the part of planners of the limitations imposed upon their role by the complexities and pluralism of metropolitan areas. Fagin offers the following summary of this outlook:

> Gone with the one-sheet one-shot plan illusion is the conceit—happily never widespread among planners despite the full implications of our one-time theories—that a single mind or a single plan can or should control the flow of future urban development. Rather today's planners are keenly aware of the multiplicity of persons and governmental units that make important plans. It is clear enough that any attempt to render these plans wholly consistent in intention of impact would be unreasonably costly and would be bound to fail in any event, given the extreme complexity and magnitude of urban life and the bewildering specialization of its manifold activities.[36]

Planning theory appears to be generally moving away from the unitary design or the ideal tool for the implementation of plans and design schemes to a far more flexible concern with optimizing "choice," "opportunity," minimizing conflict, performing "advocate" functions, and, generally, to a more "sub-optimizing" approach to planning. There is still a concern with changing existing systems and processes; but this is tempered by the recognition that social change takes place unevenly and incrementally, and that to be effective, planning must be connected with the decision-making process and the compromises it entails.

To return to the relationships between current new town development and metropolitan governmental structure, the reality appears to be that, rather than providing a means for simplifying the governance of metropolitan regions, new towns have often compounded the problem, or at best have been a mixed blessing. For example, although there is fairly widespread consensus among students of local government that special districts have become a problem because of their number and entrenchment, private new towns have probably aggravated this trend. Because they tend to be located in the outer reaches of metropolitan areas, new towns are often in localities where there is inadequate governmental machinery and services to accommodate large-scale urban construction. As a consequence, developers have tended (because of the importance of time), to seek out the most expedient means of providing needed governmental services for their prospects. In most cases this has resulted in the establishment of new special districts, either because there were no existing districts, or the arrangements or time involved in the annexation to an existing district has been unsatisfactory to the developer. The Advisory Commission on Intergovernmental Relations states that

> Developer-formed special districts have been able to issue revenue bonds, and in some cases, when given taxing powers, to issue general obligation bonds. Funds were then available for construction of water supply and sewerage disposal systems, streets and roads, and parks and recreational facilities. The powers and structure of these districts varied considerably. Some were limited to single purposes and could issue only revenue bonds, while

235

others had broad powers and constituted almost a limited-purpose local government with authority both to charge fees and to levy taxes.[37]

Such practices can result in a wide variety of problems. From a practical point of view, there is the question whether private new towns can generate enough construction and sufficiently balanced tax bases to retire district bonded indebtedness on schedule. Much of this problem derives from the inherent riskiness of new town development. One student of the governmental difficulties occasioned by private new towns argues that:

> The use of special districts, without sufficient discretionary controls exercised by and upon it can often induce the less scrupulous firms into the business of new town development. Many of the poor experiences in California with new town development were the result of this lack of discretion. Developers were allowed to use the special districts to sell municipal bonds at an interest rate comparable to what is available to California cities. However, the risks that these developers were taking were so high that they could not get adequate financing from any private source.

> The development of large subdivisions or large scale new community developments usually removes more revenue from a county than it contributes. This is predominantly because of the high costs of providing urban services to this development. These costs are not balanced by the increase in revenue from the area. This problem shifts the burden of taxes upon the industrial concerns in the community, providing any have been induced to locate in the community.[38]

Beyond these basically fiscal matters there is also the question of the use of the credit standing of the state for private profit. In at least one instance in California the state legislature created by special act a multi-purpose special district to perform a wide range of municipal services, thereby providing the landowner-developers with extensive banking ability. Called the Estero Municipal Improvement district, it raises not only the question of a government subsidy for private profit, but also, since two of the district's three directors are elected by property owners on the basis of assessed valuations, it places the developer in almost complete control of a number of crucial governmental services of the community. Some of these developer practices appear inconsistent with the claims of some new town advocates that new towns can result in an improved sense of community identity and citizen participation. If anything, owing to the fact that special district governing board members are appointed or elected on the basis of land ownership, residents of new towns have less voice in their local governmental affairs than others. There is some indication that this is a matter of citizen concern even in the American new town most heralded for its social planning. A national news magazine reported the following after an interview with a Columbia family:

> To Irwin Auerbach, the most frustrating drawback is the lack of participation in the community's management. The only forum for voicing protest is the "village association," and the residents have no legal right to shape policy. "We are powerless," says the 42-year old Medicare policy analyst. "The real control is in the hands of the developers. I think no man or corporation can own a city. A city belongs to its people."[39]

Some studies have recommended modified or new legislation to assist states and localities in dealing with these problems. [40] Such recommendations include the establishment of local commissions to review establishment of special districts, special multi-purpose districts, inter-local contracting, interim city status, and a variety of other devices and measures which, it is hoped, will protect both the developer and the public interest.

Nevertheless, these responses by local government are far off from the claims by some proponents of new towns that they offer unique opportunities for metropolitan planning. If anything, most localities have had to plan to deal with new towns because initiative had already been taken by the developer, and local governments have had to contend with the problems which they created. In many cases, this buden has landed upon local governments ill-equipped to deal with new towns. True, once legislation is developed which can deal more effectively with the special problems of new towns, and after there is more experience with them, these problems of adjustment may lessen. But the point central to this discussion is that, rather than emerging as a tool by which states and localities can direct and shape growth, new towns appear to constitute another, unique problem in providing urban services to urbanizing areas. The governmental devices which have been employed or recommended to deal with these new towns do not constitute any revolutionary process for planning and guiding urban development. On the contrary, they have been more adaptive than directive, and, by and large, appear to consist primarily of adaptations of existing devices employed in suburbanizing areas.

The Socially Balanced Community

One of the major characteristics of the modern urban malaise has been what might be termed the socioeconomic "imbalance" of the metropolis. The familiar characterization of the cities populated by increasing proportions of non-whites, the aged, and other minority groups surrounded by the more affluent suburbs shows no significant signs of reversal.[41] Public policies designed to entice the middle class back to the city or to alter the trend of out-migration have been relatively insignificant as against the forces of the market and the attractions of suburbia. What is generally clear is that the modern metropolis offers unprecedented locational choice and opportunity for large segments of the population. For some groups—those with the effective ability to exercise this choice—suburban areas have provided the opportunity to select among alternative environments. The city of the past was necessarily socially balanced, since it contained largely within the borders of one unit of government, and in a relatively compact form, all those groups which had reason to be in the city. The modern metropolis has not only permitted a locational selectivity, but also a selectivity among units of government.

As explained in an earlier chapter, the notion of "social balance" in new towns is indicated largely in two general but interrelated ways: that new towns should be built to provide for different socioeconomic groups; or, in terms of the land use components of new towns, that housing and facilities should be provided for different socioeconomic groups. The rather consistent appearance of this notion in literature describing what new towns are meant to be, or should be, demonstrates it to be an integral element of the new town concept. One prominent new town planner states, "If a new town cannot be large enough to include a normal cross-section of American people . . . the bad effects might easily outweigh the benefits."[42]

Furthermore, social balance has emerged as the principal rationale and pre-condition for the support of the new town concept and new towns legislation from a variety of groups, organizations, and bodies. For example, the Douglas Commission reported that

> Without such a requirement [of housing for low- and moderate-income families] effectively enforced, there is considerable doubt as to the public interest to be served which would justify the guarantee or subsidy. Certainly, the propriety of such a program would be very low on the general scale of values. It would be ironic, indeed, if the Government were to guarantee the obligation of new towns where there was no housing for low-income Americans while refusing to insure loans for housing in the slum and blighted areas of our central cities.[44]

However, there appear to be two somewhat different perspectives on the notion of socially balanced communities. The first, and perhaps the more long-standing, is the more subjective—that new towns should serve to integrate various socioeconomic groups. This perspective, which is tinged with elements of "physical determinism", appears to rest heavily upon the assumption that proximity among such groups would result in an improved social climate.[43] The second perspective is based more upon democratic principles. In this view, it is recognized that prevailing attitudes and governmental and institutional structure militate against socially balanced communities, and that the new town concept should be employed to overcome some of the obstacles to equal opportunity. Thus, one interpretation perceives the socially, economically, and racially integrated community as necessary to achieve the assumed integrative advantages of "social balance," while the other appears to be more concerned with "desegregation" of the metropolis. Although they are somewhat interrelated, the former perspective is the more long-standing in new town literature and receives greater attention in the following discussion.

For all the importance often attached to it, there is surprisingly little elaboration of the benefits which it is assumed would accrue from socially balanced new towns. It is clear that there would be widespread consensus regarding the notion that new towns should be "open communities." However, beyond that it appears that new town enthusiasts regard social balance or cross-section of socioeconomic groups and types and price-ranges of housing as integral to the satisfaction of the new town concept. It is usually implied that this physical mixing of different socioeconomic and racial groups can or would result in positive social interaction, presumably breeding tolerance, understanding through increased exposure and a socially and economically uplifting atmosphere for lower status groups. In the planning of Stevenage, the first new town constructed under the British New Towns act of 1946, the aim was not simply to incorporate different socioeconomic groups in the community, "but to get them actually mixing together." The Ministry of Housing and Local Government adopted the policy that, "unless they do mix, and mix freely in their leisure and recreation, the whole purpose of . . . mixed community disappears."[45]

One of the uniquely appealing features of the new town concept is that fact that as de novo developments they would appear to avoid many of the established social and political structures which have thwarted and resisted physical and social changes in established areas. On the physical side, this feature of new towns development may have some merit; there is obviously greater freedom for innovation in community design and land use arrangements when developement is planned from the ground up. However, not a few planners are of the opinion that new towns confer opportunities to shape social relationships from the ground up. Contini affirms that:

> In the new cities there will be no resistance from pre-existing patterns of population distribution, there will be no status quo to defend. Its urban structure will be so conceived as to make racial and economic integration a taken-for-granted reality—in fact, a beneficial reality—from the very beginning. Thus, many ghosts may dissolve on their own, as the Army example has proved, and the working example derived from a fresh start will be available as a model to be followed elsewhere.[46]

Social balance is open to question and criticism from a number of points of view. How valid are some of the assumptions of the socially balanced community? For example, Contini's Army reference is more appropriate to the pre-automobile city, where there was, of necessity, a greater physical proximity among all social groups. But even then there appears to have been little positive social interaction. Glazer offers that

> . . . geographical proximity may lead to very little social contact. *Dead End,* in which the slum kids interact with the swells, is still fiction; most of such interaction occurs through the intermediary of the police. Puerto Ricans and Negroes in the shadows of expensive apartment houses in New York scarcely have any interaction with the wealthy—they generally use different stores, schools, churches, and open spaces.[47]

Even if it were true that such groups interacted, understood, and tolerated each other on the basis of physical proximity, the example is far less relevant today. The forces behind suburbanization have provided the freedom for large segments of the urban population to be more selective in terms of the neighbors with which they choose to associate, the schools which they choose to support, and the housing which they choose to inhabit. New towns in suburban areas would not serve to reconstitute the "enforced" pattern of settlement which dictated the compact pre-metropolitan city, or the enforced social interaction which necessarily takes place, as Contini claims, in the Army.

The general conclusions of some students of suburban social life and community formation would also seriously question the implicit physical determinism in Contini's assertion. Although there is still much to be learned of the behavioral effects of alternative community designs and spatial relationships, there is sufficient evidence that planners have probably over-emphasized and oversimplified the relationship. Gans contends, for example, that "while physical propinquity does effect some visiting patterns, positive relationships with neighbors and the more intense forms of social interaction, such as friendship, require homogeneity of background, or of interests, or of values.[48] Furthermore, Gans suggests that attempts by planners to induce social mixing at the smaller residential scales, such as the block level, can be dysfunctional to the aims of social balance. He notes, for example, that the potential for neighborhood tension is lessened in homogeneous residential areas because families within the same socioeconomic group are more likely to employ similar methods and objectives in child-rearing.[49] Differences in attitudes and values toward fundamental concerns of the community may result in tensions with respect to the types of public services which should receive emphasis, particularly schools.[50] In his suggestions for the social planning of Columbia, Gans stressed some of the potential conflict in neighbor relations.

Conflict between neighbors is ever present, and since they are spatially tied to each other, it must be minimized. As noted before, much conflict is based on class differences. Block homogeneity is necessary; putting well-educated with poorly educated people or working-class with upper-middle-class people creates such conflicts. One cannot segregate by education or by child-rearing values, so price, which reflects income, is the only form of leverage. Mixing rich with poor puts terrible pressures on the latter to keep up, especially since children make demands they learn on the block.[51]

The relevance of social balance in general has also been challenged in terms of the scale of metropolitan areas. Melvin Webber claims that the importance of "place" and propinquity in the modern metropolis has been diminished by advances in transportation and communication, but that planners will be unable to realize the planning opportunities in the "non-place urban realm"

unless they are able to free themselves from the obsession with placeness and unless they can come to view the urban communities as spatially extensive, processual systems in which urbanites interact with other urbanites wherever they may be. For it is interaction, not place, that is the essence of the city and city life.[52]

Glazer has also suggested that metropolitan scale may not signal the decline of meaningful interaction among different socioeconomic and racial groups.

Geographical proximity may lead to little of that social interaction which we try to achieve when we press for communities with representatives of different economic levels and racial groups. On the other hand, the new monumental scale of our metropolitan areas and sub-areas does not necessarily isolate economic and racial groups more. Interaction between our larger ghettos and larger suburban communities may be in some ways more intense than when low-income and middle-income groups share the same small community. This interaction today occurs through politics, the press and the mass media, through riots and demonstrations. It may be an interaction appropriate to our new urban scale.[53]

In some respects, the foregoing critique of the nation's deterministic assumption of the socially balanced community has been borne out in the experience of new town planning and development. In the British towns, part of the problem of effectuating balanced communities and their objectives has revolved around the industrial composition of the towns. Several of the new towns have been particularly attractive to certain types of industries, or have been developed around particular types of industries. Stevenage contains high proportions of "professional and technical men and women" because of the preference given to scientific and technical establishments.[54] Peterlee was developed around coal mining, and hence is dominated by groups engaged in that activity.

Although the industrial composition of the new towns appears to be the primary determinant of their social composition, their location is also considered important other than its direct effects upon the types of activity attracted. For example, towns in the London region appear to have been more attractive to retired people or those who wish to commute to employment in London.[55]

Some of the British new towns have been more successful in attracting a more diversified industrial base, but this potential appears largely dependent upon the choice of industrial applications which the development may select from, or the policies of the development corporation itself toward industry. Still, there is the question whether the objectives of the policy toward social balance can be satisfied even where the industrial mix is permissive. Osborn notes that attempts at social mixture through housing mixture proved unpopular in Welwyn and Letchworth.

> It has been found that whatever the town planner may desire, people have a marked tendency to segregate themselves by class or income. An area in which there are some noticeably large and poor families comes to be regarded as lacking in "social tone." The better-off tenants (whether they are clerical workers or the more highly-paid factory workers) spontaneously move to streets in which, even if the houses are no larger, the social atmosphere is regarded as superior. In the less favored parts, rents fall, and in the

more favored parts rents rise, and this intensifies the distinction . . . once an area loses prestige it is extremely difficult to prevent the movement from it of better-off people to an area they like better . . . [56]

More recently, Eldredge has observed that:

Class mixtures envisaged by the Garden City idealists have had no striking success in the new towns. The multi-class "balanced" community has not emerged; most British new towns seemingly are largely lower middle class and upper working class. Middle class and working class have not intermingled easily, although the "bourgeoisation" of the latter is patently taking place.[57]

Private developers of new towns in the United States are probably more acutely aware of the forces of natural segregation, since the relationship of these forces and attitudes to the marketing process is a critical one. Even the most socially motivated developers admit that marketing concerns must take precedence if new towns are to be financially sound investments. In response to a query from Representative Widnall of the House Subcommittee on Housing as to whether there would be "economic segregation" in Columbia, Rouse replied

You can look at the word "segregation" through two ends of a telescope. It is segregation if it is compelled and it is clustering if it is voluntary. I believe—and this is a kind of pragmatic set of rules I am expressing, not a scientific one—but I believe if you could produce a truly open community in which there really were no doors closed, then I think that there would be a kind of voluntary clustering by economic level, by intellectual interests and activity and I believe that this clustering would occur in relatively small neighborhoods.

We know perfectly well that when you attempt to market a $50,000 house alongside a $20,000 house you don't do very well. On the other hand, Columbia will be a system of villages of 10,000 to 15,000 people each. And each village consists of neighborhoods of 500 to 700 houses each. Within the neighborhoods there might be quite a narrow economic band, but within a village there can be quite a wide band of income levels and certainly within a village there would be racial integration.[58]

Robert H. Ryan, Reston's new development manager, has also taken the position that, although new development strategies will place more emphasis upon lower-priced housing, the community will not attempt social experiments involving the mixing of people of different incomes.[59]

The majority of current new town developers in the United States could not be considered to be seriously pursuing the development of socially balanced communities as the term is commonly defined in traditional new town literature. For the most part, the private new towns appear to be concentrating primarily upon the mixture of single-family residences aimed at middle- and upper-income groups. Zuckerman reports, for example, that the ". . . price range in El Dorado Hills is now $22,000 and up; Sunset, Sacramento, $23,500 to $50,000."[60] Although non-profit corporations are currently building some low-income units in Reston and Columbia, the vast majority of new towns do not appear to be following suit, mainly because of the risk of upsetting sales in expensive housing. Studies conducted in two California new towns have shown that purchasers tend to view the mixtures of different types and price ranges of housing unfavorably, even when this price range is rather narrow. Werthman, Mandel and Dienstfrey point out generally that most purchasers are primarily concerned about the effects which they fear lower-priced housing may have upon the value of their investment in their home. They also note that residents were also sometimes seriously concerned about the effects of nearby lower-priced subdivisions. In one case, they state that

> These Lynn Ranchers were initially so upset about the proximity of the Eichlers that they tore down signs leading potential buyers to the Eichler models as fast as the signs could be put back up, and many began directing Eichler customers to the freeway when they stopped and asked for directions. (In desperation, the Janss Corporation finally decided to sink an Eichler sign in a cement foundation, and this too was sawed down.)[61]

Although such tactics are cited as an extreme reaction, they do illustrate some of the difficulties which developers and

246

builders may confront even in the mixing of high-priced housing (the Eichler homes at issue were priced from $30 to $35 thousand; some of the Lynn Ranch homes were priced as high as $75 thousand, but others were in the $35 to $45 thousand range).[62] It would seem reasonable to assume that greater differences in price ranges within a given area of the community would occasion increased marketing difficulties.

On the other hand, Norcross suggests that such attitudes toward mixed-price housing may not be unilateral. In his study of marketing techniques and problems in fifteen "open space communities" one of the conclusions states that

> Blue-collar families are ... suspicious of moving into a new community which they feel is above them socially. They won't go where they don't feel at home. They want friendly neighbors, with the same income and education as themselves. This may be a problem for large, open space communities, or new towns that want a mixture of all classes. It is also a problem for the community which introduces new planning ideas. Blue-collar families are far less willing to accept new ideas than better-educated people.[63]

Both studies suggest that for all socioeconomic groups the primary consideration in the purchase decision is the dwelling unit itself, although there may be significant class differences with regard to the influence of planning. Planning features and amenities offered by the developer to enhance house sales may be less relevant to the major concerns of lower socioeconomic groups than to upper socioeconomic groups. As Norcross observes, lower-income families "... buy 'the house' more than 'the community.' "[64] Werthman, Mandel and Dienstfrey generally corroborate this finding:

> The *upper working class* buyers ... as represented in Janss/Conejo by the Dutch Haven residents, were primarily interested in "more [housing] *space* for the money ..."
> The *lower middle class* and *solid middle class* buyers in College Park, Horizon Hills, and Shadow Oaks clearly felt that "more home for the money" and "natural locational advantages" were more important than either the financial or social aspects of "planning."[65]

Upper-income groups, who are less seriously affected by longer commuting distances and are affluent enough to be concerned more about and willing to pay for architectural styling and open and recreational spaces, are more attracted to the "planned community."* In general, they tend to see "planning" as providing and ensuring a "class image."

The Relevance of Social Balance

The general conclusion of this discussion is that the concept of social balance as put forth by many advocates is highly questionable. First, the behavior which is assumed to result from the physical juxtaposition of different socioeconomic groups has not resulted in new towns where it has been tried. A "natural" physical and social segregation take place. Furthermore, this is reflected in the market complexities of private new towns, and public policies which attempt to induce social "intermixing" will run afoul of the market and prevailing patterns of social interaction. This does not mean, as Gans suggests, that new towns might not be socially balanced as a whole, rather than at the neighborhood or block level. But these distinctions may be insufficient to allay the fears of class-conscious and/or bigoted middle- and upper-income home buyers. Like most cities, new towns will probably have or evolve a situation in which there is to some extent "the other side of the tracks."*

Developers are not pursuing social balance, and in fact some may be basing their investments on the fact that many

---

*In practice, developers may prefer to program development for lower-priced housing. Since the developer takes his profit for the sale of building lots to builders, if lower-priced units can be sold at higher densities, he may not only be able to sell more lots, but also reduce costs per unit for roads and utilities. However, since builders take their profit from the sale of housing rather than building lots they may prefer more expensive housing. Much, of course, depends upon the market characteristics of the area, but the different objectives of the developer and builder suggest that developers are probably initially forced to concentrate upon higher-priced housing during the phases of development.

*Or, the other side of the road, as this writer discovered in visiting Rancho Bernardo, where lower-priced neighborhoods appear to be on one side of an interstate highway.

people want some assurance that communities will remain socioeconomically or racially homogeneous. A description of one new town outside Washington, D.C., does not create images of an "open" community!

> One reason that families like Crofton is because it gives them a feeling of security. Many poeple are frightened for themselves and their children. Crofton looks to them like a safe place to live and bring up their children. There are gates on most entrance roads and later these will be locked at 9 PM except one, which will have a security guard. Weekend visitors to Crofton drive past a security car painted in Crofton colors and with a Crofton insignia and are welcomed by a uniformed guard. They also see other security officers driving around. They like this.[66]

The development is 21 miles from both Washington and Baltimore, and 14 miles from Annapolis.

Another basic issue raised here is whether new towns are suitable measures to provide greater housing opportunity for disadvantaged groups. The above discussion suggests that under current new town development practices such an objective would be highly infeasible. But, perhaps more importantly, such a policy (despite the type of program) would be questionable in terms of the needs of the groups which it would seek to assist. The move to better housing in new towns, particularly before employment opportunities developed in the community, would tend to be offset by problems of disruption of existing low-income communities (if the policy were linked to urban renewal), problems of adjustment, economic hardships of commuting, and diminished choices for employment.

Moreover, the socially balanced community could be considered to be an inefficient means for obtaining better housing for low-income groups. What such a policy might mean, in effect, is that because socially balanced communites are considered by new town proponents to be desirable, the more immediate goal of improved housing for those groups in the greatest need would be linked to a policy which necessarily supports housing for higher-income groups in less need. Put differently, if the integrative advantages of socially balanced communites are questionable, so is a policy which aims to create better housing for low-income groups which is linked to and somewhat dependent upon the creation of physically proximate housing for middle- and upper-income groups. Further, there is the question of whether low-income housing in new towns would offer greater housing choice to low-income groups when those choices might be limited primarily to inner-city locations, or the remote locations of new towns.

Requirements for a "proper balance of housing for families of low and moderate income" in Title IV may not only result in limited usage of the program,[67] but even where they do result in the physical proximity of different socioeconomic groups, the hoped-for behavioral and attitudinal changes are unlikely to occur. In fact, there appears to be increased potential for conflict in such neighborhoods. Fava suggests that socioeconomic balance is perhaps more difficult than racial balance within a socioeconomic level.

> The most difficult kind of residential balance to achieve is integration of *both* racial and economic groups. In its baldest and broadest application this means that middle-income white Americans may under certain circumstances accept significant numbers of Negroes of the same level as co-residents, but will not accept significant numbers of low-income Negroes. Yet precisely this kind of racial and economic integration is sought in the prescription of "balance" for New Towns.[68]

As planner Marshall Kaplan contends, planners have probably placed too much faith in physical determinism and the general plan, and adds that "both are out of tune with the complexities of city life, but both lend themselves quite well to the New Community."[69] Nowhere is this more evident than in the assumptions of the socially balanced community. However, there are indications that while others appear to be adopting the physical determinism of social balance, some planners have joined in criticism of it. It is interesting, for example, that one of the staunchest supporters of new towns,

Wyndham Thomas, has recently commented critically on the basis and assumptions of the socially balanced community.

> The disadvantages of suburban life exist mainly in the minds of intellectual planners and social engineers. They apply their own criteria in judging the quality of life and conclude that, because they would not like it for themselves, it must be bad for everyone else. They dislike the long distance commuting more than do the commuters. They find a density of five to six houses to the acre too low, while the residents themselves find it too high and would like larger lots with more privacy. . . . They praise the heterogeniety and exposure-to-life values of the big city while ignoring the reality that most city blocks or small neighborhoods are homogeneous, and that middle-class city parents protect their children against exposure to the seamier sides of city life.[70]
>
> Yet it is still the underlying assumption of some architects and planners . . . that people's habits and attitudes can be molded by ordering their environment in a particular way. The architect's ideal of "urbanity" is held to be synonymous with the social engineer's ideal of "togetherness."
>
> . . . the assumption is, of course, unwarranted. Community is a function of common cause and combined interest, not of forced physical propinquity.[71]

Lastly, if public policy is to pursue the objective of increasing housing choice for the low-income and the poor, there is some question whether new towns, or, more broadly, housing is the variable to be maximized. Improved housing has failed in many ways to eliminate some of the social maladies which have been traditionally associated with poor housing.[72] There appears to be increasing consensus that higher incomes, better education, more jobs, and the elimination of resistence to free choice in housing are the keys to genuine residential mobility and choice both in terms of the location and quality of housing. It appears, therefore, that "balance" is only valid to the extent that lower socioeconomic groups benefit from it. This may be so where it carries with it the expansion of real opportunities in education, employment, and housing. But there are probably more effective and more expedient ways to accomplish these objectives than through new towns.

251

New Towns and Metropolitan Balance

Every commission or body which has studied urban problems has stressed that one of the principal facts of metropolitan ecology is that central cities are increasingly inhabited by the poor and the black, and that whites are fleeing to the suburbs. This is related to and somewhat paralleled by the exodus from central cities of economic activities, particularly manufacturing. The syndrome is now familiar: the job and tax base declines, the city arrives at a financial bind and is unable to raise sufficient revenue to remodel and support soaring poor-related public services.

Integrated and black new towns are seen as one means of ameliorating these problems, principally by providing suburban relocations by which the poor and black have better access to jobs and housing in suburbs, thereby relieving pressure on the central city.* In general, these proposals are aimed at employing new towns to correct the social "imbalance" of the metropolis.

The major limitation on the feasibility of an extensive building of "black new towns" appears to come from the low support among Negroes for black separatism. From a review of a number of surveys and polls of blacks' attitudes toward alternative residential locations, Fava points out that the majority of blacks surveyed indicate a strong preference for "integrated neighborhoods."[73] The Kerner Commission and a *Fortune* poll have reported that 6 percent or less of Negro respondents are in favor of total black separatism, and therefore would probably be opposed to black new towns.[74] Although 6 percent represents a large number of Negroes, it is still doubtful that there would be sufficient numbers in many (if any) metropolitan areas to constitute a sizeable new town. Furthermore, blacks favoring separatism are represented by a diverse and sometimes conflicting leadership, and a large number would probably prefer a largely black, or all-black central city, or a rural location to a suburban new

---

*The other variation of this argument, the location of new towns in rural and depressed areas, is treated separately below.

town. Consequently, black new towns will probably be few in number and of little significance toward "re-balancing" metropolitan areas.

Still, the prospects for integrated new towns may be more limited than has been assumed by some new town proponents. Again, Fava points out that

> Although the scattered data indicate wide support among Negroes for neighborhood integration it is important they do not indicate much support for living in largely white areas. Only 4 percent in the Marx survey indicated a preference for living in "mostly white" neighborhoods and only one percent of those in the National Advisory Commission survey. While racial "balance" has not been spelled out in percentage terms for New Towns the proportion of Negroes in existing New Towns is very low and it is likely that "balance" will often come to mean 10 percent, in approximation of national racial composition... The "pool" of Negroes interested in living in New Towns under those circumstances is relatively limited and is particularly limited among low-income and newly-urban Negroes.[75]

Policies aimed at the decentralization of Negroes from cities are also likely to be regarded with skepticism by those groups who see the betterment of the Negro community linked to the political capture of the central city. For example, some black leaders are opposed to plans for metropolitan government because it would dilute existing or emerging black majorities in the central city. (Self-government, incidentally, is the central rationale of some proponents of black new towns.) The relocation of large numbers of Negroes to suburban new towns might be viewed as a measure to slow or halt such a process. The wisdom of opposition on these grounds to black or integrated new towns is highly debatable, but some of the black leadership will undoubtedly see this and other "opportunity costs" in black and integrated new town proposals. A central theme of Fava's research is the lack of consultation with black leadership on various new town programs and proposals.

Policies aimed at relocation of minority groups from the

central city would also have to be concerned with other trade-offs and special circumstances of such groups. One such concern, which has been defended primarily by sociologists and psychologists, is with the effects of relocation upon established community structures in blighted and slum areas. Some of the studies of housing for lower socioeconomic groups in both the United Kingdom and the United States suggest that the factor of adjustment must also be considered for low-income or racial groups who might be relocated to new towns. In the often quoted study conducted by Young and Willmott in East London,[76] in which the effects of the relocation of a group of families from a London "slum" to a new suburban housing project upon patterns of neighboring and social life were analyzed, the authors found "the relative unimportance of good housing and advanced design as against other things in people's lives."[77]

With implications for both new towns and renewal policies, the study disclosed not only that the subjects led an active social life in their slum environment, but also that, although they were better off in terms of housing in an improved physical environment, "social-life became relatively impoverished. Most of them lammented the loss of the old community. The authors conclude that "the social groups to which people belonged were more important than the physical setting in which they lived."[78]

Studies of the social and psychological effects of relocations from urban renewal projects in Boston and Washington parallel those cited above. Basically, these studies re-emphasize the conclusion that the social and psychological stresses which result from relocations of residents of slum areas have not been adequately weighed against the intended physical advantages. In Boston's West End, which has since undergone urban renewal, one study disclosed that "most residents experienced profound satisfaction from living in the [slum] area."[79] In both Boston and Washington relocation was found to create "grief" and other communal and familial stresses among relocatees. The Washington study stated as a major conclusion that, "Relocation is a crisis in the life of the family that has lived in a neighborhood which it considers home, even though substandard. No matter how dirty, inadequate, and unsanitary the old Southwest was, it was home for families that had been there for a long time."[80]

All of these studies suggest the greater economic and psychological sensitivity to change of lower socioeconomic groups and that the physical benefits of relocation must be weighted against the social stresses likely to inure. It would seem, for example, that the problems which attend the spatial aspects of relocation would probably be aggravated by the relatively distant move to a new town in the suburbs. In any type of relocation there is a high risk of destruction of the pre-existing community fabric; but relocations into distant suburban areas would make other community services and institutions of the city which had supported relocated groups less accessible.

There are other indications that the move to new towns could be stressful for lower socioeconomic groups from inner city communities. Some initial impressions of the Mark I British new towns resulted in charges that the towns created a phenomenon labeled as the "new towns blues," which paralleled some of the findings of early studies of American suburban communities.[81] Subsequent research in both the United States and United Kingdom indicates that there exists some "period of adjustment" for all socioeconomic groups, but that they may be transitory;[82] however, since lower socioeconomic groups have less experience in suburban life, such "periods of adjustment" would undoubtedly be more difficult and lengthy. Moreover, for lower-income groups the economic hardships of relocation would also probably be aggravated. The distances of new towns from central cities necessitates a heavy reliance upon the private automobile, which must be weighed against the greater likelihood of available mass transit in inner-city locations. Although new towns will undoubtedly create demands for service activities which could utilize low-income workers, it is unlikely that

255

the supply and diversity would match that of existing cities.

Public programs designed to relocate low-income groups into new towns will also have to contend with the problems of providing the specialized services required for such groups. Low-income and aged groups would require services such as special classes in schools and geriatric clinics, and such programs would have to be equipped to coordinate and finance the development of these services in addition to simply providing low-income housing. Moreover, these needs will tend to aggravate the difficulties of establishing balanced communities since middle- and upper-income residents may be hesitant to assume the burdens of eventually providing these services, possibly to the disadvantage of the services which they prefer to maximize.

Some enthusiastic advocates of the new communities program have been cautious in appraising the potentials for creating social balance in the suburbs. Former Secretary Weaver admits, for example, that

> Although I am a firm and long-time advocate of open occupancy and economic diversification in housing and have repeatedly emphasized the importance of such patterns in suburbia, I cannot delude myself into the belief that new communities will be a principal or the exclusive means of achieving these objectives.[83]

Gladstone also feels that "It is unrealistic to expect that new communities are inherently capable of changing this pattern without energetic application of a variety of other programs.[84]

There are also indications that the values and attitudes of some new town developers may not be consistent with the needs and values of some socioeconomic groups. Reston developer Robert Simon, for example, states that

> As for public demand for our promise of a new way of living, I am sure there will be 24,000 families in the Washington area by 1980 who will have the intellectual and educational level to understand and want what Reston offers. Our success will not depend on catering to the beer drinker who is content to sit and watch his

TV set, but rather to people who have a wide range of active interests.[85]

The Self-Contained Community

Even the most enthusiastic supporters of the new town concept would probably concede that a completely self-contained community is an impossible objective. But this has not deterred proponents from advocating that it is an objective worth attempting to pursue.[86] However, the reasons self-containment is considered a desirable objective are somewhat mixed and vague. Generally, it appears that the notion is related in part to the location of new towns some miles distant from established areas (also considered desirable because of cheaper land costs and the avoidance of urban sprawl). The more remote the new town, therefore, the more it would have to be capable of providing for more of the range of needs of its inhabitants. Self-containment also implies that the urban economy might be divided into somewhat fixed and self-sufficient units. The principal benefit claimed is that self-containment would render savings as a result of the elimination of long-distance commuting throughout the metropolitan region.[87] It is also suggested that local employment would enhance community identity.

The self-contained new town appears to be a questionable objective from several points of view. For example, urban economic stability tends to increase with the size of the urban settlement. Larger urban areas tend to possess greater variety in economic activity, more diversified labor pools, more entrepreneurial ability, and more adaptability.[88] Self-contained new towns, then, because of their smaller and more controlled size, would probably result in less stable urban economies than larger cities, particularly as they are further removed from established areas. As Alonso puts it:

> . . . seeking closure at a small scale may economize on certain inputs (such as those of commuting) but results in lower per capita production (and lower disposable income after accounting

for commuting costs) as well as the risks of instability and low adaptability which affect small cities. In small cities a declining firm can be a local disaster, new firms are less likely to develop because of the sparseness of linkages, a dismissed worker has fewer chances for re-employment, a boy has fewer career opportunities, a woman fewer choices for shopping, and so on. In short, trying to save on transportation costs may be penny-wise and pound-foolish.[89]

Furthermore, the economies which it is claimed would result from the elimination of long-distance commuting would probably be offset by the higher development costs associated with location beyond established areas.[90]

Some new town advocates counter some of these criticisms by alluding to Howard's scheme for groups of new towns that would constitute a larger economy. But, as discussed earlier, metropolitan planning bodies do not possess adequate land use control powers to direct the locations of new towns into such arrangements. Furthermore, private developers would probably look with disfavor on such schemes, since, in reducing inter-new town commuting distances, projects would be brought so close as to be competing with each other.

Even in nations with powerful and centrally directed new town policies, it has been difficult to create self-contained new towns. Ogilvy concludes from his analysis that:

... it is doubtful whether any of the new towns can be called self-contained, even in respect of employment. Large numbers of new town residents travelled out to work in other areas, and large numbers of new town jobs were filled by people who lived elsewhere. Cross movements in and out of new towns were still considerably higher than the small amounts necessary to balance numbers of jobs and working population. It was not the influence of London which was decisive, although all the new towns were within the sphere of influence of London. The attractive force of towns much smaller and nearer was responsible for most of the cross-travelling, the amount of which could be explained as a response to the size and siting of each town in relation to its circle of neighbouring towns within about ten miles. The analysis suggests that the daily interchange of population between new towns and surrounding districts is likely to increase in the future, in the same way that work-travel movements have increased in recent years around the new towns. There is growing awareness that the words 'self-sufficiency' are no longer appropriate.[91]

Commutation patterns in which large numbers of new town residents travel outside the community to jobs and non-residents commute in are also observed in such new towns as Tapiola, Finland, and Don Mills, Canada. Alonso is of the opinion that new towns within metropolitan regions might have effects on commuting distances opposite from those intended.

> It is extremely doubtful that new towns fairly near metropolitan or other urban areas could maintain self-contained labour markets, with their residents making only occasional trips to the larger cities for special services and facilities. Yet, if the new towns are not independent or self-contained, the space that intervenes between them and other opportunities can only lengthen travel and make it more costly.[92]

In general, it appears that the notion of the self-contained new town is inconsistent with the scale of the modern metropolis and the modern urban economy. Metropolitan areas and metropolitan economies continue to expand because their diversity increases their range of job choices and opportunities and they come to generate much of their growth internally. In fact, this is why most private new towns are being developed in the fastest growing regions and within the commuting orbits of large metropolitan centers.

To some extent, the notion of self-containment is tinged with the romanticized ideal of the small, place-oriented community. In this respect it is somewhat anachronistic. In the modern metropolis people are more footloose, they move more frequently (or the job rotation policies of their companies require them to), and they have less attachment to a particular local community and its institutions.[93]

New Towns and National Settlement Policies

The latter half of the 1960's has seen an increasing number of calls for a national urban growth policy, or a national settlement strategy, to cope with basically two conditions: the increasing growth of already large urban regions, and an expected national population increase of between 70 and 100 million by the year 2000. The various proposals may differ in their details and recommendations; however, they all tend to a similar line of reasoning. First, the continued growth of already large urban areas is seen as a process which should be abated or relieved. Second, a national settlement policy is required to distribute existing and future populations according to some sort of "rural and urban balance." A principal component of such policies would be the new towns concept.[94] In a number of respects these proposals translate the notion of the self-contained community into a policy proposal.

The claim that the nation needs a national urban growth policy (sometimes also referred to as a national land policy), is not new, but it has been rejuvenated somewhat with the widespread discussion of new towns. However, beyond the purpose of slowing the growth of larger urban regions and rural settlement policies, these proposals have never been very clear with respect to their consistency with other national policies and programs such as those concerned with agriculture, highways, the locations of governmental facilities, and national economic growth in general. This analysis cannot consider the vast number of questions surrounding the matter of a national urban growth policy. However, it seems reasonable to say that some of the assumptions of such policies as they are phrased in the literature cited above appear somewhat overdrawn in terms of our ability to coordinate centrally all of the factors which influence settlement patterns and locations.

First, the requirement for a national settlement policy is usually based upon the highest estimates of U.S. population increase by the year 2000.[95] Downs believes that these projections are rather high.

> Among urban futurists, a prevalent cause of alarm is the "explosion" of urban population they foresee. Extreme estimates indicate that the total U.S. population will *double* from 1960 to the year 2000, rising from 180.7 million to 361.4 million. This gain of 180.7 million in forty years is derived from the U.S. Census Bureau's highest-fertility projection (Series A), which assumes fertility rates typical of the peak postwar years. But since 1957, U.S. fertility rates have plummeted 30 percent. Hence, they are already down to the level of the Census Bureau's lowest-fertility projection (Series D), which indicates a gain of 101.9 million from 1960 to 2000. If fertility rates keep on falling (as I believe they will), then even this projection may be too high. For comparison, I have made a crude calculation based upon the assumption that fertility rates will continue to fall steeply for another decade, then level off until 2000. My rough approximation shows this would reduce the total population gain between 1960 and 2000 to 68.8 million.[96]

Alonso argues that even if the 100 million figure is accepted, the number of new towns called for by the National Committee on Urban Growth Policy (100 new towns of at least 100,000 population, and 10 new towns at 1 million each), "would affect only a small part of our population and an even smaller part of our housing production." He maintains that:

> ... the year 2000 would see only 7% of the 300 million population residing in these new settlements and 80% of the foreseen growth in existing ones. If replacement of one-third of the existing dwellings is taken into account, almost 90% of new housing would be produced in existing urban areas.
>
> Further, it would seem that, within the uncertain state of our knowledge, we cannot say that existing urban centers can absorb 80 but not 100 million persons. If each of our smallest two hundred metropolitan areas took in a half million persons, we could hold the 100 million without any of these areas exceeding two and a half million.[97]

Proposals for national urban growth policies also call for creation of some sort of "rural-urban balance" through the construction of new towns in declining and depressed areas. Basically, these proposals stress the creation of urban advantages where they do not presently exist. The pooling of labor and infrastructure would appear to make economic development more feasible than under the scattered conditions which characterize erstwhile agricultural and mining areas.

Still, these areas are often plagued by an over-aged and unskilled population, because the young leave for the large urban centers as soon as they are able. Although new towns might serve to bring some of the attractions of large urban areas to declining regions, there is no guarantee that they will not be used as a stepping stone for a move to other areas. The same may apply to attracting and holding industry in declining regions. Such areas are often inadequate in terms of rail and highway linkages, schools, hospitals, and other social and economic overhead. The regions would be urbanizing late and, in general, be at a tremendous competitive disadvantage for capital and other resources.

A related argument is that new towns in rural or declining areas would function as interceptors for migrants from rural to urban areas. Again, the proposal may be somewhat late. Migration figures suggest that the large majority of in-migration is originating from outside the country. Migration from farms has dropped off to an insignificant amount, simply because of the scarcity of farmers. Most of the migration of Negroes into metropolitan areas now comes from smaller urban places rather than farms.[98]

Assuming that a national urban growth policy were developed, it would probably be extremely difficult to implement. There are, of course, a large number of ways in which the national government might (and does) influence population distributions and urban patterns.[99] But it is difficult to discern whether these influences are even related to a policy or policies, or whether Federal programs are more adaptive (to state and local exigencies) than directive. Furthermore, although there are a number of Federal programs which can influence the direction and character of local growth, these programs often can operate only through local initiative. Other problems associated with Federal control over the "carrot" type of program abound in the history of the urban renewal program. In short, individual localities can determine whether many Federal programs operate at all.

The lack of urban goals at the metropolitan level is mirrored at the national level. A national urban growth policy would require an unprecedented degree of coordination and cooperation, both among and between the Federal agencies and localities. It is difficult to find a great deal of coordination at any level, and, in fact, one may find more conflict between programs and between the operations of different agencies. Some students of urban affairs maintain that the idea of a national urban policy is uncharacteristic of decision-making in America. Campbell and Burkhead are unequivocal on the point:

> In the polemics surrounding urbanism and metropolitanism there is a persistent demand for a unified federal urban policy. It is argued that no such policy exists today, and that the present attacks on urban problems are piecemeal, fragmented, inconsistent, and uncoordinated. An overriding urban policy would make possible, it is believed, the meshing of specific programs into a meaningful framework. Such a condition will never exist. The American decision process simply does not work that way. Policy changes are incremental, not sweeping. New directions are tried, but with caution.[100]

It is already evident that there would be differences among those who agree that a national urban growth policy is necessary as to the principal means by which such a policy might be implemented. A major area of contention would be the extent to which government in general, and the Federal government in particular, should be directly involved in the operations of such a policy, especially with respect to the relationship between the policy and local home rule and private ownership of property.[101]

Lastly, there is reason to argue that a national urban policy, to the extent that one might be attempted, might be more appropriate to today's most pressing urban problems if it were cast in a more direct framework than an essentially spatial policy. For example, in listing ten points of urban policy, Daniel Moynihan does not include the necessity for a national settlement strategy, but maintains that urban policy should be directed to specific problems in urban areas, particularly poverty, unemployment, outmoded governmental structures, and fiscal stresses.[102]

New Towns and Urban Innovation

As discussed under the case for new towns, one of the features of the new town concept that appears to generate wide appeal is that, as de novo developments, new towns permit opportunities for innovation and experimentation. However, the extent to which a given aspect of the planning and development of a new town is innovative, the extent to which this innovative freedom extends to the social dimensions of new towns, and the extent to which private developers are interested in the risks which innovation and experimentation create, have yet to be determined or are somewhat debatable. Eichler and Kaplan argue that the riskiness of private new town development makes it particularly unsuited to innovation.

> In the process of development, the community builder necessarily becomes a land manager trying to maximize the value of his unused holdings. His essential job is to conserve, to make sure that nothing goes on the land which will have a harmful effect in the future. This is hardly a climate from which unusual physical forms are likely to emerge. In fact, one may well find community builders rejecting novel proposals because of the uncertain effect they will have on the value of the land.[103]

Most frequently, reference is made to the increased capabilities for innovation in site planning and urban design, particularly the ability to employ concepts such as cluster development. But there is some question as to whether cluster concepts can any longer be considered genuine innovation, or whether their application depends upon new town development, especially since more and more zoning ordinances permit clustering, and on rather small sites. Still, others are of the opinion that the potential for innovation extends well beyond land development and planning.[104] Perhaps the most extensive and ambitious attempt to explore this potential is the Minnesota Experimental City Project. The principal goal of the project is to establish an "open city" by:

1. The application of technology in the service of people; and
2. The encouragement of continuing experimentation—social, economic, and physical—to give appropriate direction to the new techniques.

The "new" aspect of the city provides the first real opportunity for a total systems experiment, impossible in today's complex and interacting urban systems. The bits and pieces of experiments possible in existing communities are no substitute for a total systems study at full-city scale. In existing cities, both citizens and their institutions are deeply committed to the status quo. Thus, a new city is desirable. . . .[105]

While these are laudable and worthwhile objectives, there is some reason to question the relevance of the approaches to be employed. In recent years there has been increasing discussion of the potential applications to urban problems of the problem-solving and work-programming techniques developed in business, aerospace, and defense. The degree of applicability might be gauged by the extent to which the city—a complex of interacting local, national, and international systems—resembles a missile system or other system to which the systems approach has been successfully applied. Although there may be some similarities with the physical systems of the city, one must conclude that the differences are far greater, a principal difference being that cities are not closed systems. Secondly, cities do not possess the well-defined goals (fundamental to the systems approach) which have been established for defense systems and moon shots. Third, urban planners and administrators do not possess a degree of control over the factors affecting their areas of responsibility that is anywhere comparable to the control enjoyed by defense and aerospace planners.

General Electric has apparently already discovered some of these differences, especially that community development is constrained significantly by different external conditions from those encountered in the development of fuel cells for space vehicles or product improvement. Models and simulations of cash flow have been largely unable to account for fluctuations in market political climate generated externally. One General Electric researcher notes, for examples, that

> After careful consideration and investigation of the lack of progress in meeting problems of building and development, it became clear that progress was essentially blocked by interaction of proliferating, restrictive, inflexible planning and zoning regulations; archaic, conflicting codes and inspection practices; union work rules and limitations; the highly fragmented character of the construction industry (thousands of small firms with limited financial capacity and unequal bargaining power); unwillingness of mortgage lenders to support builders who might want to innovate and experiment.[106]

The corporation has since announced that it is abandoning "city building" because of its inability to exert control over many of the above-cited conditions.[107]

Assuming that large corporations were able to exert sufficient control over the inputs to community development, it would seem reasonable to question whether innovations and experiments could be extrapolated to existing urban areas. If new towns are to function as laboratories for urban innovation, they must not be so sterilized of the constraints affecting existing communities as to render such innovations infeasible elsewhere. It may be possible to change the rules under certain conditions, such as for experimental or demonstration projects; however, achieving widespread institutional change is quite another matter.

Most of the discussion of the experimental potentials of the new town concept appear to refer to technological innovation. But the description of the Experimental City Project is also tinged with elements of physical determinism. In stating that ". . . both citizens and their institutions are deeply committed to the status quo . . ," it is implied at least that the clean slate of a new town will enhance innovations in the social dimensions as well. This may be possible to a limited extent; but new town inhabitants will not be antiseptic lab mice. Rather, their values, attitudes, and institutional relationships will already have been well set by the larger society and by previous experiences.[108] All this is not to suggest that attempts at social innovation should not be encouraged or will be fruitless; only that the possibilities provided by new towns as well as the applicability of the systems approach to the solution of social problems may be overrated.

From another perspective, the fervor of some for creating "the new city" raises the question of whether the city created by the systems approach will lack some of the qualities of existing cities. Will there be room in the pre-planned, efficient city of tomorrow for the accidents, contrasts, diversities, and even the conflicts that are the substance of urbanity? Whyte, for one, doubts it:

> In another respect, the new towns lack self-sufficiency. There's to be no sin in them. Despite the claim that the new towns are to have all the attraction of the city, there are no provisions for night clubs, bookie joints, or any but the mildest of vices. The new towns are to cater to the widest possible range of tastes, but there is not to be any bad taste. There will be no raffishness, no garish "strip," no honky-tonks.

> The bars are to be genteel, too: In the new towns of England some of the pubs are so prim they look as though they should be called alcohol dispensaries, and the ones over here are not real bars but the cocktail lounges of adjoining restaurants, the kind

with Muzak. All this is understandable enough, and new towns are not to be scorned for their wholesomeness: It's one of the reasons they would be nice places to live in. But who would want to visit them?[109]

The following quotation makes a similar point:

The question arises: Are the new towns to be cities or suburbs? Not long ago a Baltimore symphony director, conferring with a Columbia executive, raised that question.

"Columbia will be a city," was the answer.

"Well, are you going to have things like a burlesque house?"

"No," said the Columbia man. "If people want that, they can go into Baltimore."

"Then," said the symphony director, "you're a suburb."[110]

The purpose of this chapter has been to question some of the central sub-concepts which comprise the new town concept as to their relevance and feasibility to American metropolitanism and its problems. It was necessarily selective and, owing to the variety of assumptions considered, does not readily lend itself to summary. What it has attempted to clarify, however, is that a number of the central assumptions encompassed by the new town concept are seriously questioned, if not in some cases disqualified, by a variety of findings in the relevant social science disciplines, as well as by some of the early research on the limited empirical base of American new towns. It therefore, in turn, raises questions as to the validity of public policies and expenditures based upon these assumptions.

Notes

1. The following line of questioning by no means exhausts the points from which the new town concept and new town policy merit examination. See, e.g., John Garvey, Jr., "New, Expanding and Renewed Town Concepts: Part I," *Assessors Journal,* July 1969, pp 49-53.

2. *Housing and Community Development Legislation U.S., Congress, House, Hearings* before the subcommittee on Housing of the

Committee on Banking and Currency, 88th Cong., 2nd Sess., 1964, p. 613.

3. R. O. Harvey and W. A. V. Clark, "The Nature and Economics of Urban Sprawl," *Land Economics*, XLI, No. 1 (February 1965), 5.

4. Harvey and Clark point out, for example, that lending institutions prefer not to risk high concentrations of loans in particular geographic areas, or among single developers, builders and projects. They add, "Most lenders supporting subdivision development demand that projects be organized in completable units which will not extend beyond one or, at best, three building seasons."

5. H. R. Woltman et al., *The Economic Feasibility of Decentralized Metropolitan Regions* (Los Angeles: Planning Research Corporation, 1965), p. 5; See also William L. C. Wheaton, "Operations Research for Metropolitan Planning," *Journal of the American Institute of Planners*, XXIX, No. 4 (November 1963), 255; and Lloyd Rodwin, "Economic Problems in the Development of New and Expanded Towns," *Round Table Conference on the Planning and Development of New Towns* (New York: United Nations, 1964).

6. As a result of theoretical and technical limitations, discussions of alternative urban configurations are often very limited in scope and highly generalized. See, for example, Catherine Bauer Wurster, "The Form and Structure of the Future Urban Complex," *Cities and Space*, ed. Lowden Wingo (Baltimore: Johns Hopkins, 1963), pp. 73-101.

7. For example, the U.S. Public Health Service indicates that public sewage disposal systems cannot be normally justified economically where residential populations are less than 2,500 persons per square mile, or a building density of more than 1/2 acre lots. *Environmental Health Planning Guide,* Public Health Service Publication No. 823 (Washington, D.C.: U.S. Government Printing Office, 1962), p. 38. This situation can exist temporarily within neighborhoods in new towns, but its occurrence can be minimized by controls over the location of incoming development and neighborhood phasing.

8. Advisory Commission on Intergovernmental Relations, *Intergovernmental Responsibilities for Water Supply and Sewage Disposal in Metropolitan Areas,* Report A-13 (Washington, D.C.: U.S. Government Printing Office, 1962), pp. 24-26. Also, U.S. Department of Health Education and Welfare, *Manual of Septic Tank Practice,* Public Health Service Publication No. 526 (Washington, D.C.: U.S. Government Printing Office, 1957).

269

9. Some illustrations of these advantages are provided by Webb S. Fiser, *Mastery of the Metropolis* (Englewood Cliffs: Prentice-Hall, 1962), pp. 66 f.

10. Edward P. Eichler and Marshall Kaplan, *The Community Builders* (Berkeley: University of California Press, 1962), p. 197.

11. Davis Shaw, "New Towns vs. Trends: Comparative Costs," *AIP Newsletter,* III No. 8 (August 1968), 11. See also Howard County Planning Commission, *Howard County 1985,* General Plan Technical Report No. 1 (April 1967).

12. E. C. Brazell, "Comparative Costs for Open Space Communities: Rancho Bernardo Case Study," *Land Use Controls,* I, No. 4 (1967), 35-36. Brazell, Vice-President of the development company, points out that in the case of Rancho Bernardo, planned unit developments have proven to be more expensive to develop than conventional subdivisions at densities of less than twelve units to the acre.

13. However, under Title IV provisions, the developer would be required to provide for all ranges in housing prices during each phase of the development. U.S. Department of Housing and Urban Development, *Title 24-Housing and Housing Credit* (Washington, D.C.: U.S. Government Printing Office, 1970), Sec. 31.6 (c) (3).

14. R. Bruce Ricks, "New Town Development and the Theory of Location," *Land Economics,* XLVI (1970) 7-11.

15. A recent addition to municipal cost revenue research suggests that the aversion to single-family, middle-income suburban housing by many new town enthusiasts cannot be generalized upon. A report on the research concludes that interstate differences in tax practices and the assignment of responsibility for educational expenditures are highly significant in explaining whether housing in a given price range will or will not pull its weight in local revenue production. Urban Land Institute, "Do Single Family Houses Pay Their Way?" *Urban Land,* XXVII, September 1968.

16. Some observers, although still in a minority, would argue that sprawl is far from a crisis in urban development and have attempted to defend the process on limited grounds. Lessinger argues, for example, that "scatteration" allows for areas of "infill" in suburban development which will reduce the tendency for the formations of large areas which become obsolete at the same rate. "The Case for Scatteration," *Journal of the American Institute of Planners,* XXVIII, No. 3 (August 1962), 159-169. Harvey and Clark, taking the same initial premise, argue that "sprawl" provides the suburban dweller with greater "choice" and that

it should not be considered economically unsound because people are ostensibly "willing" to pay for the costs of a "sprawl" environment (op. cit., pp. 8-9). Although both points of view provide some balance to the sprawl debate, they tend to suffer from a similar lack of calculation of costs and benefits which precludes resolution of the issues involved.

17. New towns have been recommended or proposed in plans in a variety of regions and in a variety of forms. For example, in the metropolitan regions in the state of New York and in a state-wide plan there have been a variety of new town proposals. The New York City region in particular has been the focus of several proposals. See, for example: Roger Willcox, "Trend of Development in the New York Region;" *Planning 1948 (Chicago: American Society of Planning Officials, 1948), Ronald Sullivan, "City of 300,000 is Urged for Meadows," The New York Times,* May 15, 1967, pp. 1, 20; Steven V. Roberts, " 'New Town' Urged on Staten Island," *The New York Times* November 9, 1967, p. 41; and Arthur T. Row, *A Consultant's Report to the Tri-State Transportation Committee on the Reconnaissance of the Tri-State Region* (1965). See also New York State Office for Regional Development, *Change, Challenge and Response, A Development Policy for New York State* (1964); and Department of City Planning, Syracuse, New York, *General Plan, Plans and Policies, Syracuse, New York* (1967), pp. 73-75.

18. Maryland—National Capital Park and Planning Commission, *On Wedges and Corridors,* (Silver Spring, 1964) p. 21.

19. . . . *On Wedges and Corridors,* p. 18.

20. *The Nation's Capital—A Plan for the Year 2000* (Washington, D.C.: National Capital Planning Commission, 1961), p. 46.

21. Victor Gruen, *The Heart of Our Cities* (New York: Simon and Schuster, 1964), p. 205.

22. In a comparative study of suburban development in the United States and England, H. E. Bracey points out that the withdrawal of land for open space around some English cities is partly responsible for considerably higher land prices than those in the United States *Neighbors: Subdivision Life in England and the United States* (Baton Rouge: Louisiana State University Press, 1964), pp. 32-34.

23. Nathan Glazer, "Housing Problems and Housing Policies," The Public Interest, No. 7 (Spring 1967) 50.

24. Derk de Jonge, "Applied Hodology," *Landscape,* XVII, No. 2 (Winter 1967/68), 10.

26. Philip Carter, "Year 2000 Plan Outdated," *The Washington Post,* December 29, 1969, p. B2.

27. Edward C. Banfield, "The Uses and Limitations of Metropolitan Planning in Massachusetts," *Taming Megalopolis,* ed. H. W. Eldredge (New York: Praeger, 1967) II, 712.

28. Regional Plan Association, *Public Participation in Regional Planning* (New York: Regional Plan Association, 1967), p. 32.

29. Lyle C. Fitch, "Goals for Urban Development," *Urban America: Goals and Problems,* (Washington, D.C.: U.S. Government Printing Office, 1967), p. 25.

30. Banfield, op. 'cit., p. 713.

31. Advisory Commission on Intergovernmental Relations, *Performance of Urban Functions: Local and Area-wide* (Washington, D.C.: U.S. Government Printing Office, 1963), Report M-21, pp. 215-16.

32. Edward C. Banfield and James Q. Wilson, *City Politics* (Cambridge: Harvard University Press, 1965), p. 197. The problems associated with acceptance of the plan have prompted one planning theorist to remark that "After more than a half century of experience, the conventional master plan is accepted by the legislature so rarely that it becomes top planning news when one is followed." Dennis O'Harrow, "Proposals for New Techniques for Shaping Urban Expansion," *Urban Expansion—Problems and Needs* (Washington, D.C.: Housing and Home Finance Agency, 1962), p. 139.

33. O'Harrow, op. cit., pp. 138-139. The scale at which planners have tended to view the city has been questioned from a number of directions. Some feel that planners plan at too large a scale, whereas others claim that they have not recognized the importance of the new scale of urbanism. Compare for example, Jane Jacobs, *The Death and Life of Great American Cities* (New York: Random House, 1961), and Melvin Webber, "Order in Diversity: Community Without Propinquity," *Cities and Space,* ed. Lowden Wingo, Jr. (Baltimore: Johns Hopkins Press, 1963), pp. 23-54.

34. Quoted from Henry Fagin, "Planning Organization and Activities Within the Framework of Urban Government," *Planning and the Urban Community,* ed. Harvey S. Perloff (Pittsburgh: University of Pittsburg Press, 1961), p. 120.

35. Keith R. Blunt et al., *Implementation of an Ordered Sprawl Urban Configuration,* prepared for the Office of Civil Defense, (Los Angeles: Planning Research Corporation, 1967), pp. 79-80. The study configuration referred to consists of a constellation of new towns surrounding a decentralized metropolitan center and separated from

one another by from four to seven miles of open space, called "ordered sprawl." Ibid., pp. 2-6.

36. Henry Fagin, "The Evolving Philosophy of Urban Planning," *Urban Research and Policy Planning*, ed. Leo Schnore and Henry Fagin (Beverly Hills, Calif.: Sage Publications, 1967), p. 318.

37. Advisory Commission on Intergovernmental Relations, *Urban and Rural America: Policies for Future Growth*, Report A-32 (Washington, D.C.: U.S. Government Printing Office, 1968), p. 91.

38. John Gliege, *New Towns: Policy Problems in Regulating Development*, Papers in Public Administration No. 17. (Tempe Institute of Public Administration, University of Arizona, 1970), pp. 20-21.

39. *Newsweek*, "Growing Pains of a New Town," July 14, 1969, p. 51.

40. *Urban and Rural America* and Gliege, op. cit.

41. The extent of this condition varies significantly with the age, size, and regional location of metropolitan areas. Generally, the larger, older, and more "northeasternly" SMSA's fit the description best. See Leo Schnore, *The Urban Scene* (New York: The Free Press, 1965), Chapter 11.

42. Clarence Stein, *Toward New Towns for America* (New York: Reinhold, 1967), p. 61.

43. See Herbert Gans, "The Balanced Community: Homogeneity or Heterogeneity in Residential Neighborhoods," *Journal of the American Institute of Planners*, XXVII, No. 3 (August 1961), 117. See also Herbert Gans, *The Levittowners* (New York: Pantheon, 1967), Chapter 8.

44. Douglas Commission, *Building the American City*, Report of the National Commission on the Urban Problems to the U.S. Congress, 91st Cong. 1st Sess., (Washington, D.C.: U.S. Government Printing Office, 1968), pp. 178-179.

45. Harold Orlans, *Utopia Ltd.* (London: Rutledge and Kegan, 1952), pp. 81-82.

46. Edgardo Contini, "New Perspectives for Urban America," *Urban America: Goals and Problems* (Washington, D.C.: U.S. Government Printing Office, 1967), p. 266.

47. Glazer, op. cit., p. 47. See also Harvey Molotoch, "Racial Integration in a Transition Community," *American Sociological Review*, XXXIV, December 1969, pp. 878-893.

48. Herbert J. Gans, "Planning and Social Life: Friendship and Neighbor Relations in Suburban Communities," *Journal of the American Institute of Planners*, XXVII, No. 2 (May 1961), 134; see also

Irving Rosow, "The Social Effects of the Physical Environment," *Journal of the American Institute of Planners,* XXVII, No. 2 (May 1961), p. 127.

49. Gans, "The Balanced Community," pp. 177-178.

50. From a somewhat different perspective Dobriner has described the tensions which emerge when relative homogeneity is upset in existing communities. William Dobriner, *Class in Suburbia* (Englewood Cliffs: Prentice-Hall, 1963), Chapter 5.

51. Herbert Gans, *People and Plans,* (New York: Basic Books, 1968), p. 189.

52. Melvin Webber, "The Urban Place and the Nonplace Urban Realm," *Explorations into Urban Structure,* (Philadelphia: University of Pennsylvania Press, 1964), p. 147.

53. Glazer, op. cit., p. 46.

54. Orlans, op. cit., p. 82.

55. J. H. Nicholson, *New Communities in Britain* (London: The National Council of Social Service, Inc., 1961), p. 54.

56. F. J. Osborn, *Green-Belt Cities* (London: Faber, 1946), pp. 92-93.

57. H. W. Eldredge, "Lessons Learned from the British New Towns Program," *Taming Megalopolis* (New York: Praeger, 1967), II, p. 827. See also B. J. Heraud, "New Towns: The End of a Planner's Dream," New Society, XI (July 1968), pp. 46-49; and B. J. Heraud, "Social Class and the New Towns," *Urban Studies,* V (February 1968), pp. 33-58.

58. U.S. Congress, House, *Demonstration Cities, Housing and Urban Development, and Urban Mass Transit,* Hearings, 89th Cong. 2nd Sess. (Washington, D.C.: U.S. Government Printing Office, 1966), p. 1055. Rouse's land use strategy conforms to Gans's conclusions on the socially balanced community: "Communities must be planned to provide . . . block homogeneity and community heterogeneity . . . which allows for compatible neighbors, yet makes room for all kinds of people in the community as a whole . . ." *The Levittowners,* p. 432. Gans was a member of the advisory panel on the planning of Columbia.

59. *Business Week,* "Can 'New Towns' Meet a Budget?" (November 18, 1967), No. 1994, p. 104.

60. Statement of Mortimer B. Zuckerman in U.S., Congress, Senate, *Housing and Urban Development Legislation of 1968,* Hearings Before the Subcommittee on Housing and Urban Affairs of the Committee on Banking and Currency, 90th Cong., 2nd Sess. (Washington, D.C.: U.S. Government Printing Office, 1968), p. 801.

61. Carl Werthman et al., *Planning and the Purchase Decision: Why People Buy in Planned Communities,* Preprint No. 10 of the Community Development Project, Institute of Urban and Regional Development, Center for Planning and Development Research (Berkeley: University of California, 1965), p. 228. The references to "Lynn Ranchers" and "Eichlers" are to the residents of the respective subdivisions.

62. Ibid., pp. 17-18. These findings also tend to support the contention, made in Chapter 6, that the more builders involved in a particular new town, the greater the likelihood of market conflicts and manageability problems for the developer.

63. Carl Norcross, *Open Space Communities in the Market Place . . . A Survey of Public Acceptance,* Bulletin No. 57 (Washington, D.C.: Urban Land Institute, 1966), p. 85.

64. Ibid., p. 84.

65. Werthman et al., op. cit., pp. 223-224.

66. Carl Norcross, "A Look At Crofton, Maryland," *Urban Land,* XXIII, No. 11 (December 1964), 5.

67. A number of loopholes and opportunities for tokenism appear to be built into the administrative procedures for Title IV. The standards are quite variable and vague, particularly as to priority.

> The following factors, among others, will be considered in determining the sufficiency of housing mix: (1) Existing and projected distribution of families by income and size for the region in which the project is located; (2) Existing and projected housing supply and demand, particularly for low- and moderate-income housing, in the region and market area of the project; and (3) Income and family characteristics of persons likely to be employed in the new community. Existing housing in standard condition or proposed to be rehabilitated within the new community, as well as new construction, may be considered in determining adequacy of housing balance.

Department of Housing and Urban Development, *Title 24-Housing and Housing Credit,* Sec. 31.6 (3) (C). See also John E. Keegan and William Rutzick, "Private Developers and the New Communities Act of 1968," *The Georgetown Law Journal,* IVII, No. 6 (June 1969), pp. 1154-55.

68. Sylvia F. Fava, "New Towns in the United States: Some Sociological Aspects of Policies and Prospects," forthcoming in *Essays in Urban Sociology in Memory of Patrick Geddes,* ed. Department of

Sociology, University of Bombay, India, in honor of the 50th anniversary of Geddes' founding of the Department, 1970, p. 30 (Mimeographed).

69. Marshall Kaplan, "The Roles of the Planner and Developer in the New Community," *Washington University Law Quarterly,* MCMLXV, No. 1 (February 1965), 100.

70. Wyndham Thomas, in untitled book review of Gans's *Levittowners,* in *Official Architecture and Planning,* XXXI, No. 2 (February 1968), 225.

71. Thomas, "New Town Blues," *Planning 1964,* (Chicago: American Society of Planning Officials, 1964), p. 189.

72. Glazer, op. cit., p. 22.

73. Fava, op. cit., pp. 21-22.

74. Ibid., and relevant note.

75. Ibid., p. 24. See also Gary Marx, *Protest and Prejudice* (New York: Harper Torchbooks, 1967).

76. Michael Young and Peter Willmott, *Family and Kinship in East London* (Glencoe: The Free Press, 1957).

77. Quoted from P. Willmott and E. Cooney, "Community Planning and Sociological Research: A Problem of Collaboration," *Journal of the American Institute of Planners,* XXIX, No. 2 (May 1963), 123.

78. Ibid.

79. Marc Fried and Peggy Gleicher, "Some Sources of Residential Satisfaction in an Urban Slum," *Journal of the American Institute of Planners,* XXVII, No. 4 (November 1961), 305. See also, Generally, Herbert Gans, *The Urban Villagers* (New York: The Free Press, 1962).

80. Daniel Thursz, *Where Are They Now?* (Washington, D.C.: Health and Welfare Council of the National Capital Area, 1966), pp. 100, 105. See also, on the Boston renewal project, Marc Fried, "Grieving for a Lost Home," *The Urban Condition,* ed. L. Duhl (New York: Basic Books, 1963), pp. 131, 171.

81. Thomas, "New Town Blues," pp. 184-189.

82. See, for example, Lucy Thoma and Erich Lindemann, "Newcomers' Problems in a Suburban Community," *Journal of the American Institute of Planners,* XXVII, No. 3 (August 1961); and Peter Willmott, "Social Research and New Communities," *Journal of the American Institute of Planners,* XXXIII, No. 5 (November 1967), 388; and William Michelson, "Urban Sociology as an Aid to Urban Physical Development: Some Research Strategies," *Journal of the American Institute of Planners,* XXXIV, No. 2 (March 1968), 107.

276

83. Robert C. Weaver, *Dilemmas of Urban America* (Cambridge: Harvard University Press, 1965), p. 29.

84. Robert M. Gladstone, "New Towns Role in Urban Growth Explored," *Journal of Housing,* XXXII, No. 1 (January 1966), p. 34.

85. Robert W. Murray, Jr., "New Towns for America," *House and Home,* XXV, No. 2 (February 1964), p. 126.

86. A. A. Ogilvy, "The Self-Contained New Town: Employment and Population," *The Town Planning Review,* XXXIX, No. 1 (April 1968), p. 38.

87. A. M. Katz, "Lower Rent Costs: A Net Social Gain Through the Creation of New Towns," *Land Economics,* XLIV, No. 2 (May 1968), pp. 273-275.

88. These factors are stressed throughout Part I of Wilbur Thompson, *A Preface To Urban Economics* (Baltimore: Johns Hopkins, 1965).

89. William Alonso, "What Are New Towns For?" *Urban Studies,* VII, No. 1 (January 1970), 44.

90. Anthony Downs, "Alternative Forms of Urban Growth in the United States," *Journal of the American Institute of Planners,* XXXVI, No. 1 (January 1970), 5-7.

91. Ogilvy, op. cit., p. 52.

92. Alonso, op. cit., p. 45.

93. See, for example, William H. Whyte, Jr., *The Organization Man* (Garden City: Doubleday, 1957). See also Maurice R. Stein, *The Eclipse of Community* (New York: Harper Torchbooks, 1960); and Webber, op. cit.

95. See "Report of the National Committee on Urban Growth Policy," in Donald Canty (ed.) *The New City: A Program for National Urbanization Strategy,* (New York: Praeger, 1969), pp. 169-174; Neil Gallagher, "The Next 100,000,000: Where Will They Live?" *Journal of the American Institute of Architects,* (January 1969), pp. 30-37; James L. Sundquist, "Where Shall They Live," *The Public Interest,* No. 18 (Winter 1970), pp. 88-100; Bernard Weissbourd and Herbert Channick, "An Urban Strategy," *The Appraisal Journal* (January 1970), pp. 100-117; ACIR, *Urban and Rural America.*

94. See, for example, Gallagher, op. cit., p. 36, and *Report of the National Committee on Urban Growth Policy,* p. 170.

96. Downs, op. cit., p. 4.

97. Alonso, op. cit., p. 40.

98. Alonso, "The Mirage of New Towns," pp. 6-7.

99. There is no question that government possesses the potential to

establish an effective settlement strategy. All private development is ultimately dependent upon a permissive governmental framework. Government already possesses the powers, incentives and leverages to direct urban development into new towns. It can impede or aid construction of the facilities needed for development, order the type of development through land use control powers, direct the locations of highways and development of public utilities in a manner which promotes nucleated patterns, etc. The Federal and state governments possess substantial powers and resources which could be applied to promote and create new towns, ranging from direct mechanisms to tax incentives for industry. State governments exercise the power of eminent domain. But even if they could be coordinated, there would still be the issue of where, in what manner, and to what degree they should be employed. See ACIR, *Urban and Rural America,* pp. 94, 125.

100. Alan K. Campbell and Jesse Burkhead, "Public Policy in Urban America," in Lowden Wingo (ed.), *Issues in Urban Economics* (Baltimore: Johns Hopkins Press, 1968), p. 637.

101. Contrast, for example, the emphasis placed on the role of government in *Planners for Equal Opportunity,* op. cit.; and the emphasis on private enterprise in J. P. Pickard, "Is Dispersal the Answer to Urban 'Overgrowth'?" *Urban Land,* XXIX, No. 1 (January 1970), pp. 8, 10.

102. Daniel Moynihan, "Toward a National Urban Policy," *The Public Interest,* No. 17 (Fall 1969), pp. 3-20.

103. Eichler and Kaplan, op. cit., p. 176.

104. Confer Chapter 4, "Urban Development Laboratories".

105. University of Minnesota, Experimental City Project, *The Minnesota Experimental City Progress Report,* 2nd Ed., (May 1969), p. x.

106. George T. Bogard, "The Role of Large-Scale Enterprise in the Creation of Better Environment," *Environment for Man,* ed. W. R. Ewald, Jr. (Bloomington: Indiana University Press, 1967), p. 270.

107. *Progressive Architecture,* Corporations as New Master Builders of New Cities," (May 1969), pp. 154-156.

108. See, for example, Bennett M. Berger, "Suburbia and the American Dream," *The Public Interest,* No. 2 (Winter 1966), 80-92.

109. William H. Whyte, Jr., *The Last Landscape* (New York: Doubleday, 1968), pp. 233 and 234.

110. James Welsh, "New Towns: Made to Order, But How Do They Fit?" *Think,* XXXIV No. 2 (March/April 1968), p. 20.

8   The New Town Concept and American Urban Public Policy

The structure of this analysis is such that it does not render hard and fast conclusions or recommendations. The inherent cloudiness of the new town concept seems to require constant clarification and qualification. As was pointed out in Chapter 3, the relatively fixed principles of the new town concept appear to hold to the notion of development of future communities in terms of wholes, or units, according to a pre-determined plan for the community; a socially, physically, and economically balanced composition, and a process of development keyed to single-ownership or control. However, the attributes upon which one chooses to place the emphasis can make a significant difference as to one's ultimate perception of the utility, potential, and feasibility of new towns. Some, for example, emphasize the development process associated with new town building; others stress social balance or other substantive aspects of the process. Some observers view the concept primarily in aesthetic terms, or in technological terms, or emphasize its advantages in terms of the interal structure of the new town or in terms of the scope of the metropolitan area. Some emphasize physical roles for the concept; others, social roles. One might conclude from this that the new town concept is in fact simply a collection of ostensibly complementary sub-concepts. The emphasis which these sub-concepts receive depends upon the context in which the new town is to be viewed. Consequently, the new town concept is, and probably always will be, a shifting one which defies precise definition. It will change, as it has, to fit what are perceived to be the urban problems of the times.

Still, implicit in the notion that new towns are desirable is the idea that existing cities should not be permitted to continue to expand indefinitely, that the characteristics of existing growth are lack of organization and control. In this regard, the new town rationale is based on a form of organic analogy which perceives that cities at some (undefined) stage in their growth should begin to subdivide in the fashion of cellular division—each part retaining all the attributes of the original. There may have been a time in which the city (or society) was much closer to the organic analogy, but that time is long past. Today's metropolis is a bewildering complexity of meshed systems in which there are forms of order and control which do not fit prior conceptions or scales. This is not to say that there is not disorder and lack of control, only that there are new structures which should be evaluated against some other standards than past cities and social orders. This new structure and scale, Webber suggests, is beyond simple spatial or scale definitions.

> Only in the limited geographical, physical sense is any modern metropolis a discrete, unitary, identifiable phenomenon. At most, it is a localized node within the integrating international networks, finding its significant identity as contributor to the working of that larger system. As a result, the new cosmopolites belong to none of the world's metropolitan areas, although they use them. They belong, rather, to the national and international communites that merely maintain information exchanges at these metropolitan junctions.[1]

This should not be interpreted to mean that the new town idea is completely out of scale with modern urban society.

Aspects of the concept may be valuable in articulating the local conditions in which we all reside. But as a national or metropolitan organizational structure it may be far less relevant. There are probably a variety of "desirable" or optimum scales for the different dimensions of urban life (government, economy, social life, etc.), which are non-coterminous and non-coincident, and consequently out of scale with the notion of the self-contained community.

Another factor which inhibits solid conclusions is the limited American experience with new towns. A basic issue, which will remain unresolved for some time (if not indefinitely), centers around the significance and potential of the private new town efforts. Some observers are of the opinion that many of the private new towns contain the necessary elements to produce all the heretofor unfulfilled promises of suburban life; others see them as at least a step in the right direction. Still others view them as a cosmetic or gimmicky treatment of the standard suburban style of development. Much depends upon the degree of optimism or skepticism of the observer, or what he feels the new towns should attempt to achieve.

As is true of the issue as to what really constitutes a "genuine" new town, assessments of the actual or potential achievements of the current American new towns are colored by different perspectives and value judgments. Architects and many planners who have taken a dim view of conventional suburban development have generally tended to welcome some of the design features of the private new towns. Those who have concentrated on their investment potential have been more cautious in their appraisal. Eichler and Kaplan view the new towns in some ways as a distinctly new phenomenon in urban development, but have judged that, in terms of priorities, public policies should be focused upon the more urgent problems of the central cities and widening of housing choice for lower socioeconomic groups. Generally they appear convinced that the new towns currently under development are not intended to serve either of these purposes.[2]

Lyford, on the other hand, like many other proponents of new towns, views the new town concept in terms of potential rather than on the basis of the current examples of private developers alone. He states, for example, that

> In America the new town *could* ... provide living space and shelter for racial minorities who are constantly being evicted and dispossessed in our cities. The new towns would also offer an opportunity for poor white families from the city and rural areas who have also had great difficulty in procuring adequate housing and employment. The new towns would offer them an opportunity to join in voluntary and racially integrated communities designed especially to meet their needs and encourage the development of their resources.
>
> The new towns would be a quite normal response to the disappearance of jobs from our great urban centers because of automation and the dispersion of new industrial establishment. And they would be consistent with the native tradition in which oppressed men united have provided the impetus for.[3]

It is quite clear that Lyford's advocacy of new towns is based upon his assessment of the potential achievements of the concept in the solution of central city problems, whereas Kaplan and Eichler have formed their opinions on the basis of the current manifestation of the concept.

To date, there is little evidence that the private new town trend on the whole represents any significant shift in attitudes in the private sector toward the solution of our most serious and difficult urban problems. Rather, it appears that Federal support was generated largely on the basis of the plans and objectives of two projects, Reston and Columbia, which have stressed not only improved physical planning but a concern for the social aspects of the communities as well. However, most American new towns show, aside from the process of development, little if any significant distinction from the characteristics of development in other suburban areas. The basis for Federal support, then, has rested largely on what has been construed as a reasonable potential for injecting public objectives into private new towns through financial assistance.

As discussed in Chapter 5, the feasibility of private new town development revolves basically around three interrelated factors: location, financing, and sales rates. Although there is high profit potential in new town development, most studies of the factors involved indicate that its risks are commensurate with that potential. There are already illustrations of the risks involved: at least one new town has been taken over by its backers (Reston), and even large corporations have begun selling off land accumulated for eventual new town development.[4] However, of the successes and failures, it will be difficult to determine for some time the relative importance of the various factors which are critical to new town development. Indications are that the Reston takeover is a result of ill-conceived marketing strategies; however, other new towns may fail as a result of location, slow sales rates, inability to attract builders, impatient backers, lack of sustained cooperation from local governments, or various permutations of these factors. A number of exogenous factors could also spell disaster for a new town venture, principally the failure of a plant to locate within or nearby the development, or a change in a highway routing or interchange location.

Title X and Title IV assistance therefore appears to be directed at fundamental problems for most private new town developers. However, as discussed above, it does not appear to affect significantly the other major variables which are critical to the financial success of private new towns. Most important, the inadequacy of these programs is linked to the fact that initiative for development rests entirely with the developer, and, therefore, the critical factors in the development process—location, acquisition, and favorable zoning and planning—would be already largely determined. Generally, it appears that the programs are incapable of effectuating many of the primary objectives which they are designed to serve. Although they are intended to speed up activity in the private development of new towns, requirements for numerous approvals and the achievement of social balance will limit their attractiveness. Although the legislation stresses the importance of location, it provides no means for guiding location. The programs attempt to minimize risk but in many ways add to or shift risks.

There are those who are of the opinion that the objectives of the new town concept cannot be achieved without more direct public involvement, particularly at the phases described above. Few would appear to support the proposal of a British-style program; however, there does appear to be considerable support (in addition to legislative proposals) for a program which would emulate the urban renewal process.[5] There is greater assurance that a publicly directed program would result in greater satisfaction of the "public purposes" for new towns than would probably be possible under enticement programs like Title X and Title IV. Moreover, public powers of land acquisition would probably allow for options in project location, particularly closer to the central city or even within it. For these reasons, publicly directed programs appear preferable to enticement programs.

Even if these legal and operational factors would produce a more efficacious program, much of the discussion of the preceding chapter would suggest that they would be employed in pursuit of questionable, and, in some cases, infeasible and irrelevant objectives, particularly some of those related to social balance and self-containment.

Generally, it appears that many proponents of new towns have placed unwarranted faith in physical determinism and the ability of the new town concept to effect desired changes in the social and economic structure of the metropolis. As discussed in the preceding chapter, prevailing social attitudes have been difficult to change even under forceful new towns policies. These appear to be factors which are not controllable by the level of public involvement in the program or the particular types of assistance mechanisms employed. Basically, then, the major problem for a new towns policy would appear to revolve around the manner in which most people ostensibly prefer to live, work, socialize, and govern themselves. Ultimately this has been the test for all urban policies, and appears to have a somewhat compounded effect upon a

284

concept which intends to interrelate compatibly several aspects of urban life and components of urban areas.

On this last point, it seems appropriate to question the strategic difficulties which might be posed by the packaging of goals under one development form or program. Such a program, while admittedly perhaps creating a better climate for coordination, increases the likelihood of a feasible goal being operationally tied to the satisfaction of an infeasible goal. Some goals might be better or more quickly achieved by not being tied to a complex program. The wide-ranging rationale for new towns mixes urgent social and economic problems, such as the pressing needs of minority groups, with less urgent if not in some cases dubious "problems," such as the widespread preference of private over public transportation and single family homes over multiples. The mixing of the goals of innovation and the minimization of risk have already been mentioned.

However, in essence, the major obstacle to a new towns policy is the fact the United States possesses no concerted urban public policy, if in fact there is any possibility for one. The formation of urban public policy has been ambivalent towards the metropolitan phenomenon. Even if the validity of the new town concept were in less dispute, the history of governmental response to urban problems and the political arena in which policy is formulated is overwhelming evidence of its improbability. For the most part, that history is characterized by an ad hoc, incremental, and cautious approach to urban problems and reflects the fact that there is no widespread agreement as to what urban problems require attention, or how they should be attended, or in what order or priority. They are also reflective of the fact that such policies are formulated in an atmosphere of competition and compromise among various interests, ideologies, and levels of government.

Thus, it seems that the new town concept may not only be inconsistent in many ways with the dominant forces shaping the form and composition of the metropolis, but also with the manner in which public policy has responded to the metropolitan phenomenon. In this light, one should not be too critical of the initial public responses to private new town development. Although there are numerous inconsistencies and pitfalls in its reasoning, its cautiousness and low-keyed approach are probably commensurate with its political ramifications and the uncertainties which surround the new town issue. Moreover, it is again an illustration of the fact that sweeping social change is inconsistent with the pluralism of the American political system, its processes of policy formulation, and our inability to predict with assurance the affects of changes induced into it.

Moreover, new town proponents have probably overemphasized the importance of the Federal role in new town development. This may have been influenced by the fact that other nations generally have centrally directed new towns programs, as well as the desire for establishment of a national growth policy.[6]

Although the Federal government creates legislation to deal with urban problems and needs, local interests are more acutely involved in the effectuation and often redefinition of policies and programs, particularly where policy formulated by higher levels of government involves optional participation by lower levels.

Some Federal urban programs illustrate the nature of this interaction and may have particular relevance to new towns policy. Although public housing, urban renewal, and urban planning assistance have passed the policy formation stage, participation in the programs which offer assistance for these activities rely primarily upon local initiative.* The degree to which such programs, once established at the Federal level, are implemented depends upon local responsiveness. Although requirements are set by the higher levels of govern-

*With recent legislation requiring area-wide planning as a prerequisite for highway assistance programs, and for the review of local applications for certain types of Federal assistance programs by area-wide planning bodies, various Federal assistance programs have become more interrelated. To a certain extent, then, requirements such as the Workable Program for Community Improvement force localities to undertake other types of programs.

ment as to the manner in which different types of assistance programs are to be utilized, the goals of a program may become blunted by their interpretation at the local level. Thus, a local urban renewal program may be employed primarily to further the objectives of downtown businessmen, or the urban planning assistance program to assist in the development of an exclusionary zoning ordinance. Thus, the formulation of a policy or program at the Federal level is no guarantee that the program will be implemented, or implemented according to the objectives it was designed to serve (when it is an enticement type of program), or that major elements of the program's operation are in the control of localities or private developers.

The fragmented governmental structure of the metropolis serves to explain a variety of the impediments to satisfaction of the objectives of the new town idea. It has made difficult if not impossible the kind of metropolitan planning and land use controls which can effectively guide and control growth at an area-wide level, and which is a prerequisite to the effectuation of many of the metropolitan plans which have employed the new town concept.

In summary, it appears that the American new town developers are attempting to turn Howard's basic idea (that the appreciation in land value arising from urban development should be returned to the community) into private profit. The resemblance of the majority of developers' practices to the tenets of the new town concept is tenuous at best and is principally concerned with the physical and procedural aspects. Those public programs which have been established to date appear inadequate to further the satisfaction of the major objectives of the new town concept. And, finally, even if adequate public programs could be developed, such programs would be in pursuit of a number of highly questionable goals basic to the new town concept. Several of these goals are infeasible and irrelevant to the political, economic, and social structure of the modern metropolis, and in this respect the new town concept may well be an idea whose time has passed.

Notes

1. Melvin Webber, "The Post-City Age," *Daedalus,* XCVII, No. 4, (Fall 1968), p. 1097.

2. Both Eichler and Kaplan were onetime active supporters of new town development. Kaplan played a part in the drafting of new communities legislation while at Housing and Home Finance Agency. Eichler testified in favor of the proposals in 1964. See Edward P. Eichler and Marshall Kaplan, *The Community Builders,* (Berkeley: University of California Press, 1967), Chapter 10; and Edward P. Eichler, "Why New Communities?" ed. Bernard Frieden and W. Nash, *Shaping An Urban Future* (Boston: M.I.T. Press, 1967), pp. 95-114.

3. Statement submitted in testimony on the U.S. Congress, Senate, *Federal Role in Urban Affairs,* Hearings, 89th Cong., 2nd Sess. and 90th Cong., 1st Sess. (Washington, D.C.: U.S. Government Printing Office, 1966, 1967), p. 1334. *Landscape* (Winter 1967-69), XVII, No. 2, 5. reports that the president of the Organization of Afro-American Unity "is directing a drive to establish black colonies which will eventually depopulate the urban ghettos. The first colonies will be located on a 1,000 acre tract in New York State." The colonies are intended to become "self-supporting."

4. *House and Home,* XXXIII, No. 2 (February 1968), 10.

5. In addition to sources already cited, see William L. Slayton, "A Critical Evaluation of New Towns Legislation," *Planning 1967* (Chicago: American Society of Planning Officials, 1967), pp. 172-174.

6. In Canada, new towns legislation appears to be developing at the provincial level. See John R. McFarland, "The Administration of the Alberta New Towns Program," *Duquesne University Law Review,* V (Spring 1957), 377-391.

Appendixes

New Towns in the United States, Proposed and Under Development
(By Region)

Name of Town	Developer	Location	Acres (thousand)	Population (thousand)
Far West				
Albertson Ranch, Calif.	Daniel K. Ludwig	Ventura & L.A. Co.	11.5	100
Calabasas Park, Calif.		L.A. & Ventura Co.	3.0	15
California City, Calif.		Kern Co.	101.1	
Camarillo Ranch, Calif.	Great Lakes Properties	Near Pomona	4.6	12
Cedar Hills, Ore.				
Clear Lake City, Tex.	Humble Oil–Del Webb Co.	S. of Houston	15.0	200
Colorado City, Colo.	N.K. Mendelson et al.	S. of Pueblo	5.0	30
Columbine, Colo.		Denver		
Crummer Ranch, Calif.	Home S & L Assoc.	L.A. Co.	6.3	50
Diamond Bar, Calif.	Transamerica Development Co.	L.A. Co.	8.0	75
El Dorado Hills, Calif.	Allan Lindsey & Co.	Sacramento Co.	9.8	75
Foster City, Calif.	T. Jack Foster	San Mateo Co.	2.7	35
Green Valley, Ariz.	Maxon Construction Corp.	S. of Tucson	11.0	25
Hamilton, Calif.		S. of San Jose	11.5	100

Place	Developer	Location		
Hawaii-Kai, Hawaii		Honolulu Co.	6.0	56
Hearst Ranch, Calif.	Hearst Corp.	Near San Simeon	88.0	65
Horizon City, Tex.	Horizon Land Corp.	E. of El Paso	65.0	100
Huntington Beach, Calif.	Huntington Beach Corp.	Orange Co.	1.0	10
Irvine Ranch, Calif.	The Irvine Co.	Orange Co.	93.0	500
Janss/Conejo, Calif.	Janss Corp.	Ventura Co.	11.0	87
Kearny, Ariz.		Pinal Co.	1.3	4
La Costa, Calif.	Adelson et al.	N. of San Diego	2.7	—
Laguna Niguel, Calif.	Laguna Niguel Corp.	Orange Co.	7.1	90
Lake Havasu (Ariz.)	McCulloch Oil Co.	E. of L.A., Cal. (235 mi.)	16.6	60
Lake San Marcos, Calif.		San Diego Co.	1.7	80
Litchfield Park, Ariz.	Goodyear Tire & Rubber Co.	W. of Phoenix	13.0	75
Marincello, Calif.	Thomas Frauge	Marin Co.	2.1	—
Marin City, Calif.	Sunset Int'l Petroleum	Marin Co.	2.0	15
Mililani Town, Hawaii		Honolulu Co.	3.0	56
Mission Viejo, Calif.		Orange Co.	11.3	80
Montbello, Colo.		Denver	3.0	35
Mountain Park, Calif.	Lazard Freres & Co.	L.A. Co.	10.7	60
New Tucson, Ariz.	Horizon Land Co.	E. of Tucson	16.5	100
Northglen		Adams Co.	2.7	30

Padilla Bay, Wash.	—	75 mi. N. of Seattle	6.6	40
Paradise Hills, N.M.	Horizon Land Corp.	W. of Albuquerque	8.5	60
Pike's Peak Park, Colo.	Spraul Homes	Colorado Springs	4.3	30
Porter Ranch, Calif.	Macco Realty	L.A. Co.	4.1	43
Rancho Bernardo, Calif.	Hawn and Summers	San Diego Co.	5.4	33
Rancho California, Calif.	—	San Diego Co.	87.0	—
Redwood Shores, Calif.	—	Adj. to Redwood City	6.1	60
Rico Rico, Ariz.	Gulf American Land Corp.	N. of Nogales	55.0	—
Robart's Landing, Calif.	—	San Francisco Bay Area	—	—
Rossmoor, Calif.	Ross Cortese	Contra Costa Co.	2.1	15
Rossmoor Leisure World, Calif.	Ross Cortese	Orange Co.	3.6	30
San Carlos, Calif.	Sunset Int'l Petroleum	San Diego Co.	5.0	35
San Manuel, Ariz.	—	Pinal Co.	.7	6
San Ramon Village, Calif.	—	Alameda and Contra Costa Co.	4.5	72
Sea Ranch, Calif.	—	N. of San Francisco	5.0	—
Seven Hills, Calif.	E. Belvilaqua	Alameda Co.	6.0	60
Sharpstown, Tex.	—	Houston	4.0	35
Somerset West, Ore.	H.R. Watchie	W. of Portland	6.6	40

Sun City, Calif.	—	Riverside Co.	1.7	11
Sun City, Ariz.	Del Webb Co.	N.W. of Phoenix	16.5	60
Sunset, Calif.	Sunset Int'l Petroleum	Sacramento Co.	—	150
Sunset City, Calif.		Placer Co.	12.0	110
Tierra Linda, Calif.		L.A. Co.	4.0	250
Tucson Green Valley, Ariz.		Pima Co.	2.9	15
University City, Calif.	—	San Diego Co.	13.0	—
University Village, Calif.	Kaiser Industries et al.	Santa Barbara Co.	4.0	250
Vail Ranch, Calif.	California Land Co.	Near L.A.	87.0	
Valencia, Calif.	Robert Hayutin	L.A. Co.	44.0	200
Village East, Colo.	American-Hawaiian Land Co.	E. of Denver	1.0	10
Westlake Village, Calif.		Ventura and L.A. Co.	12.0	70
Unnamed (Calif.)	Oceanic Properties	Near San Jose	11.0	
Unnamed (Calif.)	Sunset Int'l Petroleum	Near Santa Monica	3.5	—

South

Canaveral, Fla.	Canaveral	S.W. of Cape Kennedy	2.5	43
Carol City, Fla.				
Chapel Hill, Ga.	General Builders	Atlanta	1.1	12

Place	Developer	Location		
Coral Springs, Fla.	Western Electric	N.W. of Ft. Lauderdale	15.0	60
Deltona, Fla.	CKP–Deltona	S.W. of Daytona	15.0	41
East New Orleans, La.	Krattner Corp.		5.0	20
EPCOT (Disney World), Fla.	Walt Disney Enterprises	Near Orlando	27.4	20
Lake St. Louis, La.		N. of New Orleans (35 mi.)	2.6	20
Leigh Acres, Fla.	Lee Ratner	N. of Ft. Myers	60.0	80+
Margate, Fla.				
Miami Lakes, Fla.	Sengra Development Corp.	N. of Miami	3.0	6
New Orleans East, La.	Murchison—Wynne	E. of New Orleans	32.0	175
North Palm Beach, Fla.		Palm Beach Co.	9.6	25
Oxmoor, Ky.	Bullitt Trust	W. of Louisville	1.1	15
Palm Beach Gardens, Fla.		Palm Beach Co.	6.1	70
Palm Beach Lakes, Fla.	Perini Land & Development Corp.	W. of Palm Beach	7.0	70
Peachtree City, Ga.	General Builders	S. of Atlanta	15.0	
Port Charlotte	Princeton Land Co.	N. of Punta Gorda,	92.7	100+
Princeton				
Sea Pines (N.C.)	Charles Fraser	N. of Savannah (40 mi.)	5.2	

Spring Hill, Fla.	—	Hernando Co.	10.0	75
Strike City, Miss.				
Unnamed (Fla.)	Deltona Corp.	N. of Tampa	22.0	50
Mid-Atlantic				
Alcoa, Tenn.				
Belair, Md.	—	Prince George's Co.	3.8	30
Bemis, Tenn.				
Churchill Estates, Md.	B. N. Seigel	Montgomery Co.	3.3	35
Columbia, Md.	Community Research & Development	Howard Co.	15.1	110
Crofton, Md.	Crawford Corp.	Ann Arundel Co.	1.3	15
Dale City, Va.		N. Va.		
Fairless Hills, Pa.	—			
Germantown, Md.		Montgomery Co.		
Joppatowne, Md.	Panitz & Co.	Harford Co.	1.2	15
Marlboro Meadows, Md.	—	Prince George's Co.	1.2	31
Marlton, Md.		Prince George's Co.	2.3	48
Mill Creek, Del.	Mill Creek Ventures	N. of Wilmington	1.3	13
Montgomery Village, Md.		Montgomery Co.	2.0	30
Northampton, Md.	Disc, Inc.	Prince George's Co.	2.8	35
Pike Creek Valley, Del.	—	New Castle Co.	1.2	20

Location	Developer	County / Area		
Potomac Valley Estates, Md.	———	Montgomery Co.	3.0	21
Reston, Va.	R. E. Simon Enterprises	Fairfax Co.	6.8	75
St. Charles, Md.	Chord Development Corp.	Charles Co.	8.0	75+
Stafford Harbor, Va.	Chord Development Corp.	Stafford Co.	5.0	35
Willingboro, N. J.	———	Burlington Co.	4.5	50
Unnamed (Md.)	———	Frederick Co.	2.0	———
Unnamed (Md.)	———	Howard Co.	1.0	———

Northeast

Location	Developer	County / Area		
Jefferson Valley, N. Y.	E. Hanslin Assoc.	Westchester Co.	3.0	16
New Seabury, Mass.	———	S. E. of Cape Cod	———	4.5
Rockland Village, N. Y.	———	———	———	———
Roxborough, N. Y.	———	———	———	———
Shanks Village, N. Y.	———	———	———	———
Sterling Forest, N. Y.	City Development Corp.	N. Y. Metropolitan Region	20.0	———

Midwest

Location	Developer	County / Area		
Bloomfield Heights, Ill.	———			
Elk Grove, Ill.	Centex Co.	N. of Chicago	3.0	35
Forest Park, Ohio	———	Hamilton Co.	4.0	35

Name	Location	Developer	Acres (×1,000)	Population (×1,000)
Grant Park, Ohio	Clermont Co.	——	7.5	50
Jonathan, Minn.	Hennepin Co.	George Henkle	2.2	50
Kingswood, Ohio	N. of Dayton		1.7	
Lincoln Village, Ohio			——	10
Oak Brook, Ill.	W. of Chicago	Butler Co.	3.6	25
Park Forest, Ill.		American Community Builders		31
Park Forest South, Ill.	Will Co.	——	1.6	60
Silver Bay, Minn.			——	5.5
Weston, Ill.	W. of Chicago	Riley Management Co.	4.7	50

This list of new towns in the United States includes developments of over 1,000 acres. Several may not be considered by some as "genuine" new towns, but they are included because they are sometimes referred to as new towns. A few which have been included are actually second-home and retirement communities. Information for this table was obtained from several sources. Data marked by an asterisk indicate estimates by the source. A dash indicates information unknown to the compiler at this writing. The developer column does not necessarily indicate the only developer: those mentioned by the source have been used. The population column indicates projected population.

New Town Development Legislation and Legislative Proposals

Year of Introduction	Type of Legislation	Action Taken
1964	Mortgage insurance for land development of new subdivisions and new communities.	Not enacted
1965	Mortgage insurance for land development of new subdivisions and new communities.	Only subdivisions provisions enacted
	Loans to state land development agencies for land acquisition for new communities.	Not enacted
1966	Mortgage insurance for land development of new communities (Title X).	Enacted
	Loans to public land development agencies for land acquisition for new communities.	Not enacted
1967	Loans to state land development agencies for land acquisition and land development.	Not enacted
1968	Federally guaranteed bonds, debentures, notes, and other securities (New Communities Act of 1968).	Enacted

TITLE IV—LAND DEVELOPMENT AND NEW COMMUNITIES

Experimental Mortgage Insurance Program for New Communities

Sec. 401. (a) Title X of the National Housing Act is amended by inserting after section 1003 the following new section 1004 and redesignating the remaining sections accordingly:

"New Communities

"Sec. 1004. (a) New communities consisting of developments, satisfying all other requirements under this title, may be approved under this section by the Secretary for mortgage insurance if they meet the requirements of subsection (b) of this section.

"(b) A development shall be eligible for approval as a new community if the Secretary determines it will, in view of its size and scope, make a substantial contribution to the sound and economic growth of the area within which it is located in the form of—

"(1) substantial economies, made possible through large-scale development, in the provision of improved residential sites;

"(2) adequate housing to be provided for those who would be employed in the community or the surrounding area;

"(3) maximum accessibility from the new residential sites to industrial or other employment centers and commercial, recreational, and cultural facilities in or near the community; and

"(4) maximum accessibility to any major central city in the area.

"(c) No development shall be approved as a new community by the Secretary under this section unless the

---

Source: U.S. Congress, *Demonstration Cities and Metropolitan Development Act of 1966,* pp. 17-19.

construction of such development has been approved by the local governing body or bodies of the locality or localities in which it will be located and by the Governor of the State in which such locality or localities are situated: *Provided,* That if such locality or localities have been delegated general powers of local self-government by State law or State constitution, as determined by the Secretary, the approval of the Governor shall not be required.

"(d) The aggregate amount of mortgages insured under this title with respect to new communities approved under this section and outstanding at any one time shall not exceed $250,000,000."

(b) No mortgage shall be insured under title X of the National Housing Act with respect to a new community approved under section 1004 of such Act (as added by subsection (a) of this section) after October 1, 1972, except pursuant to a commitment to insure entered into before that date.

Mortgage Amount and Term

Sec. 402. (a) Section 1002(c) of the National Housing Act is amended by striking out "$10,000,000" and inserting in lieu thereof "$25,000,000".

(b) Section 1002(d) (1) of such Act is amended to read as follows:

"(1)contain repayment provisions satisfactory to the Secretary and have a maturity not to exceed seven years, or such longer maturity as the Secretary deems reasonable (A) in the case of a privately owned system for water or sewerage, and (B) in the case of a new community approved under section 1004;".

Encouragement of Small Builders

Sec. 403. The section of the National Housing Act redesignated as section 1005 by section 401 of this Act is amended by inserting "particularly small builders," after "broad participation by builders,".

Water and Sewerage Facilities

Sec. 404. The section of the National Housing Act redesignated as section 1006 by section 401 of this Act is amended to read as follows:

"Water and Sewerage Facilities

"Sec. 1006. After development of the land it shall be served by public systems for water and sewerage which are consistent with other existing or prospective systems within the area, except that—

"(a) in the case of systems for water, the land may be served by privately or cooperatively owned systems which are consistent with other existing or prospective systems within the area; are approved as adequate by the Secretary; and are regulated or supervised by the State or political subdivision or an agency thereof, or (in the absence of such State or local regulation or supervision) are otherwise regulated in a manner acceptable to the Secretary, with respect to user rates and charges, capital structure, methods of operation, rate of return, and conditions and terms of any sale or transfer; and

"(b) in the case of systems for sewerage, the land may be served by—

"(1) existing privately or cooperatively owned systems (including reasonable extensions thereto) which are approved as adequate by the Secretary, and which are regulated or supervised by the State or political subdivision or an agency thereof, or (in the absence of such State or local regulation or supervision) are otherwise regulated in a manner acceptable to the Secretary; or

"(2) if it is necessary to develop a new system and the Secretary determines that public ownership of such a system is not feasible, an adequate privately or cooperatively owned new system (A) which he finds consistent with other existing or prospective systems within the area, (B) which during the period of such ownership will be regulated or supervised by the

State or political subdivision or an agency thereof, or (in the absence of such State or local regulation or supervision) will be otherwise regulated in a manner acceptable to the Secretary, with respect to user rates and charges, capital structure, methods of operation, and rate of return, and (C) regarding which he receives assurances, satisfactory to him, with respect to eventual public ownership and operation of the system and with respect to the conditions and terms of any sale or transfer."

Federal National Mortgage Association
Special Assistance for New Communities

Sec. 405. Section 302(b) of the National Housing Act is amended by inserting after "or title VIII," in the proviso the following: "or under title X with respect to a new community approved under section 1004 thereof,".

Urban Planning Grants

Sec. 406. Section 701(a) (4) of the Housing Act of 1954 is amended by inserting before the semicolon at the end thereof the following: ", or for areas where rapid urbanization is expected to result on land developed or to be developed as a new community approved under section 1004 of the National Housing Act".

Public Facility Loans

Sec. 407. Section 202(b) (4) of the Housing Amendments of 1955 is amended by adding before the period at the end of the second sentence the following: ", or (iii) to be provided in connection with the establishment of a new community approved under section 1004 of the National Housing Act".

TITLE IV—GUARANTEES FOR FINANCING NEW COMMUNITY LAND DEVELOPMENT

Citation

Sec. 401. This title may be referred to as the "New Communities Act of 1968".

Purpose

Sec. 402. It is the purpose of this title, by facilitating the enlistment of private capital in new community development, to encourage the development of new communities that—

(1) contribute to the general betterment of living conditions through the improved quality of community development made possible by a consistent design for the provision of homes, commercial and industrial facilities, public and community facilities, and open spaces;

(2) make substantial contributions to the sound and economic growth of the areas in which they are located;

(3) provide needed additions to the general housing supply;

(4) provide opportunities for innovation in housing and community development technology and in land use planning;

(5) enlarge housing and employment opportunities by increasing the range of housing choice and providing new investment opportunities for industry and commerce;

(6) encourage the maintenance and growth of a diversified local homebuilding industry; and

(7) include, to the greatest extent feasible, the employment of new and improved technology, techniques,

Source: U. S. Congress, *Housing and Urban Development Act of 1968*, pp. 38-43.

materials, and methods in housing construction, rehabilitation, and maintenance under programs administered by the Department of Housing and Urban Development with a view to reducing the cost of such construction, rehabilitation, and maintenance, and stimulating the increased and sustained production of housing under such programs.

Guarantee Authority

Sec. 403. To carry out the purposes of this title the Secretary is authorized to guarantee, and enter into commitments to guarantee, the bonds, debentures, notes, and other obligations issued by new community developers to help finance new community development projects. The Secretary may make such guarantees and enter into such commitments, subject to the limitations contained in sections 404 and 405, upon such terms and conditions as he may prescribe, taking into account (1) the large initial capital investment required to finance sound new communities, (2) the extended period before initial returns on this type of investment can be expected, (3) the irregular pattern of cash returns characteristic of such investment, and (4) the financial and security interests of the United States in connection with guarantees made under this title.

Eligible New Community Development

Sec. 404. No guarantee or commitment to guarantee may be made under this title unless the Secretary has determined that—

(1) the proposed new community (A) will be economically feasible in terms of economic base or potential for growth, and (B) will contribute to the orderly growth and development of the area of which it is a part;

(2) there is a practicable plan (Including appropriate time schedules) for financing the land acquisition and land development costs of the proposed new community and for improving and marketing the

land which, giving due consideration to the public purposes of this title and the special problems involved in financing new communities, represents an acceptable financial risk to the United States;

(3) there is a sound internal development plan for the new community which (A) has received all governmental approvals required by State or local law or by the Secretary: and (B) is acceptable to the Secretary as providing reasonable assurance that the development will contribute to good living conditions in the area being developed, will be characterized by sound land use patterns, will include a proper balance of housing for families of low and moderate income, and will include or be served by such shopping, school, recreational, transportation, and other facilities as the Secretary deems satisfactory; and

(4) the internal development plan is consistent with a comprehensive plan which covers, or with comprehensive planning being carried on for, the area in which the land is situated, and which meets criteria established by the Secretary for such comprehensive plans or planning.

Eligible Obligations

Sec. 405. (a) Any bond, debenture, note or other obligation guaranteed under this title shall—

(1) be issued by a new community developer, other than a public body, approved by the Secretary on the basis of financial, technical and administrative ability which demonstrates his capacity to carry out the proposed project;

(2) be issued to and held by investors approved by, or meeting requirements prescribed by, the Secretary, or if an offering to the public is contemplated, be underwritten upon terms and conditions approved by the Secretary;

(3) be issued to finance a program of land development

(including acquisition or use of land) approved by the Secretary: *Provided,* That the Secretary shall, through cost certification procedures, escrow or trusteeship requirements, or other means, insure that all proceeds from the sale of obligations guaranteed under this title are expended pursuant to such program;

(4) involve a principal obligation in an amount not to exceed the lesser of (A) 80 per centum of the Secretary's estimate of the value of the property upon completion of the land development or (B) the sum of 75 per centum of the Secretary's estimate of the value of the land before development and 90 per centum of his estimate of the actual cost of the land development;

(5) bear interest at a rate satisfactory to the Secretary, such interest to be exclusive of any service charges and fees that may be approved by the Secretary;

(6) contain repayment and maturity provisions satisfactory to the Secretary; and

(7) contain provisions which the Secretary shall prescribe with respect to the protection of the security interests of the United States (including subrogation provisions), liens and releases of liens, payment of taxes, and such other matters as the Secretary may, in his discretion, prescribe.

(b) The outstanding principal obligations guaranteed under this title with respect to a single new community development project shall at no time exceed $50,000,000.

Fees and Charges

Sec. 406. The Secretary is authorized to establish and collect fees for guarantees made under this title and may make such charges as he considers reasonable for the analysis of development and financing plans and for appraisals and inspections related to new community development projects. On or before January 1, 1970, the Secretary shall make a report to the Congress concerning the fees and other charges under this title that he estimates will be adequate to provide income sufficient for a self-supporting program.

Guarantee Fund

Sec. 407. (a) To provide for the payment of any liabilities incurred as a result of guarantees made under this title, the Secretary is authorized to establish a revolving fund which shall be comprised of (1) receipts from fees and charges; (2) recoveries under security or subrogation rights or other rights, and any other receipts obtained in connection with such guarantees; and (3) such sums, which are hereby authorized to be appropriated, as may be required for program operations and nonadministrative expenses and to make any and all payments guaranteed under this title.

(b) The full faith and credit of the United States is pledged to the payment of all guarantees made under this title with respect to both principal and interest, including (1) interest, as may be provided for in the guarantee, accruing between the date of default under a guaranteed obligation and the payment in full of the guarantee, and (2) principal and interest due under any debentures issued by the Secretary toward payment of guarantees made under this title.

(c) Notwithstanding any other provision of law relating to the acquisition, handling, improvement, or disposal of real and other property by the United States, the Secretary shall have power, for the protection of the interests of the guarantee fund authorized under this section, to pay out of such fund all expenses or charges in connection with the acquisition, handling, improvement, or disposal of any property acquired by him under this title; and notwithstanding any other provision of law, the Secretary shall also have power to pursue to final collection by way of compromise or otherwise all claims acquired by him in connection with any security, subrogation, or other rights obtained by him in carrying out this title.

(d) The aggregate of the outstanding principal obligations guaranteed under this title shall at no time exceed $250,000,000.

Incontestability

Sec. 408. Any guarantee made by the Secretary under this title shall be conclusive evidence of the eligibility of the obligations for such guarantee, and the validity of any guarantee so made shall be incontestable in the hands of a qualified holder of the guaranteed obligation except for fraud or material misrepresentation on the part of such holder.

Encouragement of Small Builders

Sec. 409. The Secretary shall adopt such requirements as he deems necessary to assure that new community construction assisted under this title will encourage the maintenance of a diversified local home-building industry and broad participation by builders, particularly small builders.

Labor

Sec. 410. All laborers and mechanics employed by contractors or subcontractors in land development assisted under section 403 shall be paid wages at rates not less than those prevailing on similar construction in the locality as determined by the Secretary of Labor in accordance with the Davis-Bacon Act, as amended (40 U.S.C. 276a—276a-5). No assistance shall be extended under section 403 for land development without first obtaining adequate assurance that these labor standards will be maintained upon the construction work involved in such development. The Secretary of Labor shall have, with respect to the labor standards specified in this section, the authority and functions set forth in Reorganization Plan Numbered 14 of 1950 (64 Stat. 1267), and section 2 of the Act of June 13, 1934 (40 U.S.C. 276c).

Real Property Taxation

Sec. 411. Nothing in this title shall be construed to exempt any real property that may be acquired and held by the

Secretary as a result of the exercise of lien or subrogation rights from real property taxation to the same extent, according to its value, as other real property is taxed.

Supplementary Grants

Sec. 412. (a) The Secretary is authorized to make supplementary grants to State and local public bodies and agencies carrying out new community assistance projects, as defined in section 415(c), if the Secretary determines that such grants are necessary or desirable for carrying out a new community development project approved for assistance under section 403, and that a substantial number of housing units for low and moderate income persons is to be made available through such development project.

(b) In no case shall any grant under this section exceed 20 per centum of the cost of the new community assistance project for which the grant is made; and in no case shall the total Federal contributions to the cost of such project be more than 80 per centum.

(c) In carrying out his authority under this section the Secretary shall consult with the Secretary of Agriculture with respect to new community assistance projects assisted by that Department, and he shall, for the purpose of subsection (b), accept that Department's certifications as to the cost of such projects.

(d) There are authorized to be appropriated for grants under this section not to exceed $5,000,000 for the fiscal year ending June 30, 1969, and not to exceed $25,000,000 for the fiscal year ending June 30, 1970. Any amounts so appropriated shall remain available until expended, and any amounts authorized for any fiscal year under this subsection but not appropriated may be appropriated for any succeeding fiscal year commencing prior to July 1, 1970.

General Provisions and Rules and Regulations

Sec. 413. In the performance of, and with respect to, the functions, powers, and duties vested in him by this title, the Secretary shall (in addition to any authority otherwise vested in him) have the functions, powers, and duties (including the authority to issue rules and regulations) set forth in section 402, except subsections (c) (2), (d), and (f), of the Housing Act of 1950: *Provided,* That subsection (a) (1) of section 402 shall not apply with respect to functions, powers, and duties under section 412 of this title.

Audit by General Accounting Office

Sec. 414. Insofar as they relate to any grants or guarantees made pursuant to this title, the financial transactions of recipients of Federal grants or of developers whose obligations are guaranteed by the United States pursuant to this title may be audited by the General Accounting Office under such rules and regulations as may be prescribed by the Comptroller General of the United States. The representatives of the General Accounting Office shall have access to all books, account, records, reports, files, and all other papers, things, or property belonging to or in use by such developers or recipients of grants pertaining to such financial transactions and necessary to facilitate the audit.

Definitions

Sec. 415. As used in this title—

(a) The term "land development" means the process of grading land, making, installing, or constructing water lines and water supply installations, sewer lines and sewage disposal installations, steam, gas, and electric lines and installations, roads, streets, curbs, gutters, sidewalks, storm drainage facilities, and other installations or work, whether on or off the site, which the Secretary deems necessary or desirable to prepare land for residential, commercial, industrial, or other uses, or to provide facilities for public or common use. The term "land development" shall not include any building unless it is (1) a building which is needed in connection with a water supply or sewage disposal installation or a steam, gas, or electric line or installation, or (2) a building, other than a school, which is to be owned and maintained jointly by the residents of the new community or is to be transferred to public ownership, but not prior to its completion.

(b) The term "actual costs" means the costs (exclusive of rebates or discounts) incurred by a new community developer in carrying out the land development assisted under this title. These costs may include amounts paid for labor, materials, construction contracts, land planning, engineers' and architects' fees, surveys, taxes, and interest during development, organizational and legal expenses, such allocation of general overhead expenses as are acceptable to the Secretary, and other items of expense incidental to development which may be approved by the Secretary. If the Secretary determines that there is an identity of interest between the new community developer and a contractor, there may be included as a part of actual costs an allowance for the contractor's profit in an amount deemed reasonable by the Secretary.

(c) The term "new community assistance projects" means projects assisted by grants made under section 702 of the Housing and Urban Development Act of 1965, section 306(a) (2) of the Consolidated Farmers' Home Administration Act, or title VII of the Housing Act of 1961.

Conforming Amendments

Sec. 416. (a) Section 202(b) (4) of the Housing Amendments of 1955 is amended by adding before the period at the end of the second sentence "or under title IV of the Housing and Urban Development Act of 1968".

(b) The first paragraph of section 24 of the Federal Reserve Act is amended by striking out all that follows "national banking association" in the fourth sentence and adding "may make loans or purchase obligations for land development which are secured by mortgages insured under title X of the National Housing Act or guaranteed under title IV of the Housing and Urban Development Act of 1968.".

(c) The paragraph which, prior to the amendments made by this Act, was the next to last paragraph of section 5(c) of the Home Owners' Loan Act of 1933 is amended by adding at the end thereof the following new sentence: "Without regard to any other provision of this subsection, an association may invest in loans or obligations, or interests therein, as to which the association has the benefit of any guaranty under title IV of the Housing and Urban Development Act of 1968, as now or hereafter in effect, or of a commitment or agreement therefor, and such investments shall not be included in any percentage of assets or other percentage referred to in this subsection."

Bibliography

Books

Adams, Thomas. *Outline of Town and City Planning.* New York: Russell Sage, 1935.

Banfield, Edward C. *The Unheavenly City.* Boston: Little, Brown, 1970.

Banfield, Edward C. and James Q. Wilson. *City Politics.* Cambridge, Mass.: Harvard University Press, 1965.

Bollens, John C., and Henry J. Schmandt. *The Metropolis.* New York: Harper, 1965.

Bracey, H. E. *Neighbors: Subdivision Life in England and the United States.* Baton Rouge: Louisiana State University Press, 1964.

Canty, Donald (ed). *The New City: A Program for National Urbanization Strategy.* New York: Praeger, 1969.

Carver, Humphrey. *Cities in the Suburbs.* Toronto, Ontario: University of Toronto Press, 1962.

Chermayeff, Serge, and Christopher Alexander. *Community and Privacy.* New York: Doubleday, 1963.

Churchill, Henry S. *The City is the People.* New York: Norton, 1962.

Community Builders Council. *The Community Builders Handbook.* Washington, D.C.: Urban Land Institute, 1960.

Conkin, Paul K. *Tomorrow a New World: The New Deal Community Program.* Binghamton: Cornell University Press, 1959.

Dahir, James. *Communities for Better Living.* New York: Harper Bros, 1950.

Dobriner, William. *Class in Suburbia.* Englewood Cliffs: Prentice-Hall, 1963.

Duhl, L. (ed). *The Urban Condition.* New York: Basic Books, 1963.

Eichler, Edward P., and Marshall Kaplan. *The Community Builders.* Berkeley: University of California Press, 1967.

Eldredge, H. W. *Taming Megalopolis.* 2 Vols. New York: Praeger, 1967.

Fiser, Webb S. *Mastery of the Metropolis.* Englewood Cliffs, N.J.: Prentice-Hall, 1962.

Fulmer, O. Kline. *Greenbelt.* Washington, D.C.: American Council on Public Affairs, 1941.

Gallion, Arthur and Simon Eisner. *The Urban Pattern.* Princeton, N.J.: Van Nostrand, 1960.

Gans, Herbert. *The Levittowners: Ways of Life and Politics in a New Suburban Community.* New York: Pantheon, 1967.

Gans, Herbert. *People and Plans.* New York: Basic Books, 1968.

Gans, Herbert. *The Urban Villagers.* New York: The Free Press, 1962.

Gordon, R. E., K. K. Gordon, and M. Gunther. *The Split-Level Trap.* New York: Dell, 1960.

Gruen, Victor. *The Heart of Our Cities.* New York: Simon and Schuster, 1964.

Gutkind, E. A. *The Expanding Environment.* London: Freedom Press, 1953.

Hadden, Jeffrey, Louis Massotti, and Calvin Larson, eds. *Metropolis in Crisis.* Itasca, Ill.: Peacock, 1967.

Higbee, Edward. *The Squeeze.* New York: Morrow, 1960.

Hiorns, Fredrick. *Town-Building in History.* London: Harrap, 1956.

Howard, Ebenezer. *Garden Cities of Tomorrow.* London: Faber, 1945; 3rd ed., Cambridge: M.I.T. Press, 1965.

Jacobs, Jane. *The Death and Life of Great American Cities.* New York: Random House, 1961.

Keats, John. *The Crack in the Picture Window.* Boston: Houghton Mifflin, 1957.

Kyle, John H. *The Building of TVA.* Baton Rouge: Louisiana State University Press, 1958.

London County Council. *The Planning of a New Town.* London: London County Council, 1961.

Mace, Ruth L. *Municipal Cost-Revenue Research in the United States.* Chapel Hill: University of North Carolina Press, 1961.

Marx, Gary. *Protest and Prejudice.* New York: Harper Torchbooks, 1967.

Mumford, Lewis. *The Culture of Cities.* New York: Harcourt, 1939.

Nicholson, J. H. *New Communities in Britain*. London: The National Council of Social Service, Inc., 1961.

Orlans, Harold. *Utopia Ltd*. London: Routledge and Kegan, 1952.

Osborn, F. J. *Green-Belt Cities*. London: Faber, 1946.

Osborn, F. J., and A. Whittick. *The New Towns*. New York: McGraw-Hill, 1963.

Planners for Equal Opportunity, *New Cities for Black and White*. New York: Planners for Equal Opportunity, 1970.

Rodwin, Lloyd. *The British New Towns Policy*. Cambridge, Mass: Harvard University Press, 1956.

Schnore, Leo. *The Urban Scene*. New York: The Free Press, 1965.

Spectorsky, A. C. *The Exurbanites*. New York: Lippincott, 1955.

Speirengen, Paul D. *Urban Design: The Architecture of Towns and Cities*. New York: McGraw-Hill, 1965.

Spiegel, Erika. *New Towns in Israel*. Stuttgart, Germany: Verlag, 1966.

Stein, Clarence. *Toward New Towns for America*. New York: Reinhold, 1957.

Stein, Maurice R. *The Eclipse of Community*. New York: Harper Torchbooks, 1960.

Stewart, Cecil. *A Prospect of Cities*. London: Longmans-Green, 1952.

Thompson, Wilbur. *A Preface to Urban Economics*. Baltimore: Johns Hopkins, 1965.

Thursz, Daniel. *Where Are They Now?* Washington, D.C.: Health and Welfare Council of the National Capital Area, 1966.

Tunnard, Christopher. *The City of Man*. New York: Scribner's, 1953.

Weaver, Robert C. *Dilemmas of Urban America*. Cambridge, Mass.: Harvard University Press, 1965.

Webber, Melvin et al. *Explorations Into Urban Structure*. Philadelphia: University of Pennsylvania Press, 1964.

Weber, Max. *The City*. New York: Collier, 1962.

White, Morton and Lucia. *The Intellectual Versus the City.* New York: Mentor, 1962.

Whyte, William H., Jr. *Cluster Development.* New York: American Conservation Association, 1964.

———— *The Last Landscape.* Garden City, N.Y.: Doubleday, 1968.

———— *The Organization Man.* Garden City, N.Y.: Doubleday, 1957.

Wingo, Lowden. *Issues in Urban Economics.* Baltimore: Johns Hopkins, 1968.

Wood, Robert C. *Suburbia, Its People and Its Politics.* Boston: Houghton Mifflin, 1958.

Young, M., and P. Willmott. *Family and Kinship in East London.* Glencoe, Ill.: Free Press, 1957.

Articles in Periodicals

Alonso, William. "The Mirage of New Towns," *The Public Interest,* No. 19 (Spring 1970), 3-17.

———— "What are New Towns For?" *Urban Studies,* VII, No. 1 (January 1970), 37-55.

Amdursky, Robert S. "A Public-Private Partnership for Urban Progress," *The Journal of Urban Law,* XLVI, No. 2, 119-216.

American City. "What's Needed for New Cities," LXXXIV, No. 2 (April 1967), 104, 148.

American Society of Planning Officials Newsletter. "New Town News," XXXIII, No. 5 (June 1967), 71.

Architectural Forum. "Industry Builds Kitimat," CI, No. 1 (July 1954), 128-147.

Architectural Forum. "New Town in Town," CXXVII, No. 3 (October 1967), 28.

Architectural Forum. CXXIV, No. 6 (June 1966), 87.

Architectural Record. "Park Forest, Illinois," CIX, No. 5 (May 1951), 94-110.

Atkinson, J. R. "Washington New Town, England," *Washington University Law Quarterly,* MCMLXV, No. 1 (February 1965), 56-70.

Augur, Tracy. "The Dispersal of Cities as a Defense Measure," *JAIP,* XIV (Summer 1948), 29-35.

Baily, Anthony. "Through the Great City—III," *The New Yorker* (August 5, 1967), pp. 32-63.

Berger, Bennet M. "Suburbia and the American Dream," *The Public Interest*, No. 2 (Winter 1966), 80-92.

Bland, K. W. "Private-Enterprise Housing in New Towns," *Town and Country Planning*, XXXVI, Nos. 1 & 2, (January/February 1968), 101-105.

Brazell, E. C. "Comparative Costs for Open Space Communities: Rancho Bernardo Case Study," *Land Use Controls*, I, No. 4 (1967), 35-40.

Business Week. "Master Builder With a New Concept," No. 1929 (August 20, 1966), 106, 110.

Business Week. "Where City Planners Come Down to Earth," No. 1929, (August 20, 1966), 101, 102, 104.

Business Week. "Can 'New Towns' Meet a Budget?" No. 1994, (November 18, 1967), 103-104.

Business Week. "Can FHA Switch for Slum Housing Problem," (December 9, 1967), 146-147.

Clawson, Marion. "Suburban Development District," *JAIP*, XXVI, No. 2 (May 1960), 69-83.

Conklin, W. J. "Planning Approaches to New Towns," *Building Research*, III, No. 1 (January/February 1966), 18-20.

Contini, Edgardo. "New Cities for America," *The Center Magazine*, I, No. 1 (October/November 1967), 42-102.

Current Municipal Problems. "A New Concept in Pre-City Planning," X, No. 3 (February 1969), 253-264.

Davis, Kingsley. "The Urbanization of the Human Population," *Scientific American*, CCXIII, No. 3 (September 1965), 41-53.

de Jonge, Derk. "Applied Hodology," *Landscape*, XVII, No. 2 (Winter 1967/68).

Dienstfrey, Ted. "A Note on the Economics of Community Building," *JAIP*, XXXIII, No. 2 (March 1967), 120-123.

Downs, Anthony. "Alternative Forms of Future Urban Growth in the United States," *Journal of the American Institute of Planners*, XXXVI, No. 1, (January 1970), 3-11.

Drachman, Roy. "The High Cost of Holding Land," *Urban Land*, (October 1968), 10.

Faltermayer, E. K. "We Can Cope With the Coming Suburban Explosion," *Fortune*, LXXIV, No. 4 (September 1966), 147-151.

Feiss, Carl. "New Towns for America," *JAIA*, XXXIII, No. 1 (January 1960), 85-89.

_____ "USA: New Communities—or Their Simulacrum," *Town and Country Planning*, XXXV, No. 1 (January 1967), 34-35.

Finley, W. E. "New Towns of the Future," *Building Research*, III, No. 1 (January/February 1966), 24-27.

Fischer, John. "A Possibly Practical Utopia," *Harper's*, CCXXX, No. 1394 (July 1966, 16-25.

_____ "Notes from the Underground," *Harper's*, (February 1970), 12-22.

Foard, A. A., and H. Fefferman. "Federal Urban Renewal Legislation," *Law and Contemporary Problems*, XXV, No. 4 (Autumn 1960), 635-684.

Foley, Donald L. "Idea and Influence: The Town and Country Planning Association," *JAIP*, XXVIII, No. 1 (February 1962), 10-17.

Fried, Marc, and Peggy Gleicher. "Some Sources of Residential Satisfaction in an Urban Slum," *Journal of the American Institute of Planners*, XXVII, No. 4 (November 1961), 305-317.

Friedlander, Gordon. "Birth of a New City: An Exciting Creation," *IEEE Spectrum*, IV, No. 4 (April 1967), 70-82.

Galantay, Ervin. "Black New Towns: The Fourth Alternative," *Progressive Architecture*, XLIX, No. 8 (August 1968), 126.

Gallagher, Neil. "The Next 100,000,000: Where Will They Live?" *Journal of the American Institute of Architects* (January 1969), 30-37.

Gans, Herbert J. "The Balanced Community: Homogeneity or Heterogeneity in Residential Areas," *JAIP*, XXVII, No. 3 (August 1961), 176-184.

_____ "Planning and Social Life: Friendship and Neighbor Relations in Suburban Communities," *JAIP*, XXVII, No. 2 (May 1961), 134-140.

_____ "The Sociology of New Towns: Opportunities for Research," *Sociology and Social Research*, XL (March/April 1956), 231-239.

_____ "The White Exodus to Suburbia Steps Up," *The New York Times Magazine*, January 7, 1968, 25, 85, 88-97.

Garvey, John Jr. "New, Expanding and Renewed Town Concepts: Part I," *Assessors Journal*, (July 1969), 49-57.

Geer, David S. "Oak Ridge: A World War II New Town," *JAIA*, XV, No. 1 (January 1951), 16-20.

Gladstone, Robert M. "Does Building a City Make Economic Sense," *Appraisal Journal*, XXXIV, No. 3 (July 1966), 407-412.

_____ "New Towns Role in Urban Growth Explored," *Journal of Housing*, XXXII, No. 1 (January 1966), 29-35.

Glazer, Nathan. "Housing Problems and Housing Policies," *The Public Interest*, No. 7 (Spring 1967), 21-51.

Gruen, Victor, Associates. "Valencia, A Planned City," *Arts and Architecture*, XXXVIII, No. 10 (November 1966).

Harris, Thomas G., Jr. "Howard County Plans Its Future: Columbia," *American County Government*, XXXII, No. 5 (May 1967), 20-23.

Harvey. R. O., and W. A. V. Clark. "The Nature and Economics of Urban Sprawl," *Land Economics*, XLI, No. 1 (February 1965), 1-9.

Heraud, B. J. "New Towns: The End of a Planner's Dream," *New Society*, XI (July 1968), 46-49.

_____ "Social Class and the New Towns," *Urban Studies*, V (February 1968), 33-58.

House and Home. "Suburban Sprawl," XVIII, No. 2 (August 1960), 114 ff.

House and Home. "El Dorado Hills: New Model for Tomorrow's Satellite Cities," XXIII, No. 3 (March 1963), 107-115.

House and Home. "Land Legislation: Inflationary Time Bomb?" XXV, No. 4 (April 1964), 105.

House and Home. "Land Loans: Congress is Cool," XXV, No. 4 (April 1964), 6-7.

House and Home. "Land Planning: New Way to Attract Tenants," XXV, No. 5 (May 1964), 90-98.

House and Home. "New Towns: Are They the Best Answer to the Land Use Problem," XXVI, No. 3 (September 1964), 64-70.

House and Home. "New Towns: Are They Just Oversized Subdivisions—With Oversized Problems?" XXIX, No. 6 (June 1966), 93-103.

House and Home. XXVII, No. 4 (October 1965), 12.

House and Home. XXXIII, No. 2 (February 1968), 10.

Hurd, R. M. "City Problems Require Building New Towns," *Urban Land,* XXV, No. 3 (March 1966), 1, 16.

Huxtable, Ada Louise. " 'Clusters' Instead of 'Slurbs,' " *The New York Times Magazine,* February 9, 1964, p. 37-44.

Kain, John F. "Coping with Ghetto Unemployment," *Journal of the American Institute of Planners,* XXXV, No. 2 (March 1969), 80-89.

Kaplan, Marshall. "The Roles of the Planner and Developer in the New Community," *Washington University Law Quarterly,* MCMLXV, No. 1 (February 1965), 88-106.

Katz, A. M. "Lower Rent Costs: A Net Social Gain Through the Creation of New Towns," *Land Economics,* XLIV, No. 2 (May 1968), 273-275.

Keegan, John E., and William Rutzick. "Private Developers and the New Communities Act of 1968," *The Georgetown Law Journal,* LVII, No. 6 (June 1969), 1119-1158.

Klaber, Eugene H. "Who Needs New Cities," *Architectural Forum,* CXXIV, No. 3 (April 1966), 68, 69.

Kristol, Irving. "It's Not a Bad Crisis to Live In," *The New York Times Magazine,* January 22, 1967, pp. 22 f.

Lalli, Frank. "Builders Public Appeal Fails to Gain Support for New Town," *House and Home,* XXVIII, No. 4 (October 1965), 12.

Landscape. XVII, No. 2 (Winter 1967-68), 5.

Langewiesche, Wolfgang. "Look at America's 'New Towns,' " *Reader's Digest,* March 1967, pp. 140-145.

Lemkau, Paul V. "Human Factors in the New Town," *Building Research*, III, No. 1 (January/February 1966), 29-32.

Lessinger, J. "The Case For Scatteration," *JAIP*, XXVIII, No. 3 (August 1962), 159-169.

Lowe, Jeanne R. "Race, Jobs, and Cities: What Business Can Do," *Saturday Review*, (January 11, 1969), p. 27.

Mandelker, Daniel. "Some Policy Considerations in the Drafting of New Towns Legislation," *Washington University Law Quarterly*, MCMLXV, No. 1 (February 1965), 71-86.

Mathewson, Kent. "Skip Annexation," *Nation's Cities*, V, No. 10 (October 1967), 41-44.

Mayer, Albert. "A New Town Program," *JAIA*, XV, No. 1 (January 1951).

McFarland, John R. "Administration of the Alberta New Towns Program," *Duquesne University Law Review*, V (Spring 1967), 377-391.

_____ "Administration of the English New Towns Program," *Washington University Law Quarterly*, MCMLXV, No. 1 (February 1965), 17-55.

_____ "Administration of the New Deal Greenbelt Towns," *JAIP*, XXXII, No. 4 (July 1966), 217.

Mehran, Masud. "The Pros and Cons of a Planned Community," *Current Municipal Problems*, V (November 1963), 99-102.

Metropolitan. "Must a new town be run as a benevolent oligarchy ... or may citizens participate?" LXI, No. 5 (September 1965), 47-49.

Metropolitan Digest. "UDC to Develop Welfare Island." XII, (November/December 1969), 1.

Michelson, William. "Urban Sociology as an Aid to Urban Physical Development: Some Research Strategies" *JAIP*, XXXIV, No. 2 (March 1968), 105-108.

Molotoch, Harvey. "Racial Integration in a Transition Community," *American Sociological Review*, XXXIV (December 1969), 878-893.

Moynihan, Daniel. "Toward a National Urban Policy," *The Public Interest,* No. 17 (Fall 1969), 3-20.

Murray, Robert W., Jr. "New Towns for America," *House and Home,* XXV, No. 2 (February 1964), 123-130.

Newsweek. "Growing Pains of a New Town," (July 14, 1969), p. 51.

Nolen, John. "New Towns vs. Existing Cities," *JAIP,* II, No. 2 (1926), 69-78.

Norcross, Carl. "A Look at Crofton, Maryland," *Urban Land,* XIII, No. 11 (December 1964), 3-7.

Official Planning and Architecture. XXX, No. 2 (February 1967), 266.

Ogilvy, A. A. "The Self-Contained New Town: Employment and Population," *The Town Planning Review,* XXXIV, No. 1 (April 1968), 38-54.

O'Harrow, Dennis. "New Towns or New Sprawl," *American Society of Planning Officials Newsletter,* XXX, No. 9 (October 1964), 105.

Osborn, F. J. "Just How Dense Can You Get," *Town and Country Planning,* XXXIII, No. 3 (March 1965), 113-114.

Perkins, G. H. "New Towns for America's Peacetime Needs," *JAIA,* XV, No. 1 (January 1951), 11-15.

Perloff, Harvey S. "New Towns Intown," *JAIP,* XXXII, No. 3 (May 1966), 155.

Petersen, William. "The Ideological Origins of Britain's New Towns," *JAIP,* XXXIV, No. 3 (Mary 1968), 160-170.

Pickard, J. P. "Is Dispersal the Answer to Urban 'Overgrowth'?" *Urban Land,* XXIX, No. 1 (January 1970), 3-12.

Progressive Architecture. "New Town—New Hope For Mississippi," XLVII, No. 9 (September 1966), 192-194.

Progressive Architecture. "Corporations as New Master Builders of Cities," (May 1969), 150-161.

Rapkin, Chester. "New Towns for America: From Picture to Process," *The Journal of Finance,* XXII, No. 2 (May 1967), 208-219.

Ricks, R. Bruce. "New Town Development and the Theory of Location," *Land Economics,* XLVI (1970), 5-11.

Ricks, R. Bruce. "A Tool for Managerial Analysis in Land Development," *JAIP*, XXXIII, No. 2 (March 1967), 117-120.

Ridgeway, James. "New Cities Are Big Business," *New Republic* (October 1, 1966), pp. 15-17.

Riehl, Donald R. "Caveats for Corporate Real Estate Development," *Urban Land*, (April 1970), pp. 3-8.

Rosow, Irving. "The Social Effects of the Physical Environment," *JAIP*, XXVII, No. 2 (May 1961), 127-132.

Schmitt, R. C. "Density, Health, and Social Disorganization," *JAIP*, XXXII, No. 1 (January 1966), 38-39.

Schulman, S. J. "The Public's Response: Planning for and Against Development," *Land Use Controls*, I, No. 2 (1967), 20-26.

Scott, Stanley. "The Large New Communities and Urban Growth: A Broader Perspective and Its Implications," *Folder, Public Affairs Report,* Bulletin of the Institute of Governmental Studies, University of California, Berkeley, VI, No. 6 (December 1965).

_____ "Local Government and the Large New Communities," *Folder, Public Affairs Report,* Bulletin of the Institute of Governmental Studies, University of California, Berkeley, VI, No. 3 (June 1965).

Shaw, David. "New Towns vs. Trends: Comparative Costs," *AIP Newsletter,* III, No. 8 (August 1968), 11.

Shkvarikov, V., M. Haucke, and O. Smirnova. "The Building of New Towns in the USSR," *Ekistics,* XVIII, No. 108 (November 1964), 307-319.

Silkin, Lord. "Israel's New Town Programme," *Town and Country Planning,* XXXV, No. 3 (March 1967), 146-147.

Sills, David J. "New Towns: Spectacle of Spectacular," *American County Government,* XXXII, No. 5 (May 1967), 10-15.

Simon, Robert E. "Modern Zoning for Reston," *American County Government,* XXXII, No. 5 (May 1967), 17-20.

Simon, Robert E. "Problems of the New Town Developer," *Building Research,* III, No. 1 (January/February 1966), 16-17.

Snyder, David E. "Alternative Perspectives on Brazilia," *Ekistics*, XVIII, No. 108 (November 1964), 328-330.

Steele, D. B. "New Towns for Depressed Areas," *Town Planning Review*, XXXIV, No. 3 (October 1963), 199-212.

Stollman, Israel. "Oh Yes We Can! Oh No You Can't!" *ASPO Newsletter*, XXXV, No. 2 (February 1969), 1.

Sundquist, James L. "Where Shall They Live?" *The Public Interest*, No. 18 (Winter 1970), 88-100.

Tannenbaum, Robert. "Planning Determinants for Columbia," *Urban Land*, XXIV, No. 4 (April 1965), 2-6.

Thoma, Lucy, and Erich Lindemann. "Newcomers' Problems in a Suburban Community," *JAIP*, XXVII, No. 3 (August 1961), 185-193.

Thomas, Wyndham. (Untitled book review). *Official Architecture and Planning*, XXXI, No. 2 (February 1968), 225-226.

Time Magazine. "Thistles in the New Towns," September 29, 1967, pp. 87-88.

Town and Country Planning. "Progress of the New Towns to December, 1966," XXXV, No. 1 (January 1967), 40-41.

Towne, Carroll A. "Atomic Energy Community Developments," *Landscape Architecture*, XLIII, No. 3 (April 1953), 119-123.

Trevino, Alberto F. "The New University and Community Development on the Irvine Ranch, California," *Urban Land*, XVII, No. 9 (September 1966), 1, 3-7.

U.S. News and World Report. "On a Texas Prairie—Space City for 200,000," LIV, No. 7 (February 18, 1963), 66-69.

U.S. News and World Report. "New Towns—Answer to Urban Sprawl?" LX, No. 7 (February 14, 1966), 114-116.

Urban Land Institute. "Do Single Family Homes Pay Their Way?" XXXVII (September 1968).

Von Eckardt, Wolf. "The Case for Building 350 New Towns," *Harper's*, CCXXXI, No. 1387 (December 1965), 85-94.

——— "New Towns in America," *The New Republic*, October 26, 1963, pp. 16-18.

Walker, Harry A. "Canadian 'New Towns,'" *Community Planning Review,* IV (1954), 80-87.

Webber, Melvin. "The Post City Age," *Daedalus,* XCVII, No. 4 (Fall 1968), 1091-1110.

Weissbourd, Bernard, and Herbert Channick. "An Urban Strategy," *The Appraisal Journal,* January 1970, pp. 100-117.

Welsh, James. "New Towns: Made to Order, But How Do They Fit?" *Think,* XXXIV, No. 2 (March/April 1968), 17-23.

Wendt, Paul F. "Large-Scale Community Development," *Journal of Finance,* XXII, No. 2 (May 1967), 220-239.

Wheaton, William L. C. "New Towns for American Defense," *JAIA,* XV, No. 1 (January 1951), 4-5.

Wheaton, William L. C. "Operations Research for Metropolitan Planning," *JAIP,* XXIV, No. 4 (November 1963).

Willmott, Peter. "Social Research and New Communities," *JAIP,* XXXIII, No. 5 (November 1967), 387-397.

Willmott, Peter and Edmund Cooney. "Community Planning and Sociological Research: A Problem of Collaboration," *JAIP,* XXIX, No. 2, 123-126.

Wilson, James Q. "The War on Cities," *The Public Interest,* No. 3 (Spring 1966), 27-44.

Wood, Robert C. "A Creative Partnership Between Public Goals and Private Means," *Mortgage Banker,* XXVII, No. 1 (October 1966), 28-30.

Other Articles

Abrams, Charles. "Business Welfare and the Public Interest," U.S. Congress, Joint Economic Committee, *Urban America: Goals and Problems.* Materials compiled and prepared for the Subcommittee on Urban Affairs, 90th Cong. Washington, D.C.: U.S. Government Printing Office, 1967, pp. 235-254.

_____ "A Land Development Program for California," *Taming Megalopolis,* ed. H. W. Eldredge, II. New York: Praeger, 1967, 848-854.

Arnold, David S. "What New Towns Ought To Be," *New Towns—A New Dimension of Urbanism* Chicago: International City Managers Association, 1966, pp. 52-54.

Augur, Tracy. Untitled paper on New Towns in a *Report of the Milwaukee Proceedings,* 46th Annual Conference of the AIP (February 1964), pp. 158-162.

Banfield, Edward C. "The Uses and Limitations of Metropolitan Planning in Massachusetts," *Taming Megalopolis,* ed. H. W. Eldredge, II. New York: Praeger, 1967, 710-718.

Baranov, N. V. "Building New Towns," Background Paper No. 11, *Round Table Conference on the Planning and Development of New Towns.* New York: United Nations, 1964.

Bogard, George T. "The Role of Large-Scale Enterprise in the Creation of Better Environment," *Environment for Man,* ed. W. R. Ewald, Jr. Bloomington: Indiana University Press, 1967, pp. 269-274.

Cartsonis, E. "New Towns: A Challenge to Partnership of Private and Public Enterprise," *Planning 1967.* Chicago: American Society of Planning Officials, 1967, pp. 174-177.

Chapin. F. S. "Existing Techniques for Shaping Urban Growth," *Urban Expansion—Problems and Needs.* Washington, D.C.: Housing and Home Finance Agency, 1962, pp. 108-130.

Contini, Edgardo. "New Perspectives for Urban America," *Urban America: Goals and Problems.* U.S. Congress, Joint Economics Committee. Materials compiled and prepared for the Subcommittee on Urban Affairs, 90th Cong., 2nd Sess. Washington, D.C.: U.S. Government Printing Office, 1967, pp. 255-271.

Duncan, O. D. "The Optimum Size of Cities," *Cities and Society.* Glencoe, Ill.: Free Press, 1957, pp. 759-772.

Dyckman, John. "The Public and Private Rationale for a National Urban Policy," *Planning for a Nation of Cities,* ed. S. B. Warner, Jr. Cambridge, Mass.: M.I.T. Press, 1966, 23-42.

Edwards, Gordon. "The Proposed Federal Program," *Planning 1964.* Chicago: American Society of Planning Officials, 1964, pp. 157-160.

Eichler, Edward P. "Why New Communities?" *Shaping an Urban Future,* ed. B. Rieden and W. Nash. Boston: M.I.T. Press, 1969, pp. 95-114.

Eldredge, H. W. "Lessons Learned from the British New Towns Program," *Taming Megalopolis,* ed. H. W. Eldredge, II. New York: Praeger, 1967, pp. 823-828.

Evans, Henry K. "Transportation Planning Criteria for New Towns," *Planned Communities,* Highway Research Record No. 97. Washington, D.C.: Highway Research Board, 1965, pp. 30-51.

Fagin, Henry. "The Evolving Philosophy of Urban Planning," *Urban Research and Policy Planning,* ed. Leo Schnore and Henry Fagin. Beverly Hills, Cal.: Sage Publications, 1967, pp. 309-328.

_____ "Planning Organization and Activities Within the Framework of Urban Government," *Planning and the Urban Community,* ed. Harvey Perloff. Pittsburg, Pa.: University of Pittsburg Press, 1961, pp. 105-120.

Fava, Sylvia F. "New Towns in the United States: Some Sociological Aspects of Policies and Prospects," forthcoming in *Essays in Urban Sociology in Memory of Patrick Geddes,* ed. the Department of Sociology, University of Bombay, India, in honor of the 50th anniversary of Geddes' founding of the Department, 1970.

Fitch, Lyle C. "Goals for Urban Development," *Urban America: Goals and Problems,* U.S. Congress, Senate. Materials compiled and prepared for the Subcommittee on Urban Affairs of the Joint Economics Committee, 90th Cong., 1st Sess. Washington, D.C.: U.S. Government Printing Office, 1967, pp. 19-42.

Fried, Marc. "Grieving for a Lost Home," *The Urban Condition,* ed. L. Duhl. New York: Basic Books, 1963, pp. 151-171.

Gladstone, Robert M. "Planned New Communities and Regional Development," *Proceedings—1965 Government*

Relations and Planning Policy Conference. Washington, D.C.: American Institute of Planners, 1965, pp. 44-50.

Kaplan, Marshall. (Untitled Comments). *Proceedings of the 1964 Annual Conference of the American Institute of Planners.* Washington, D.C.: American Institute of Planners, 1964, pp. 198-199.

Mandelker, Daniel. "A Legal Strategy for Urban Development," *Planning for a Nation of Cities,* ed. Sam Bass Warner. Cambridge, Mass.: M.I.T. Press, 1966, pp. 209-226.

Mayer, Albert. "Ingredients of an Effective Program for New Towns," *Proceedings of the 1964 Annual Conference.* Washington, D.C.: American Institute of Planners, 1964, pp. 186-192.

McDade, Thomas. "Considerations of a Federal Program for Facilitating New Community Development," *Proceedings of the 1964 Annual Conference, Newark.* Washington, D.C.: American Institute of Planners, 1964, p. 193.

O'Harrow, Dennis. "Proposals for New Techniques for Shaping Urban Expansion," *Urban Expansion—Problems and Needs.* Washington, D.C.: Housing and Home Finance Agency, 1962.

Perkins, G. H. "The Regional City," *The Future of Cities and Urban Redevelopment,* ed. Coleman Woodbury. Chicago: University of Chicago Press, 1953, pp. 26-43.

Perloff, Harvey S., and Royce Hanson. "The Inner City and a New Urban Politics," *Urban America: Goals and Problems,* U.S. Congress, Joint Economics Committee. Materials compiled and prepared for the Subcommittee on Urban Affairs, 90th Cong., 2nd Sess. Washington, D.C.: U.S. Government Printing Office, 1967, pp. 162-169.

Reps, John. "The Future of American Planning: Requiem or Renascence?" *Planning 1967.* Chicago: American Society of Planning Officials, 1967, pp. 47-65.

Rodwin, Lloyd. "Economic Problems in the Development of New and Expanded Towns," *Round Table Conference on the Planning and Development of New Towns.* New York: United Nations, 1964.

Rouse, James. "The City of Columbia, Maryland," *Taming Megalopolis,* ed. H. W. Eldredge. New York: Praeger, 1967, II, pp. 838-847.

Rubel, John H. "The Aerospace Project Approach Applied to Building New Cities," *Taming Megalopolis,* ed. H. W. Eldredge, II. New York: Praeger, 1967, pp. 854-874.

Sjoberg, Gideon. "Theory and Research in Urban Sociology," *The Study of Urbanization,* ed. Hauser and Schnore. New York: Wiley, 1965, pp. 157-189.

Slayton, W. L. "A Critical Evaluation of New Towns Legislation," *Planning 1967.* Chicago: American Society of Planning Officials, 1967, pp. 171-174.

Tankel, Stanley. (Untitled Paper) *Open Space and the Metropolis.* Selected portions of the Proceedings of the Fourth Annual Conference of the Organization of Cornell Planners, 1960, pp. 51-56.

Thomas, Wyndham. "New Town Blues," *Planning 1964.* Chicago: American Society of Planning Officials, 1964, pp. 184-189.

Thompson, Wayne E. "Prototype City—Design for Tomorrow," *New Towns: A New Dimension of Urbanism.* Chicago: International City Managers Association, 1966, pp. 38-43.

Weaver, Robert C. "Federal Proposals May Solve City Problems," *New Towns: A New Dimension of Urbanism.* Chicago: International City Managers Association, 1966, pp. 32-37.

_____ "Planned Communities," *Planned Communities.* Highway Research Record No. 97. Washington, D.C.: Highway Research Board, 1965, pp. 1-6.

Webber, Melvin. "Order in Diversity: Community Without Propinquity," *Cities and Space,* ed. Lowden Wingo, Jr. Baltimore: Johns Hopkins, 1963.

_____ "The Urban Place and the Nonplace Urban Realm," *Explorations Into Urban Structure.* Philadelphia: University of Pennsylvania Press, 1964, pp. 79-137.

Wheaton, William L. C. "Form and Structure of the Metropolitan Area," *Environment for Man,* ed. William

Ewald, Jr. Bloomington: Indiana University Press, 1967, pp. 157-184.

_____ "Some Implications of Metropolitan Decentralization," *Planning 1948.* Chicago: American Society of Planning Officials, 1948, pp. 12-14.

Whyte, William H., Jr. "Urban Sprawl," *The Exploding Metropolis,* Editors of Fortune. Garden City, N.Y.: Doubleday, 1957.

Willcox, Roger. "Trend of Development in the New York Region," *Planning 1948.* Chicago: American Society of Planning Officials, 1948, pp. 9-11.

Wirth, Louis. "Urbanism as a Way of Life," *Cities and Society,* ed. Hatt and Reiss. Glencoe, Ill.: Free Press, 1961, pp. 46-63.

Wurster, Catherine Bauer. "The Form and Structure of the Future Urban Complex," *Cities and Space,* ed. Lowden Wingo. Baltimore: Johns Hopkins, 1963, pp. 73-102.

Reports and Hearings

Advisory Commission on Intergovernmental Relations. *Urbanization and New Community Development.* (Draft), Washington, D.C.

Advisory Commission on Intergovernmental Relations. *Governmental Structure, Organization and Planning in Metropolitan Areas.* Washington, D.C.: U.S. Government Printing Office, 1961.

Advisory Commission on Intergovernmental Relations. *Intergovernmental Responsibilities for Water Supply and Sewage Disposal in Metropolitan Areas.* Report A-13. Washington, D.C.: U.S. Government Printing Office, 1962.

Advisory Commission on Intergovernmental Relations. *Performance of Urban Functions: Local and Areawide.* Washington, D.C.: U.S. Government Printing Office, 1963.

Advisory Commission on Intergovernmental Relations. *State-Local Taxation and Industrial Location.* Report A-30. Washington, D.C.: U.S. Government Printing Office, 1967.

Advisory Commission on Intergovernmental Relations. *State Legislative Program: New Proposals for 1968.* Report

M-39. Washington, D.C.: U.S. Government Printing Office, 1968.

Advisory Commission on Intergovernmental Relations. *Urban and Rural America: Policies for Future Growth.* Report A-32. Washington, D.C.: U.S. Government Printing Office, 1968.

Allen, Muriel I. (ed). *New Communities: Challenge for Today.* AIP Background Paper No. 2. Washington, D.C.: American Institute of Planners, 1968.

Baltimore Regional Planning Council and Maryland State Planning Department. *Metrotowns for the Baltimore Region—Stages and Measures.* Planning Report No. 2. Baltimore: The Department, 1962.

Blunt, Keith R. et al. *Implementation of an Ordered Sprawl Urban Configuration* (prepared for the Office of Civil Defense). Los Angeles: Planning Research Corporation, 1967.

Bowery Savings Bank. *The English New Town.* New York: Bowery Savings Bank, 1953.

Burtt, Everett J., Jr. *Plant Relocation and the Core City Worker.* Washington, D.C.: U.S. Government Printing Office, 1967.

Congressional Record, CXIII, No. 190. 90th Cong., 1st Sess. Washington, D. C., November 21, 1967.

Department of City Planning, Syracuse, New York. *General Plan, Plans and Policies, Syracuse, New York.* Syracuse, N.Y.: The Department, 1967.

Douglas Commission. *Building the American City.* Report of the National Commission on Urban Problems to the U.S. Congress. 91st Cong., 1st Session. Washington, D.C.: U. S. Government Printing Office, 1968.

Edwards, Gordon. "New Town Planning in Rapid Growth Areas," text of address by the Chief of the Planning Branch, Office of Metropolitan Development, Housing and Home Finance Agency, before the Fairfax County Federation of Citizens Associates, Annandale, Va., January 16, 1964.

Gliege, John. New Towns: *Policy Problems in Regulating Development.* Papers in Public Administration No. 17.

Tempe: Institute of Public Administration, University of Arizona, 1970.

Governor's Advisory Commission on Housing Problems. *Housing in California* (n.d.), Summary (unpaged).

Gruen, Victor (Associates). *Valencia,* Proposed Land Use Plan. California Land Co.

Highway Research Board. *Planned Communities,* Highway Research Record No. 97. Washington, D.C.: National Research Council, 1965.

Howard County Planning Commission. *Howard County 1985.* General Plan Technical Report No. 1. April 1968.

Joint Center for Urban Studies of the Massachusetts Institute of Technology and Harvard University. *The Effectiveness of Metropolitan Planning.* Prepared for the Subcommittee on Intergovernmental Relations of the Committee on Government Operations of the United States Senate. Washington, D.C.: U.S. Government Printing Office, 1964.

Kentucky, University of (Department of Architecture). *New Towns for the Appalachian Region.* Lexington: Kentucky Research Foundation, 1960.

Krasnowiecki, Jan. *Legal Aspects of Planned Unit Residential Development,* Technical Bulletin No. 52. Washington, D.C.: Urban Land Institute, 1965.

Litchfield Park Properties. *A New Kind of City.*

Litchfield Park Properties. *Litchfield Park Plan.*

Maryland-National Capital Park and Planning Commission. . . . *On Wedges and Corridors.* Silver Spring: Maryland-National Capital Park and Planning Commission, 1964.

McDade, Thomas. "New Communities in America: A New Context for Institutional Innovation," text of speech given by the Director of Urban Studies, Housing and Home Finance Agency, to the Eighth Annual Organization of the Cornell Planners, Cornell University, Ithaca, N.Y. October 17, 1964.

National Association of Home Builders. *New Towns: A Conference.* Report on a Conference at the National Housing Center. Washington, D.C.: National Association of Homebuilders, 1964.

National Capital Planning Commission and National Capital Regional Planning Council. *The Nation's Capital—A Plan for the Year 2000.* Washington, D.C.: National Capital Planning Commission, 1961.

New York State Office for Regional Development. *Change, Challenge and Response, A Development Policy for New York State.* New York: Office for Regional Development, 1964.

New York State Urban Development Corporation. *New York State Urban Development Acts of 1968.* Albany: Urban Development Corporation, 1968.

Nolen, Richard, et al. *Local Government and Pre-planned Communities in San Diego County.* San Diego: San Diego State College, Public Affairs Research Institute, 1968.

Norcross, Carl. *Open Space Communities in the Market Place . . . A Survey of Public Acceptance.* Bulletin No. 57. Washington, D.C.: Urban Land Institute, 1966.

Regional Plan Association. *Public Participation in Regional Planning.* New York: Regional Plan Association, 1967.

Row, Arthur, T. *A Consultant's Report to the Tri-State Transportation Committee on the Reconnaissance of the Tri-State Region.* New York, 1965.

Siegel, Shirley. *The Law of Open Space.* New York: Regional Plan Association, Inc., 1960.

Simon Enterprises. *Reston, Virginia* (Brochure), Fairfax, Va.

Sub-panel on Housing, Office of Science and Technology. "Better Housing for the Future," Reprinted from *International Science and Technology,* September, 1966, in U.S. Congress, Senate, Federal Role in Urban Affairs, Hearings Before the Subcommittee on Executive Reorganization of the Committee on Government Operations, 89th Cong., 2nd Sess., and 90th Cong., 1st Sess. Washington, D.C.: U.S. Government Printing Office, 1966, 1967.

United Nations. *European Seminar on Urban Development Policy and Planning, Warsaw, September, 1962 (Report).* Geneva: United Nations, 1962.

United Nations. *Report of the United Nations Symposium on the Planning and Development of New Towns.* (Moscow,

August 24-September 7, 1964), New York: United Nations, 1966.

U.S. Congress. *Demonstration Cities and Metropolitan Development Act of 1966.* Washington, D.C.: U.S. Government Printing Office, 1966.

U.S. Congress. *Housing and Urban Development Act of 1968.* Washington, D.C.: U.S. Government Printing Office, 1968.

U.S. Congress, Joint Committee on Atomic Energy. *Nevada Test Site Community.* Hearings before the Subcommittee on Legislation and Subcommittee on Communities of the Joint Committee on Atomic Energy, 88 Cong., 1st Sess., on H.R. 8003 and S. 2030. Washington, D.C.: U.S. Government Printing Office, 1963, part 1.

U.S. Congress, Joint Economic Committee. *Urban America: Goals and Problems.* Materials compiled and prepared for the Subcommittee on Urban Affairs, 90th Cong., 1st Sess. Washington, D.C.: U.S. Government Printing Office, 1967.

U.S. Congress (House). *Drafts of Bills Relating to Housing: Message from the President of the United States Relative to Drafts of Bills Relating to Housing,* 88th Cong., 2nd Sess., Document No. 206. Washington, D.C.: U.S. Government Printing Office, 1964.

U.S. Congress (House). *Housing Act of 1964,* Report No. 1703 of the House Committee on Banking and Currency, 88th Cong., 2nd Sess. Washington, D.C.: U.S. Government Printing Office, August 5, 1964.

U.S. Congress (House). *Housing and Community Development Legislation.* Hearings before the Subcommittee on Housing of the Committee on Banking and Currency, 88th Cong., 2nd Sess. Washington, D.C.: U.S. Government Printing Office, 1964.

U.S. Congress (House). *Housing and Urban Development Act of 1965.* Hearings before the Subcommittee on Housing of the Committee on Banking and Currency, 88th Cong., 1st Sess. Washington, D.C.: U.S. Government Printing Office, 1965.

U.S. Congress (House). *Housing and Urban Development Act of 1965.* Report No. 365 of the Committee on Banking and Currency, 89th Cong., 1st Sess. Washington, D.C.: U.S. Government Printing Office, 1965.

U.S. Congress (House). *Demonstration Cities and Metropolitan Development of 1966,* Report No. 1931, 89th Cong., 2nd Sess. Washington, D.C.: U.S. Government Printing Office, 1966.

U.S. Congress (House). *Demonstration Cities, Housing and Urban Development, and Urban Mass Transit.* Hearings before the Subcommittee on Housing of the Committee on Banking and Currency, 89th Cong., 2nd Sess. Washington, D.C.: U.S. Government Printing Office, 1966.

U.S. Congress (House). *Houses and Cities, Message from the President of the United States,* Document No. 261, 90th Cong., 2nd Sess. Washington, D.C.: U.S. Government Printing Office, 1968.

U.S. Congress (Senate). *Housing Legislation of 1964.* Hearings before a Subcommittee of the Committee on Banking and Currency, 88th Cong., 2nd Sess., on S. 2468 and other bills to amend the Federal Housing Laws. Washington, D.C.: U.S. Government Printing Office, 1964.

U.S. Congress (Senate). *Housing Legislation of 1966.* Hearings before a Subcommittee of the Committee on Banking and Currency, 89th Cong., 2nd Sess., on Proposed Housing Legislation for 1966. Washington, D.C.: U.S. Government Printing Office, 1966.

U.S. Congress. (Senate). *Federal Role in Urban Affairs.* Hearings before the Subcommittee on Executive Reorganization of the Committee on Government Operations, 89th Cong., 2nd Sess., and 90th Cong., 1st Sess. Washington, D.C.: U.S. Government Printing Office, 1966, 1967.

U.S. Congress (Senate). *Housing and Urban Development Legislation of 1968.* Hearings before the Subcommittee on Urban Affairs of the Committee on Banking and Currency. 90th Cong., 2nd Sess. Washington, D.C.: U.S. Government Printing Office, 1968.

U.S. Department of Agriculture. *National Growth and Its Distribution* (Symposium on Communities of Tomorrow, December 11 and 12, 1967). Washington, D.C.: U.S. Government Printing Office, 1968.

U.S. Department of Health Education and Welfare. *Manual of Septic Tank Practice,* Public Health Service Publication No. 526. Washington, D.C.: U.S. Government Printing Office, 1957.

U.S. Department of Housing and Urban Development. *Urban Renewal Project Characteristics.* Washington, D.C.: U.S. Government Printing Office, December 31, 1965.

U.S. Department of Housing and Urban Development (Federal Housing Administration). *Land Development Handbook for Title X Mortgage Insurance,* FHA Publication No. 3560. Washington, D.C.: U.S. Government Printing Office, 1966.

U.S. Department of Housing and Urban Development. *Questions and Answers on the Urban Development Bill.* Washington, D.C.: Department of Housing and Urban Development, 1966.

U.S. Department of Housing and Urban Development. *Title 24-Housing and Housing Credit.* Washington, D.C.: U.S. Government Printing Office, 1970.

U.S. Housing and Home Finance Agency (Urban Renewal Administration). *Urban Renewal Manual,* I. Washington, D.C.: U.S. Government Printing Office.

U.S. Housing and Home Finance Agency. *Urban Renewal Provisions of the Housing Act of 1949, as Amended Through August, 1955, and Excerpts from Other Federal Laws Authorizing Federal Assistance to Slum Clearance and Urban Redevelopment and Urban Renewal.* Washington, D.C.: U.S. Government Printing Office.

U.S. National Resources Committee. *Urban Planning and Land Policies,* II of the Supplementary Report of the Urbanism Committee to the National Resources Committee. Washington, D.C.: U.S. Government Printing Office, 1939.

University of Louisville (Urban Studies Center). *New Community Development as a Means for Realizing Urban and Rural Opportunities,* Louisville, 1968.

Weaver, Robert C. *Urbanization in the Middle and Late 1960's,* text of the Lorado Taft Lecture delivered by the

Administrator, Housing and Home Finance Agency, at the University of Illinois, March 8, 1964 (Washington, D.C.: Housing and Home Finance Agency, 1964).

Werthman, Carl, et al. *Planning and the Purchase Decision: Why People Buy in Planned Communities.* Preprint No. 10 of the Community Development Project, Institute of Urban and Regional Development, Center for Planning and Development Research. Berkeley: University of California, 1965.

Woltman, H. R. et al. *The Economic Feasibility of Decentralized Metropolitan Regions.* Prepared for the Office of Civil Defense. Los Angeles: Planning Research Corporation, 1965.

Woltman, H. R. and Goodrow, E. C. *Civil Defense Implications of Current and Future Urban Configurations.* Prepared for the Office of Civil Defense. Los Angeles: Planning Research Corporation, 1963.

News Articles

Anderson, R. H. "Soviet Urban Sprawl Defies Official Efforts to Curb Growth of Cities," *The New York Times,* November 13, 1966.

Bellows, Maggie. "He'd Mass Produce Whole New Cities At $1 Billion Each," *The Democrat and Chronicle.*

Carter, Philip. "Year 2000 Plan Outdated," *The Washington Post,* December 29, 1969, pp. B1, B2.

Khiss, Peter. "State Starts Plans for Two 'New Towns,' " *New York Times,* August 4, 1969, pp. 1 & 26.

Miller, Norman C., Jr. "Land Developers Form Public Districts with Right to Sell Bonds," *The Wall Street Journal,* March 14, 1962, pp. 1, 22.

New York Times. "India Unearths Old Civilization," August 30, 1964, p. 8.

New York Times. "U.S. Asked to Help Build New Cities," July 31, 1966, p. 87.

Roberts, S. T. " 'New Town' Urged on Staten Island," *The New York Times* (November 9, 1967), p. 41.

Semple, Robert B., Jr. "A Company Like Comsat to Battle Slums is Urged," *The New York Times,* November 27, 1966, pp. 1, 40.

_____ "Major Changes Due at 'New Town' of Reston, Va.," *The New York Times,* October 13, 1967, p. 42.

Spilhaus, A. "The City of Tomorrow . . ." *The Democrat and Chronicle* (Rochester, N.Y.), March 19, 1967, p. 1H.

_____ "Should We Rebuild our Cities or Build New Modern Ones?" *The Democrat and Chronicle* (Rochester, N.Y.), March 26, 1967, p. 1H.

Sullivan, Ronald. "City of 300,000 is Urged for Meadows," *The New York Times,* May 15, 1967, pp. 1, 20.

Sunday Times (London). "Shape of Towns to Come," March 22, 1964, p. 7.

U.S. Department of Housing and Urban Development. " 'Experimental City' Study Project Announced," *HUD News,* April 13, 1967.

Bibliographies

American Institute of Architects. *Selected References on Planned Communities.* Washington, D.C., 1968.

Clapp, James A. *The New Town Concept: Private Trends and Public Responses,* Exchange Bibliography No. 122. Monticello, Ill.: Council of Planning Librarians, April 1970.

Housing and Home Finance Agency. *New Communities: A Selected, Annotated Reading List.* Washington, D.C.: U.S. Government Printing Office, 1965.

U.S. Department of Housing and Urban Development, *New Communities: A Bibliography.* Washington, D.C.: U.S. Government Printing Office, 1969.

Viet, Jean. *New Towns: A Selected, Annotated Bibliography.* France: UNESCO, 1960.